New Testament Healing

Peter E. Ostrander

xulon
PRESS

New Testament Healing
by Peter E. Ostrander

Printed in the United States of America

ISBN 9781613792841

Unless otherwise indicated, Bible quotations are taken from The Holy Bible, New International Version®, NIV®. Copyright © 1973, 1978, 1984 by Biblica, Inc.™ Used by permission of Zondervan. www.zondervan.com

Front Cover Painting by Judy Gorecki
Front Cover Design by SpiritWithinDesigns.com

www.xulonpress.com

Endorsement

From the moment I met Peter Ostrander at an Order of St. Luke Healing Conference, I saw his high level of joy as he experienced fully the Kingdom of God in our midst. He is so beautifully devoted to Jesus and His ministry, especially the ministry of healing broken and hurting people. Peter has deep experience in healing and has an authority to write about it. He brings Scripture richly alive in a brand new way. If you are hungry to go higher with God and to see the works of Jesus renewed in our time, this book is for you!

Jack Sheffield

Preface

As a retired Anglican priest, involved for some years in the Christian healing ministry, I have read many healing books, attended talks on healing, and have participated in healing workshops. In the International Order of Saint Luke the Physician, we are encouraging the continuation and growth of the healing ministry of Jesus Christ and his disciples in the Church today. If we want to find out more about this ministry, there is simply no better source and authority than the New Testament itself. I want to build upon that precious foundation with good materials (1 Cor. 3: 10-15), not only by finding and using patterns for healing in the New Testament, but also by using Christian doctrine, as found in scripture and summarized in the historical creeds as my framework. For example, I believe that the death of Jesus the Christ upon the cross provided for our salvation, forgiveness, eternal life, healing and wholeness. Jesus still expects us to proclaim the good news about him in word and deed as we heal the sick and set people free. He delights in working through people like you and me.

In this book we will explore various aspects of Christian healing. We begin by observing what Jesus and his disciples said and did which led to individual or group healings. Then, we consider the reasons why Jesus healed the sick and cast out unclean spirits from them. We also look at the role of the Holy Spirit in early ministry and the faith of those who come to Jesus or are brought to him. We spend some time considering the positive or negative reactions people, including religious authorities, have to Jesus' ministry and three key issues. We also look at the ways individuals were set free from temptation, oppression, or control by demons.

At this point, I present three healing patterns from the New Testament and one contemporary, five-step model with options. I demonstrate our need for inner healing from the scriptures and find help for three common problems with a contemporary model. From there, we widen our perspective and consider prayer, obstacles to healing, and healing congregations, followed by questions and answers, and a summary. I trust that this book will provide a solid foundation for understanding and participating in Christian healing ministry.

During the renewal movements of the seventies I experienced a series of healings: a kidney stone dissolved, the loss of my twin brother resolved, the love of Abba, Father received, along with forgiveness of myself, and joy. When praying for others on a team, I was delighted and surprised when shingles faded, a disk moved, an intruding spirit left, and a smile returned. Why don't we observe Jesus, the great physician, and his early followers in the New Testament as their proclamation is accompanied by healings and miracles, then set out on the calling or mission which God has given us, knowing that God is with us, helping us touch the lives of others. Being connected with Jesus the true vine, results in good fruit and we come home rejoicing.

April 2011   Peter Ostrander

TABLE OF CONTENTS

Acknowledgments

First, I am thankful for those who not only brought me to faith in Jesus Christ but also encouraged me to receive the Holy Spirit and his good gifts for ministry in the context of the Episcopal Church. Then, many members and leaders, including past regional directors of the International Order of St. Luke the Physician (OSL) and the various speakers at conferences were very caring and healing in my life as I began to move toward greater involvement. In particular, I want to thank the members of OSL's Theophilus Chapter at Setauket, NY for their friendship, helpfulness, hard work, and perseverance. I discovered many of the same qualities among people from other OSL regions of North America and abroad. I am also thankful for my friends at Servant Song Ministries in Waynesburg, PA, where I pray on Wednesdays, do workshops, and healing services, and enjoy this spiritual community—especially Donna and Larry Koller, along with other board members. I am grateful for my intercessor and honorary mom, Meredith Kelly, who urged me to write, and then finish, this book. Thank you to Amanda McBride, who spent hours editing my words and holding my feet to the coals in her crusade for accuracy and clarity. My sister, Wendy helped me with some artistic choices.

Without my hardworking, giving, and loving wife, Polly, I would have accomplished little. I bless God for our daughter, Karin; son-in-law, Jeff; and grandson, Adam. Above all, thanks be to God who loves me beyond my imagining, draws me to himself, cleanses and heals me, and empowers me for ministry!

Chapter 1

Variety and Consistency in New Testament Healings

During a recent workshop on Christian healing, with five participants, we began by reading several healing incidents from the Gospels out loud and commenting upon them. I followed with a summary of the things which Jesus and his disciples said and did during healing ministry as I will present below. I also mentioned how God may give insight about the conditions which He would heal. When I used a painful shoulder as an example, one of the participants had that condition. After I went to her, I demonstrated the pattern I had just presented, and she was healed by our lunchtime break. A biblically based ministry can result in physical, emotional, spiritual and relational healing which moves beyond maintenance to health and wholeness. In the process we encounter the true God, who is the loving Father, grace-filled Son, and powerful Holy Spirit as we proclaim the good news in word and deed.

In addition to teaching with authority, masterfully telling stories, calling people to discipleship, and dealing with unfriendly authorities, Jesus certainly healed many people of a variety of diseases and infirmities, and set others free from demonic influence and control. In Mark, the first action-packed Gospel, if one begins counting at Jesus' baptism and ends with his triumphant entry into Jerusalem, there are 126 verses on healing or deliverance out of a total of 677 verses, or 30 percent of the gospel. In Matthew, there are 81 verses out of 681, for 12 percent. In Luke, there are 133 verses out of 861, for 15 percent, and in John, 112 verses out of 585, for 19 percent. Many scholars believe that the Gospel according to Mark was the first of these to be completed. That being the case, Matthew and Luke had access to the Gospel of Mark as well as to another sayings source, known as Q, which references two healings that Jesus performed. They also had their own resources, as indicated in Luke 1:1–4. However, the healings recorded in the Gospel of John are all unique.

In researching this book, I read every healing passage in the Gospel accounts, then translated them carefully from the original Greek and began to write down various questions which I hoped to answer through further studies and reflection. I began with this one: What did Jesus and his disciples say and do when they were healing the sick or setting people free from unclean spirits? Working from two major tables that list all healing events in the four Gospels and Acts, supplemented by lists of infirmities or diseases, we will find some answers. Expect variety, beauty, and power as we explore narratives of individual and group healings. We will find that there is no simple formula that always works in the healing ministry!

Table 1 which lists individual healing incidents, many reported in more than one Gospel, is arranged in the order given in The Healing Ministry of Jesus, the Initial Study Project for Associate Members in the International Order of St. Luke the Physician.[1] In the columns after the scriptural references, I indicate whether Jesus issued a command (**C**), declared something (**D**), responded to faith (**F**), issued or dealt with a challenge (**CH**), prayed to the Father (**P**), asked questions (**Q**), or touched the person who was in need (**T**). The resulting counts are approximate! In the third column, titled Command, I try to indicate whether Jesus commanded the relevant person (**P**), demon (**D**), or condition (e.g., illness, injury, spiritual crisis; **C**). In most other columns, a capital letter "**Y**" indicates a definite yes and a lowercase "**y**" indicates a possible yes.

The results of this exploration held some surprises for me! Although Jesus must have spent extended periods in prayer, especially before making crucial decisions, I found that the Gospels only record him praying out loud once in a healing context: before raising Lazarus from the dead (and that prayer is mainly a thanksgiving for the heavenly Father's having listened to his plea). However, I would not be surprised to learn that Jesus had been constantly interacting with the Father, observing what the Father was doing, and then per-fectly carrying out his works.

By contrast, of the twenty-six individual healing incidents that I studied, Jesus uses mild to strong commands approximately twenty-two times, and he gives the majority of these orders to the person or persons who is in need. Jesus tells the people he had cleansed of leprosy to present themselves to the priest and to give the sacri-fice required by Moses as a testimony to their cleansing. After using mud to cover the eyes of a man who had been born blind, Jesus tells him to wash his eyes at the Pool of Siloam. He also tells some individuals to act as if they were already healed, by getting up and taking their mats or by stretching out their hands. Jesus tells the Widow at Nain not to cry, then he tells her dead son to get up—and the woman's son does as he has been told! The same thing happens with the daughter of a synagogue ruler, and even with Jesus' friend Lazarus!

Table 1
Incidents of Individual and Group Healings by Jesus

Individual Healings	Scripture(s)	Command	Declare	Faith	Challenge	Pray	Question	Touch
Nobleman's son	John 4:46-54	Person	Yes	After	Yes			
Man with unclean spirit	Mark 1:21-28, Luke 4:31-36	Demon			Demon			
Peter's mother-in-law	Matt. 8:14-15, Mark 1:29-31, Luke 4:38-39	Illness						Yes
Leper	Matt. 8:1-4, Mark 1:40-45, Luke 5:12-15	Person	Yes	Yes				Yes
Paralyzed man	Matt. 9:1-8, Mark 2:2-12, Luke 5:17-26	Person	Yes	Yes men	Yes		Yes	
Invalid at Bethesda	John 5:1-17	Person			Yes		Yes	
Man with shriveled hand	Matt. 12:9-14, Mark 3:1-6, Luke 6:6-11	Person			Yes		Yes	
Centurion's servant	Matt. 8:5-13, Luke 7:1-10	Person	Yes	Yes				
Widow of Nain's son	Luke 7:11-17	Persons						Coffin
Demonized man	Matt. 8:26-34, Mark 5:1-20, Luke 8:26-39	Demon			Demon		Yes	
Woman with hemorrhage	Matt. 9:20-22, Mark 5:25-34, Luke 8:42-48	Person	Yes	Yes			Yes	Yes
Ruler's daughter raised	Matt. 9:18-26, Mark 5:22-43, Luke 8:40-56	Persons	Yes	Yes	Yes			Yes
Two blind men	Matt. 9:27-34			Yes			Yes	Yes
Mute & demonized man	Matt. 9:32-34	Demon			Yes			
Demonized daughter	Matt. 15:21-28	Person	Yes	Yes	Yes			

Individual Healings	Scripture(s)	Command	Declare	Faith	Challenge	Pray	Question	Touch
Deaf, almost mute man	Mark 7:32-37	Condition						Spit
Blind man, touched twice	Mark 8:22-26						Yes	Spit
Epileptic demonized son	Matt. 17:14-20, Mark 9:14-29, Luke 9:37-43	Demon		Yes	Yes		Yes	Yes
Man born blind	John 9: 1-38	Person	Yes	After	Yes		No	Spit, mud
Blind, mute, with spirit	Matt. 12:22-23, Luke 11:14-15	Demon?			Yes		Yes	
Bent over afflicted woman	Luke 13:10-17		Yes		Yes			Yes
Man with dropsy	Luke 14:1-6				Yes		Yes	Yes
Lazarus raised	John 11:1-47	Persons	Yes	Martha	Yes	Yes	Yes	
Ten lepers	Luke 17:11-19	Persons	Yes	Yes			Yes	
Blind man from Jericho	Matt. 20:30-34, Mark10:46-52, Luke 18:35-43	Persons	Yes	Yes	Yes		Yes	Yes
Servant of the high priest	Luke 22:50-51				Yes			Yes
Gospel Healing Summary 1	Matt. 8:16-17, Mark 1:32-34, Luke 4:40-41	Demons						Yes
Summary 2	Matt. 14:14, 35-36							Yes
Summary 3	Mark 3:10-12	Demons						Yes
Summary 4, Nazareth	Mark 6:5							Yes
Summary 5	Luke 6:17-19							Yes (people)
Other Group Healings	Matt. 4:23-25; Matt. 9:35-37; Matt. 19:2; Luke 7:21, 9:11; John 6:2							

When Peter's mother-in-law was suffering from a fever, Jesus rebukes it. When confronted with a human being who is oppressed by a demon or unclean spirit, Jesus addresses the spirit or demon, telling it to leave—with quick results! Jesus also tells unclean spirits to be silent and orders them not to reveal his identity. Likewise, he tells the individuals he has healed not to speak about their healings. With God-given authority, believers in Christ may also tell an infirmity or unclean spirit to leave.

In approximately twelve healings, Jesus declares that something is true or has happened: Jesus tells the Capernaum official, "You may go. Your son will live (John 4:40)." Similarly, Jesus tells the persistent Syro-Phoenician woman that she can leave because the demon has left her daughter. Amazed at the faith of one centurion, Jesus tells the man that what he has asked for will be done—just as the centurion had believed it would. Jesus declares the sins of a paralyzed man forgiven; he proclaims a woman who is bleeding and a blind man from Jericho to be have been healed by their own faith; and, before laying his hand on a woman whose body is bent over permanently due to a spirit, he declares her freedom.

Some of today's Christian groups have various theories about the necessity of certain levels of faith as a prerequisite for people to be healed. While noting that people who are sick or disabled, those who minister healing, and members of healing congregations may possess such faith, I cannot establish any such requirements in the New Testament. In fact, Jesus only refers to a person's faith in

10 out of 26 accounts of the individual healings he performed. On occasion, Jesus elicits or encourages an individual to express or act in faith. And at times, although Jesus seems to be standing in their way, other individuals rise to the occasion, as in the case of a foreign woman whose daughter had been demonized and a frustrated father whose son had been demonized. We will consider this important factor of faith without discouraging anyone from approaching Christ and God's throne of grace.

While Jesus' public ministry of healing, including that of deliverance, usually produced positive reactions of surprise, thanksgiving, wonder, and praise, half of these healings also elicited challenges or negative reactions from the religious authorities of Jesus' day, especially from members of the party of the Pharisees. The Pharisees even engineered situations in which Jesus' actions might have resulted in his being discredited because he had performed healings on the Sabbath. In turn, Jesus challenged the Pharisees' wrong assumptions about the Sabbath while he healed all the people who had gone to him in hopes of being healed. Jesus' growing popularity and his fellowship with sinners, outcasts, and tax collectors certainly added fuel to the fire of the Pharisees' opposition to him.

Having read and preached from many passages in the Gospels, I wasn't surprised to find that Jesus asks questions in more than half of the accounts of individual healings that I studied. When two blind men in Jericho cry out for mercy, Jesus asks, "What do you want me to do for you?" (Matt.20). Though their need is obvious, he waits for a definite request. Jesus asks the man by the pool of Bethesda whether he really wants to be made whole. That's an important question for us. Many of the questions Jesus asks and many of the parables are directed toward religious authorities, challenging their views about healing and the Sabbath or their disdain for the common people.

Also, Jesus often touches persons in need of healing or permits them to touch him, even though some may be lepers, bleeding persons, or have already died. His purity and holiness cannot be destroyed, when he mingles with ordinary people, while the Pharisees spent much of their time preserving their ritual purity from any contamination.

Healings Among Crowds

Now, when we look at the twelve accounts of group healings in the Gospels, we find relatively little information to supplement the individual accounts. They are summarized in the last section of Table 1. In two cases, Jesus issues commands to demons, who promptly obey. In five situations, Jesus either touches or is touched by people who need to be healed. For example, Jesus is aware that one particular woman has touched him with faith as the power of God flows out to heal her of her long-standing hemorrhage. His knowledge and discernment facilitated many quick healings mentioned in the summaries. We will often have to wait upon God for guidance as we listen to the person.

Table 1 only lists some of the major elements of Jesus' healing ministry. Unique words and actions of Jesus include telling lepers to obey the law to certify their cleansing, taking the initiative to raise the woman of Nain's deceased son, questioning the legion of demons, forgiving the paralytic's sins, spitting on eyes or making a mud pack with spit to cover them, and deliberately waiting until Lazarus is dead before doing anything to help him.

Jesus not only healed many people with a variety of diseases in flexible, dynamic ways; but he also set people free from the oppression or control of evil. The table below gives a simple list showing some of the conditions which the great physician faced.

Table 2
Afflictions that Jesus Healed

AFFLICTION	NUMBER OF INCIDENTS
Blindness	4
Deaf and/or unable to speak	5
Leprosy or other skin disease	2
Death (unknown cause)	3
Paralysis	2
Demonic oppression	6
Severe illness, person near death	2
Demonic possession	2
Hemorrhage (bleeding)	1
Fever	1
Withered hand	1
Dropsy (edema)	1
Inability to stand erect	1
Inability to walk	1

Healings Performed by Christian Leaders

These healings are summarized in Table 2 below, which includes two new categories and columns: **A** stands for anointing with olive oil and **N** stands for instances when the Name of Jesus is spoken. The other categories are the same as those listed in Table 1. Looking at the upper part documenting the healing of individuals first, we see that Christian leaders issue five commands: four to a person in need of healing and one to an unclean spirit. There are also three instances in which these leaders make declarations. In one instance, Paul discerns or notes the faith of a lame man at Lystra, and in a few instances prayer precedes the healing event or the raising of the dead. In three cases, leaders effectively use the name of Jesus or touch the afflicted person.

When the twelve apostles and the group of seventy two disciples go out on mission after being prepared by Jesus, as listed in the table, they carry out a ministry of preaching, healing, and casting out spirits that is similar to the ministry they had observed in Jesus. According to Mark 6:7 they did anoint many people with oil, touched them and healed them as they declared the presence of God's kingdom.

During later ministries recounted in Acts, people would be healed as Peter's shadow fell upon them or as cloths or rags that had touched the Apostle Paul during his tent making efforts were distributed. These accounts do not give us sufficient information to understand precisely how early Christians went about their healing ministries, especially those that involved group situations, but it is clear that these disciples had learned much by watching Jesus and partici- pating in ministry for almost three years. Their one notable failure in ministry, which occurred while the inner three—Peter, James and John were witnessing Jesus' transfiguration upon the mountain, was their inability to set free an epileptic boy with an unclean spirit and

Table 3
Individual and Group Healings by the Disciples

Individual Healings	Scriptures	Command	Declare	Faith	Pray	Touch	Anoint	Name/Jesus
Crippled man at temple	Acts 3:1–16	Person	Y			Y		Y
Saul receives sight	Acts 9:17–19		Y			Y		Y
Paralytic in Lydda	Acts 9:32–35 (Aeneas)	Person	Y					Y
Tabitha raised from death	Acts 9:36–42 put criers out	Person			y?	Y*		
Man crippled from birth	Acts 14:8-18	Person		Y				
Slave girl with demon	Acts 16:16–19	Demon						Y
Eutychus falls, revived	Acts 20:7-12		?			Y		
Publius' father healed	Acts 28:8-9				Y	Y		

Healing in Group Settings	Scriptures	Command	Declare	Faith	Pray	Touch	Anoint	Name/Jesus
Twelve disciples are given authority and power for their mission	Matt. 10:1 (authority given)							
Healings during the mission of the 12	Matt. 10:1–16, Mark 6:7–30, Luke 9:1–6	Demons					Y	
Healings during the mission of the 72	Luke 10:1–10	Demons	Y					
Healings in Jerusalem	Acts 5:12–16					Shadow		
Healings performed by Stephen in Judea	Acts 6:8 (wonders, signs)							
Healings performed in Samaria (by Philip and others.)	Acts 8:61–8							
Healings performed by Paul in Ephesus	Acts19:11–19 (Cloths convey healing power)					Cloths		
Healings performed by Paul in Malta	Acts 28:8-10							

*Afterward

worried father. Jesus set the boy free and told the disciples that they had needed prayer and faith for success (Matt. 17:20, Mark 9:29). By examining the 8 individual healings by the apostles, deacons and one ordinary believer, we obtain the table shown below: Although most of these conditions and those from Table 2 are found in various countries today; other diseases prevalent today, including heart disease, stroke, cancer, chronic obstructive pulmonary disease, and diabetes seem completely absent . Many of these modern scourges are related to the vast differences between our lifestyles today and those of first century Palestine, Asia Minor, Greece, and Italy.

Table 4
Afflictions Healed by Disciples Listed in the Book of Acts

AFFLICTION	NUMBER OF INCIDENTS
Blindness (after vision)	1
Crippled, lame person	3
Death (person raised)	2
Fever and dysentery	1
Paralysis	1
Oppression	1

In New Testament accounts of healing, Jesus and his early disciples most often issue commands to the person who hopes to be healed or to any unclean spirits that are inflicting sickness or injury to a person's body or spirit, and then they also make declarations about the healing or they touch the sick person. Less often, they are involved in controversies, respond to a person's faith, or ask questions. Rarely are their prayers mentioned in the context of healing. However, our studies would be enriched by noting the examples of members of New Testament churches interceding and praying for one another, with resulting healings, according to the patterns set before us in the Epistles. Such patterns are displayed in later literature through the fourth century.[2]

In chapters 2–6 we will consider several of the major points surveyed briefly here, as well as others, including the role of the Holy Spirit and evidence that Jesus and early Christians healed the sick, preached, and taught the good news. John Wilkinson, M.D., provides a detailed discussion of the medical conditions found in the New Testament and their treatment in his book *The Bible and Healing*.[3]

Chapter 2

Why Did Jesus Heal the Sick and Cast Out Demons?

G iven that Jesus not only preached and taught the good news but also embodied that message in a ministry of healing and deliverance, right up to his final week in Jerusalem, another important question to ask ourselves is, What are some of the possible explanations for why Jesus acted in this way, giving us a good example to follow as Christians? To find some answers, let us examine the Scriptures without attempting to analyze Jesus' psychology or to rank his reasons.

One reason for the healing ministry of Jesus is that it fulfilled the Hebrew Scriptures, especially the latter half of Isaiah, which features the servant of Yahweh passages. Evidently, the servant of Yahweh was a man who was obedient and righteous, a spirit-filled, persistent prophetic teacher. He had not only been humiliated and persecuted but had atoned for sin by his sacrificial death, yet he lives again and is glorified. Jesus not only provides forgiveness, redemption, and new life but also heals many by the wounds or stripes he suffered during his execution.

Even though Jerusalem had been in great trouble while its inhabitants continued to practice their religious rituals and the court prophets were effectively blind, Isaiah begins to speak of a future transformation for God's people. "In that day the deaf will hear the words of the scroll, and out of gloom and darkness the eyes of the blind will see" (Isa 29:18).

While Isaiah 34 speaks of the wilderness of Edom, Isaiah 35 describes the blooming of the desert as redeemed exiles return and experience healing: "Strengthen the feeble hands, steady the knees that give way; say to those with fearful hearts, 'Be strong, do not fear; your God will come, he will come with vengeance; with divine retribution he will come to save you.' Then will the eyes of the blind be opened and the ears of the deaf unstopped. Then will the lame leap like a deer and the mute tongue shout for joy. Water will gush forth in the wilderness and streams in the desert" (Isa 35:3–6).

Then, in the crucial, often-quoted suffering servant passage of Isaiah 52:12–53:12, we find the description of a man who not only seems to lack human attractiveness or kingly majesty but is so despised and rejected by other men, so beaten, broken, and disfigured that few can even look at him and recognize another human being. He goes to his death like a silent lamb, being wounded, pierced, crushed, and bleeding to death, and is finally buried with sinners. Though people considered him guilty and stricken or punished by God, he is actually bearing the burden and penalty of our sins, iniquities, transgressions, and guilt, so that we can be justified; treated by God as if we had never sinned. In addition, he takes up our infirmities, carries our sorrows, and by his wounds or stripes heals us. Surprisingly, this isn't the end for him! He will see the light of life, his "offspring," and the triumph of God and be highly exalted after his humiliating plunge into the depths of suffering, pain, and death (see also Psalm 22 and Philippians 2:5–11).

In the final passage taken from Isaiah 61:1–3, which Jesus reads in his hometown synagogue in Nazareth to explain his ministry agenda, we learn about an anointed one of God, probably the Messiah or Christ, the king, who has come to change the lives of people in need. As we will find later, the particular anointing of the Holy Spirit for ministry, distinct from a more general infilling or baptism with the Holy Spirit, provides power and resources for that ministry. In Isaiah's description, this ministry features the preaching or proclamation of good news to the poor, a binding up of the emotional wounds of the brokenhearted, a proclamation of freedom and light replacing darkness for those held captive, the announcement of God's timely favor, and a glorious replacement of comfort, beauty, and the oil of gladness for those who are mourning, grieving, or despairing. This passage may well indicate a future outbreak of whole-person healing to come for those willing to stand aside from the first-century legalistic program of the Pharisee party and become supple wineskins, ready to receive the new wine of the Spirit!

In reviewing these passages from Isaiah and noting where they are quoted in the New Testament, it seems evident that healing, as well as the forgiveness of our sins, eternal life, and membership in a new people of God, is included in the atonement that the servant of the Lord accomplishes through his own death. Again, Isaiah 53:4–5 reads: "Surely he took up our infirmities and carried our sorrows, yet we considered him stricken by God, smitten by him, and afflicted. But he was pierced for our transgressions, he was crushed for our iniquities; the punishment that brought us peace was upon him, and *by his wounds we are healed*" (italic added for emphasis).

In Matthew 8:17 (which follows the accounts of a leper being cleansed; the centurion's faith, which results in his servant's healing; Peter's mother-in-law being healed of a fever; and the healing and deliverance of many outside her house), Matthew states: "This was to fulfill what was spoken through the prophet Isaiah: 'He took up our infirmities and carried our diseases.'" Likewise, in 1 Peter 2:24 we find: "He himself bore our sins in his body on the tree, so that we might die to sins and live for righteousness; by his wounds you have been healed (*iaomai*[4]). These Scriptures give us hope that not only our fundamental relationships with God and one another but also the brokenness of our souls and bodies may be transformed and healed by the power of God flowing from Jesus' redemptive work. When this will occur depends on the wisdom of God and his timing for our encounters with him.

When Jesus healed the sick, he not only fulfilled the Hebrew Scriptures but also acted in accordance with divinely appointed roles as the anointed kingly Messiah, or Christ, as the good shepherd of Israel, and as a true prophet of God.

Although the prophet of Yahweh is known for speaking the word of the Lord, whether as a proclamation of the truth about God's people or as a prediction of God's future actions, early prophets, including Elijah and Elisha, are also known for their miraculous works and surprising departures from this Earth!

After quoting Isaiah 61 in his hometown synagogue, then stating that the Scripture was being fulfilled, Jesus reacts to the amazement of the people who heard him by saying that a prophet is only without honor in his hometown. When he gives the example of Elijah only providing a miraculous supply of flour and oil for a foreign widow and Elisha only healing a Syrian general of leprosy, his audience tries to kill him (Luke 4:24–30). Later, when warned that Herod is after him, Jesus retorts that he must continue to drive out demons and heal people until he reaches Jerusalem because no prophet can die outside of that city (Luke 13:34). Thus, he gives his disciples and the people reason to believe that he is a true prophet of God and is following in the footsteps of his forerunner, John the Baptist.

After hearing his authoritative teaching and observing his healing works, the people identify Jesus as a prophet (Matt. 16:14). After the widow of Nain's son is raised from the dead, onlookers realize that a "great prophet has appeared among us" (Luke 7:16) and that God has come among them to help his people. After the feeding of thousands (John 6:14), the crowd not only identifies Jesus as the prophet who is to come into the world but wants to make him king, even as he is leaving them to pray and then walk on the sea to his disciples. At a crucial moment, when Jesus asks his disciples, "Who do the people say I am?" (Mark 8:27)they reply that the people believe he is Elijah, Elisha, or one of the other prophets. When Jesus asks his disciples what they personally think, Peter identifies Jesus as the Messiah, the Son of God (Matt. 16:16). During the confrontation between the Pharisees and a man who had been born blind but can now see, the man also identifies Jesus as a prophet. After Jesus' death, two sad disciples on the road to Emmaus tell an unknown companion, "He was a prophet, powerful in word and deed before God" (Luke 24:19). Then, while the disciples are eating together, they discover that their companion is Jesus, raised from the dead! This supports the theory that Jesus' role as prophet is consistent with his healing ministry.

Within the Hebrew Scripture we may observe the spirit of God being active in the lives of heroes, prophets, priests, and kings but not often among the common people. Saul, the first king of Israel, experiences the spirit of God while meeting a group of prophets, begins to prophesy, and is temporarily turned into a different person before being overcome by another, darker spirit. When Jesse's son David is selected by God to be the next ruler and is then anointed with holy oil by the prophet Samuel, he is simultaneously anointed by the Holy Spirit for life. David will not kill his predecessor, Saul, because Saul is still God's anointed leader. Neither king is perfect, but David is a man after God's own heart. (Their successors were routinely called God's anointed, even though many of them worshipped false gods.) Though God's people had been oppressed by many Gentile empires, including Rome, they still expect God to establish his reign over the world through a special anointed one, another king like David, who will come from his hometown of Bethlehem. Soon after Jesus' birth, wise men travel from the East, seeking to worship and give gifts to the new king. This threatens Herod, the suspicious, paranoid vassal king under Rome. Zealots and even some of Jesus' disciples expect the anointed one, the Messiah (Hebrew) or Christ (Greek), to be a conquering hero who will throw the Romans out and immediately establish his rule over Earth. Although Peter at Caesarea Philippi correctly identifies Jesus as the Christ, the Son of God, he rebukes Jesus for saying that he will be rejected, tortured, and killed by Jewish leaders before rising from the dead.

According to John's Gospel, many in the crowd put their faith in Jesus and asked, "When the Christ comes, will he do more miraculous signs than this man?" (John 7:31). For some realistic or pessimistic disciples, including Thomas, the miracles they had seen were not sufficient to convince them of the miraculous event of the resurrection, until they had actually touched and seen their risen

Lord. John remarks that Jesus had performed many other miracles in the presence of his disciples. These are not recorded in John's Gospel, but those acts that have been recorded are there so that we may believe that Jesus *is* the Christ, the Son of God, and that we may have eternal life in his name (John 20:30–31). This message correlates with Isaiah 61, which speaks of an anointed one of God who performs miracles of healing. Hence, it is not unexpected that an anointed one of God, who happens to be an unusual king, without a visible throne or territory, might also be one who heals. In 1 Corinthians 1:23 Paul says, "We preach Christ (the anointed one of God) crucified: a stumbling block to Jews and foolishness to Gentiles, but to those whom God has called, Christ the power of God and the wisdom of God." For those who have eyes to see, Jesus of Nazareth is the anointed one of God whose miracles fulfill the Scriptures.

Focusing further, we realize that Jesus, born in Bethlehem to fulfill Scripture (Mic. 5:2, Matt. 2:6) and recognized by the wise men, is a new and quite different king who proclaims, inaugurates, and demonstrates a new reign of God among human beings. When Gabriel announces to Mary that she will give birth to a son, he indicates that Mary's son will be called the Son of the Most High and will receive the throne of David, then reign forever! Although many Jews expected the Messiah's reign to be like that of King David. We actually come under his gracious rule by accepting him as our Savior and Lord, then walking in obedience to him.

As soon as Jesus is baptized by his cousin John, the Forerunner, he takes up John's proclamation of good news: "Repent, for the kingdom of Heaven is near" (Matt. 4:17). He covers Galilee by visiting synagogues and preaching the good news about the kingdom, then healing every disease and sickness. When the twelve apostles are sent out on mission, they are told to announce that the kingdom of God (or Heaven) is near and to demonstrate its presence by freely driving out demons, cleansing lepers, healing the sick, and even raising the dead. When the Pharisees claim that Jesus is driving out demons by the power of another major demon, commonly known as Beelzebub or Satan, Jesus not only shows that such division would indicate a collapsing reign of evil but also suggests that he is driving out demons by the Spirit of God and that the kingdom of God is powerfully present!

At his triumphant entry into Jerusalem, Jesus arrives as a peaceful king, fulfilling Isaiah 62:11 to the acclaim of the people, who quote Psalm 118 by saying, "Blessed is the king who comes in the name of the Lord." However, when Jesus refuses to defend himself or to fulfill the hopes of the zealots, he is swiftly condemned, beaten, brought before Pilate, and then executed. It appears that the reign of this messianic pretender among his followers has been terminated after only three years of ministry. Yet, a few days later, his disciples claim that he has risen bodily from the dead! Soon they find the Holy Spirit working in their lives, and they begin to proclaim the good news of a king who has died on the cross for our sins but is now exalted to the right hand of God, to reign until all his enemies are subdued. His kingdom, his reign, is truly "not of this world" (John 18:36). One cannot perceive or enter into the kingdom of God unless he or she is born from above or born again. In the Epistles, the focus shifts toward the reign of Christ, primarily within a new people of God, the Church.

From the time of David, kings were also called shepherds. When the tribes of Israel accepted his rule, they reminded David, "The Lord said to you, 'You will shepherd my people Israel, and you will become their ruler 2 Sam 5:2).'" If later rulers in the lineage of David forsook all false gods and then served only Yahweh, they were approved in the books of Kings and Chronicles. Otherwise, they were often condemned. Because Jesus identifies himself as the good shepherd as well as the gate to the sheepfold, let us see how his shepherding with healing relates to the Scriptures. Keep in mind the reality that David himself considers God to be his shepherd, in whom he fully trusts (Ps. 23).

Jeremiah later prophesies to the rulers: "Woe to the shepherds of Israel who only take care of themselves! Should not shepherds take care of the flock? You have not strengthened the weak or healed the sick or bound up the injured. You have not brought back the strays or searched for the lost. You have ruled them harshly and brutally. So they were scattered because there was no shepherd, and when they were scattered they became food" (Jer. 34:2, 4–5). Ezekiel follows this with a promise from God: "I myself will search for my sheep and look after them. I will search for the lost and bring back the strays. I will bind up the injured and strengthen the week, but the sleek and strong I will destroy" (Ezek. 34:11–16). We discover that God will place over them one shepherd, his servant David. After that, Micah promises that out of Bethlehem will come a ruler and shepherd of his people, Israel (Mic. 2:6). When Jesus heals many, as recorded in Matthew 9, he has compassion for them because they are "harassed and helpless, like sheep without a shepherd" (Matt. 9:36).

In John 10, Jesus declares himself to be the good shepherd who lays down his life for the sheep, in contrast to hirelings who run away when they see predators coming. Consistent with rustic sheep pens, where the shepherd would lie across the opening to prevent the sheep from escaping and predators from entering, Jesus is also the gate — no one enters without going by him. He knows his sheep, and they know him. He also wants to bring in other sheep so there would be one flock and one shepherd. From these stories we can understand how Jesus fulfills prophetic promises of a strong, loving, healing, and sacrificial leader. Even for those who come out of the Great Tribulation, Jesus will be their shepherd, leading them to springs of living water and wiping away every tear from their eyes after their earthly sufferings for him are over (Rev. 7:17).

This true shepherd and king, unlike so many others, so perfectly obeys his Father that no one can successfully show that he is a sinner. Even when Satan comes to tempt, attack, and destroy Jesus, he is not able to find imperfection, guilt, or shame to use against Jesus. In this way, in his healing ministry, Jesus, the Son of Man and Son of God, is perfectly fulfilling the good will of Abba, his heavenly Father, just as he always obeyed his earthly parents. Unfortunately, we need much forgiveness, loving discipline, and healing because we have not done likewise! If we obey Jesus' commands, primarily by agápe[5] loving others, we will remain in his love, just as he has obeyed his Father's commands and has remained in his heavenly Father's love (John 15:10). Paul states that through the disobedience of Adam, many were made sinners, yet through the obedience of another man, the many will be made righteous! In a sense, Jesus experiences the cost of obedience in suffering and is further perfected, becoming the source of salvation for all who obey him (Heb. 5:8–9). Hours before his death, Jesus prays in Gethsemane that the cup of God's wrath will be taken from him; yet he continues, "Not as I will, but as you will" (Matt. 26:39).

In all his works, including healing and deliverance, Jesus depends on God the Father. Shortly after the lame man at the pool of Bethesda is healed on the Sabbath and then told to carry his mat, Jesus says: "My Father is always at his work to this very day, and I, too, am working. I tell you the truth (amen and amen), the Son can do nothing by himself; he can do only what he sees his Father doing, because whatever the Father does the Son also does. I have testimony weightier than that of John. For the very work that the Father has given me to finish, testifies that the Father has sent me" (John 5:17, 19, and 36). Even if we don't believe in Jesus directly, we should believe in the miracles so that we may realize that Jesus is in the Father and the Father is in Jesus (John 10:37). Indeed, Jesus so loves his Father that he does exactly as his Father commands, unlike us (John 14:31)! In other words, Jesus' important healing and miracle ministry is according to God's will, even when he heals on the Sabbath.

Also, by his perfect innocence and obedience, Jesus is glorifying the Father as the Father is preparing to glorify him after his humiliating death on the cross. Glimpses of the Son's glory are seen in Jesus' healings, deliverances, and nature miracles, but particularly in his transfiguration on the mountain, in company with Moses and Elijah (Luke 9:32). When Jesus hears about Lazarus' sickness, yet remains in Galilee for two days until Lazarus dies, he tells his disciples, "This sickness will not end in death. No, it is for God's glory so that God's Son may be glorified through it" (John 11: 4). Shortly after arriving at the home of Lazarus' sisters and listening to their laments and weeping, Jesus tells the sisters to take the stone away from the tomb. When they do as they have been told, Jesus prays and then tells Lazarus to walk out of the tomb, which he does! This final miracle in the Gospel according to John results both in glory being given to Jesus and the acceleration of his opponents' plans to destroy him (John 11). During this crucial season, Jesus says, "The hour has come for the Son of Man to be glorified. Father, glorify your name" (John 12:23). Then a voice comes from Heaven, saying: "I have glorified it, and will glorify it again" (John 12:28). God does this through Jesus' resurrection, appearances, ascension, and seating at the right hand of the Father. All of Jesus' works of obedience glorify the Father.

Since Jesus is perfectly carrying out the will of the Father, with whom he is in such perfect unity, and because to see the Son is to see the Father, we are correct in thinking that Jesus demonstrates the fundamental reality and nature of God's will regarding healing and wholeness. In order to confirm this, we will examine a few verses from the Hebrew Scripture.

After Israel is liberated from Egypt, but before she enters the promised land, God promises: "If you will diligently hearken to the voice of the Lord your God and will do what is right in his sight and listen to and obey his commands, I will put none of these diseases upon you. . . . Serve the Lord your God and I will take sickness from you" (Ex. 15:26, 23:25). In Deuteronomy 30, Moses invites the people to choose blessings and life rather than curses and death so that their descendants may love the Lord their God and cling to him. When Israel is facing disasters, including exile, the Israelites may humble themselves, pray, seek God, and turn from their wicked ways with the result that God will hear and forgive them, then heal their land. Admittedly, these promises are addressed to Israel collectively, and have not been fulfilled because of the Israelites' idolatry (2 Chron. 7:14). In the context of worship, Psalm 103 urges God's people to bless the Lord rather than forget all of his wonderful blessings, including forgiving their sins, healing their diseases, offering them redemption from death, and renewing their youthful vigor (Ps. 103:15). Again, the prophet Malachi says that for those who worship in the fear of God, the sun of righteousness will rise with healing in his wings, enabling them to venture out like young playful animals (Mal 4:2). The conditional nature of these promises does not give us reason to believe that every individual person within a largely obedient nation will automatically be healthy. We must remember the tragedy and consequences of the fall of the first humans, expanding through time, except by the mercy of God.

One need only look at the word "curse" to see anew the terrible effects of sin or the wonderful results of Christ's redemption. The serpent mouthpiece for Satan and the ground were cursed at the Fall. Those who blessed Abraham were blessed, while those who cursed him were cursed. Balaam was unable to curse Israel, even for money (Num. 22:6). According to Deuteronomy, Moses proclaimed a blessing or a curse, depending on the people's obedience or disobedience in regard to the law (Deut. 11:26). Anyone who carves an image or casts an idol is cursed (Deut. 27:15). God then gives a long list of blessings, which includes healing for obedience to the law, and a corresponding list of curses for disobedience (Deut. 28:15): "The Lord will send on you curses, confusion and rebuke in everything you put your hand to, until you are destroyed . . . because you did not obey the Lord your God and observe the commands" (Deut. 28:45). Later, Jeremiah says that anyone who trusts in man, who depends on flesh for his strength, and turns away from the Lord is cursed. In Malachi 3:9, the people are cursed for cheating God by sacrificing defective animals and conferring less than the tithe. Is it possible that we could be deservedly under God's curse rather than his blessing, due to similar actions or attitudes?

But Paul, the author of Galatians, has some good news for us: Christ has redeemed us from the curse of the law by becoming a curse for us, for it is written, "Cursed is everyone who is hung on a tree" (Gal. 3:13–14, Deut. 21:23). By his becoming accursed on the cross and our being united with him, Jesus has set us free from the curse of the law, unless we fall back into Judaism by trying to be made righteous through our obedience to the law. When we begin to trust in Jesus by faith, we receive all the blessings of his death for us as a divine gift. The Father looks on us and sees the righteousness of Christ, then blesses us.

Presuming that it was God's will for Jesus to heal the sick who came to him and requested healing and those whom the Father instructed him to heal, it follows that Jesus could heal because he had both sufficient authority and power to do so! These flowed from his relationship with the Father and the Holy Spirit, his identity as Son of God, Messiah, King, and Prophet, and his complete obedience.

According to Mark, when the crowds of people first hear Jesus speak in the synagogue then witness him drive a vocal but threatened demon out of a man, they are amazed! Jesus doesn't speak like an ordinary teacher of the law, always quoting the past opinions of famous rabbis or other traditions. Not only does he speak directly with authority but he also silences and rapidly ejects the demon before their very eyes. Though not a product of rabbinic schools, he has great authority and strong convictions. When faith-filled friends lower a paralyzed man in front of Jesus at Capernaum, Jesus tells the man that his sins are forgiven! When the authorities respond by grumbling and saying that only God has the authority to forgive sin, Jesus asks them which is harder—to pronounce forgive-ness or to tell the man to get up. The answer is obvious: to demon-strate the authority of the Son of Man to forgive sins, Jesus does the harder thing by telling the man to get up—and the man gets up. The awestruck people praise God because Jesus has been given such authority. The centurion with a dying servant understands authority and knows that Jesus has it—he has faith that Jesus can simply say the word and the man will be healed. Jesus, in turn, makes this soldier an example of great faith. During Jesus' final week on Earth, after he throws the money changers and animal sellers from the temple, the temple officials say to him, "Tell us by what authority you are doing these things" (Luke 20:2). He refuses to do so because they will not say whether the work of his forerunner, John the Baptist, is of God or just of man.

When Jesus sends his twelve disciples out on a mission, he gives them authority to drive out evil spirits and to heal every disease, even before they are baptized with the Holy Spirit. After his resur-rection, Jesus tells his disciples that he has been given all authority in Heaven and on Earth, so he can tell them to go out into the entire world, in widening circles, to make new Christian disciples. Jesus had the authority, the right, to say and do what he did. Not only should we call him Lord but we should actually do what he tells us to do.

Jesus also has the ability, the power (*dunamis*[6]), to actually accomplish the Father's will. In Daniel 7:14 we find a "son of man" going to God the Father on the clouds of Heaven, then being given authority, glory, and sovereign power so that all nations will worship and obey him. John the Baptist contrasts his baptism in water for repentance with baptism by the Holy Spirit, which is associated with the coming one. When Jesus returns from facing the devil's temptations in the wilderness, he walks in the power of the Spirit (Luke 4:14). Later, people try to touch him because power comes from Jesus and heals them all (Luke 6:19). After Jesus' ascension to the Father, Peter summarizes Jesus' ministry in this way: "God anointed Jesus with the Holy Spirit and power, and he went around doing good and healing all who were under the power of the devil" (Acts 10:38). That ministry resulted in Jesus' execution! As a retired physicist who believes in the healing ministry, I want to note that the power by which Jesus healed many was not the human-controlled manipulation of an impersonal force involving energy patterns, as in Reiki or Qigong, but God's personal action in our lives. Later, we will learn that this personal power is available to Christians today.

Jesus not only had abundant authority and power for his healing ministry, he also was motivated by compassion and the agape kind of love. In Psalm 72 (Psalm of Solomon), which begins with a request that God "endow the king with his justice, the royal son with his righteousness," we find a very expansive description of the king's reign, which may also point to a later ruler who will be a blessing to all nations. In verses 12–13 we read, "For he will deliver the needy who cry out, the afflicted that have no one to help. He will take pity on the weak and the needy and save the needy from death." Then, in Psalm 103:13, the Psalmist likens the compassion of the Lord for those who fear the Lord to the compassion of a (good) human father for his children. Even a mother might forget the baby at her breast and have no compassion for her child, but God will never forget his people (Isa. 49:15). Micah prophesies about a coming day when God will again have compassion on Israel by treading the sins of the Israelites underfoot and throwing their iniquities into the sea (Mic. 7:19).

So, when Jesus sees the crowds, he has "compassion on them, because they were harassed and helpless, like sheep without a shepherd and healed their sick" (Matt. 9:36). This is a deep inward response which involved his whole being. After a leprosy-afflicted man says that Jesus can heal him if he wants to, Jesus is filled with compassion and says, "I am willing" as he touches the unclean man and declares him clean. Though two blind men in Jericho first have to specify what they want from Jesus, he touches their eyes with compassion and they are healed. Jesus' parable of the prodigal son uses compassion for the way the father, representing the heavenly Father, feels about his son (Luke 15:20)!

Jesus was sent to Earth because God the Father so loved the world that he gave his only Son, who came voluntarily to live and die among us. Jesus loved his disciples, his friend Lazarus, and the rich young ruler who wouldn't part with his money in order to begin following him. As Jesus is about to die and reveal the extent of his sacrificial love for all people, Jesus tells his disciples, "Love one another, as I have loved you. Greater love has no one than this, that he lay down his life for his friends" (John 13:34, 15:13). Years later, Paul asks, "Who will be able to separate us from that love of God which is in Christ Jesus?" (Rom. 8:28). We cannot understand how wide, long, high, and deep is the love of Christ by which he made provision for our salvation, including our healing; but we are right to see healing as an expression of God's love and mercy.

The Gospels also provide numerous examples of Jesus' attitudes. He responds to the blind man/men who appeals to the son of David for mercy and, after challenging the Canaanite woman who has a demonized daughter, Jesus sets her daughter free. He also shows mercy to the distraught father who has a demonized, epileptic son. After the Gadarene demoniac is set free and restored to his right mind, Jesus tells him to proclaim to his family how much the Lord had done for him because he had mercy on him. Jesus is merciful and urges us to be merciful like his Father in Heaven: "Jesus was made like his Jewish brothers in every way, that he might become a merciful and faithful high priest and make atonement for our sins" (Heb. 2:17).

I believe that Jesus not only preached good news but also did miraculous works so that those who encounter him will believe in him, make personal commitments to him, and become his disciples, thereby coming under his gracious, loving reign. In Mark's action-packed version of the good news, which includes many uses of the word "immediately," we hear Jesus calling, "The time has come, the kingdom of God is near. Repent and believe the good news" (Mark 1:15). In his parable of the various soils, those along the hard path hear the word Jesus sows, but the devil takes away the seed before they can believe and be saved. Jesus helps the synagogue ruler whose daughter had died and the man with a demonized boy to believe before he heals their children. Jesus tells Nicodemus that whoever believes in the Son already has eternal life, but God's wrath remains on those who don't. After the sinful, isolated woman at the well hears Jesus and responds, she immediately tells the townspeople about him. They react positively, with curiosity, then fully believe that Jesus is the savior of the world (John 4:42). Later, Jesus urges other listeners to not believe unless he is doing what the Father does. If Jesus does what the Father does, then people should believe in the miracles and understand that the Father is within Jesus (John 10:37–38). Experiencing Jesus through his preaching, teaching, and miraculous healings (as well as through works of nature, which are consistent with the known nature of God) should move people toward faith and commitment in the God-man who carries them out.

Inevitably, a man who is sinless and pure, who knows even our thoughts, and who challenges our hypocrisy is noticed and attacked. The same is true today of godly, spirit-filled, evangelical disciples of Jesus. Jesus came as a light shining in darkness for those huddling in the shadow of death (Luke 1:79). Light has come into the world, but men prefer darkness, which can hide their evil deeds. When Jesus drives out demons, he does so by the Spirit of God and the finger of God, so that it is God's reign that is overcoming evil. He is the one who truly sets us free and makes us whole (John 8:36) even if we are under the power of the devil (Acts 10:38).

No one has faced such a barrage of temptation from Satan as Jesus did, but he never gave in. Even after Judas's betrayal, Peter's denial of his master, and the scattering of his flock, Jesus obeys God and dies on the cross so that we may be saved. Jesus won the crucial battle! Then, God raised him on the third day! His victory encourages Christians as they proclaim the good news, participate in healing ministry, and observe what God is doing today in our midst, even if others refuse to listen, see or perceive.

When Jesus was challenged by skeptical religious authorities who demanded some miraculous sign that they may see it and believe, after he has already healed and set so many free, Jesus refuses to cooperate. The only sign they will get will be the sign of Jonah. As the unwilling prophet was hidden in the whale, Jesus will be hidden in the ground for three days. Even when faced with the man born blind but now seeing, the Pharisees continue to call Jesus a sinner because he violated their Sabbath traditions when he healed the man. They ridicule and throw the formerly blind man out after he bests them in argument. Then, Jesus's raising of Lazarus only accelerates their plans to destroy our Savior. Some people don't or can't believe, because they refuse to be Jesus' sheep.

In their listening but not really hearing, or their obstinacy, non-believers are once again fulfilling Isaiah's words. The Gospel provides not only the words of Jesus but also accounts of God's mighty actions. Jesus expects his listeners to respond to his words and works by putting their trust in him rather than in religion. He is not an illusionist who tricks gullible people or a quack. Although amazement and awe routinely follow Jesus' healings, he expects people to react in the long run by becoming disciples, not by getting tickets for the next show. The impact of Jesus' mighty works of healing, deliverance, and provision in the wilderness validate and support the good news and thus fulfill the Scriptures.

Members of established religious parties in Jesus' day did not like him. He didn't have a degree from one of their rabbinic schools but taught authoritatively. He loved sinners, including those who were poor, marginal, or outcasts—even Samaritans! Jesus also healed people on the Sabbath day, right in the synagogues. Jesus was widely popular among the people of the land, and he routinely bested officials when responding to their challenges or offering challenges of his own! Jesus sometimes made certain that those who were healed on the Sabbath(including the man born blind) knew who he was. As a good physician who makes house calls, Jesus healed people wherever he saw the need and heard the Father's approbation. I consider the confrontations Jesus encountered with his enemies to be unfortunate consequence, the fallout of his ministry.

As I come to the end of this chapter, I understand that many people want simple answers to their questions about healing. I have not attempted to tell you what were the most important factors or rationales motivating Jesus to heal so many sick and demonized people. Yet, cumulatively, these reasons give us solid evidence for the reality and validity of his healing ministry, and point to the possibility that such a ministry not only can but should continue in the Church, which is the Body of Christ.

Chapter 3

The Holy Spirit and the Ministry of Jesus and His Disciples

The Holy Spirit and the Ministries of Jesus

When Jesus spoke and acted with authority and with God's power to heal the sick and disabled, he set people free from demonic oppression, then rebuked and stilled the storm on the Sea of Galilee. Were these mighty works primarily related to his divine nature as the Son of God, or to the person and power of the Holy Spirit? When Jesus humbled himself to be born of a virgin, he took on the form of a servant and became obedient to death (Phil. 2:5–11), even death on the cross for our sins. Had he laid aside the abilities that had already been his from the creation? I do not believe that he ceased to be the divine Son of God. I believe that his healing ministry was performed in such a way that Spirit-filled, empowered Christians, forming the Body of Christ, might do similar or even greater works, after Jesus' resurrection and ascension. Let's explore the role of the Holy Spirit in the Gospels, book of Acts, and the Epistles.

In chapter 2, we considered several explanations for why Jesus of Nazareth engaged in a healing and deliverance ministry. There are also significant Hebrew Scriptures, primarily in Isaiah, that relate the personality and ministry of the coming anointed one to the work of the Spirit of God in his life. When, through Isaiah, the threatened king Ahaz of Judah is given an opportunity to ask the Lord for a sign, whether it should come up from the depths or down from the heights, Jesus refuses to provide a sign but Isaiah is given one anyway: "The virgin will be with child and will give birth to a son, and you will call him Immanuel, meaning 'God with us'" (Isa. 7:14). The prophet then speaks of darkness in the land of Zebulun and Naphtali being replaced by God's light after heavy burdens are broken off: "For to us a child is born, to us a child is given and the government will be on his shoulders. And he will be called Wonderful Counselor, Mighty God, Everlasting Father, Prince of Peace" (Isa. 9:6–7). His just and righteous kingdom will continue forever. These epithets pointing to the divinity of the coming King were not commonly used in Israel. These words are followed by a prophecy that a shoot and branch would come up from the cut-off stump of Jesse's tree. This indicates a return of the Davidic dynasty, which seemingly ended forever during the Babylonian exile that began around 587 B.C. This new ruler would bear fruit because the sevenfold Spirit of the Lord, of Yahweh, would rest on him. The Spirit would give him wisdom, understanding, counsel, power, knowledge, and reverence for the Lord, who is his delight (Isa. 11:1–3). After the wicked are slain by the "rod of his mouth" the peaceable, safe kingdom will finally break out on the Earth. This will occur as the knowledge of God becomes universal and all the Jewish exiles are restored to their land, along with many others who are attracted by the glory of God.

It was in fact normal for leaders in Israel—kings, priests, and prophets—to not only be anointed outwardly by special preparations of olive oil with spices but also by the Holy Spirit of God. When Moses, exhausted by the burden of the people (which numbered over 500,000), complains to God, the Lord has him bring together seventy elders so that the Spirit that is on Moses can also be on them. When the Spirit comes upon sixty-eight punctual elders and two tardy elders in the camp, they prophesy. When a young man protests about the two individuals, Moses says that he wishes that all of the Lord's people would be prophets because the Spirit of God rests on them (Num. 11:29). These elders wisely deal with the bulk of legal matters and other disputes among the people. Before Moses dies in the wilderness because of his earlier disobedience, he is told to lay his hand on Joshua and commission him as the new leader of Israel. Joshua is filled with the spirit of wisdom (Num. 27:18, Deut. 34:9) and leads God's people through the Jordan River into the promised land.

After the conquest or resettlement of Canaan by the descendants of the Jews who left Egypt and the chaotic ups and downs of the time of the Judges, the people want a king. Samuel, the final judge, is not happy about this; however, the people get what they want. Saul, the Son of Kish, is chosen and not only begins to prophesy when he meets a band of prophets but is for a time changed into a different man. Later, controlled by another spirit, Saul tries to kill David, son of Jesse, out of jealousy. He refuses to wait for Samuel to carry out a sacrifice, and fails to terminate the Amalekites. Ultimately, Saul and his sons die in a battle against the Philistines.

While mourning Saul's failures, Samuel is sent by God to Jesse in order to quietly anoint the next ruler of Israel. As the sons parade by Samuel, God keeps saying no. When Samuel finds out there is one more candidate, a boy named David, who had been minding the sheep, he has Jesse get the boy. Then God tells Samuel that David is the right one. Samuel takes the horn of oil and anoints David. From that day on, the Spirit of God comes on David in power. In seventeen years, David will finally become king of all Israel. Though far from perfect, David is the best king or anointed one of God for over a thousand years. After he sins with Bathsheba and kills her husband, David prays, "Do not cast me from your presence or take your Holy Spirit from me. Restore to me the joy of your salvation and grant me a willing spirit, to sustain me" (Ps. 51:11–12). Late in life, David says, "The Spirit of the Lord spoke through me; his word was on my tongue" (1 Sam. 23:2). Many kings of Israel or Judah fell far short of David, who was a man after God's heart.

Returning to Isaiah, chapter 42, we find the first of the Servant Songs. It seems to be describing a special servant of Yahweh, rather than the nation as a whole. With pride, God says: "Here is my servant, whom I uphold, my chosen one in whom I delight; I will put my Spirit on him and he will bring justice to the nations" (Isa. 42:1). We hear this very passage again in the voice of the Father at Jesus' baptism and transfiguration. The servant of Yahweh will neither cry out loudly in the streets nor deal harshly with those who are weak and wounded, bruised, easily snapped reeds, or smoldering wicks, whose light and heat are almost extinguished. Indeed, Jesus expresses his care for the poor, marginalized, and wounded of first-century Palestine. As the suffering servant passage in Isaiah 52–53 shows, the servant would go meekly, like a voiceless lamb, to his death. This death would set us free from guilt, condemnation, shame, and our infirmities. Indeed, these passages are so serious, so grim, that few Jews think of associating them with the Messiah, whom they expect to be a victorious, military, political king like David.

Chief among the passages from Isaiah, which are applicable to Jesus, is the one that he chooses to read in his hometown synagogue. This occurs shortly after he is baptized by his cousin John and is tempted by Satan in the wilderness (Luke 4:16–20). Luke records his reading as "The Spirit of the Lord is on me, because he has anointed me to preach good news to the poor. He has sent me to proclaim freedom for the prisoners and recovery of sight for the blind to release the oppressed, to proclaim the year of the Lord's favor." In Isaiah 61, we read further: ". . . and the day of vengeance of our God, to comfort all who mourn, and provide for those who grieve in Zion—to bestow on them a crown of beauty instead of ashes, the oil of gladness instead of mourning, and a garment of praise instead of a spirit of despair" (Isa. 61:1–3). Jesus shocks his audience when he sits down to preach and then says, "Today this Scripture is fulfilled in your hearing!" In other words, Jesus is the Messiah, the Christ, the anointed one of God, the expected king. Jesus' surprised listeners are not only unable to square his statement with their memories of the carpenter's son, but they also fulfill Jesus' statement that a prophet will not be accepted in his hometown. They try to kill him after he speaks about God helping Gentiles instead of his own people. The fulfillment of Isaiah 61 might not only involve changes in the situation of poor, sick, and marginalized people in Judea (as a result of alterations in government, laws, institutions, and parties) but also involve an interior change in people as they develop a personal relationship with the Messiah, are healed physically and emotionally, and then live new lives. Though Isaiah didn't know anything about inner healing of past wounds, the passage is certainly relevant to those involved in such ministry. Jesus is the one anointed to fulfill the prophecies of Isaiah.

The same Holy Spirit that descends on Jesus as he is being baptized by John in the Jordan River had been actively involved in his conception, birth, and growth. The Spirit also influenced the lives of Jesus' family and those who eagerly awaited Jesus' coming. Zechariah and Elizabeth, well along in years and childless, had been enabled to bear a son who would be filled with the Holy Spirit from birth (Luke 1:15). When Gabriel tells Mary that she will bear a son named Jesus who will be called the Son of the Most High and will reign on David's throne, she asks how this could happen, since she is a virgin. The angel tells her that the Holy Spirit will come on her and the power of the Most High will overshadow her, so the holy one born will be called the Son of God (Luke 1:35). Mary visits her cousin Elizabeth after finding it difficult to explain what has happened to her. When she arrives, John, the future baptizer, leaps for joy within his mother. Elizabeth exclaims, "Blessed are you among women, and blessed is the child you will bear" (Luke 1:42). Mary then praises God with words enshrined as the Magnificat (Luke 1:47–55).

Joseph decides to put Mary quietly away after he learns that she is pregnant but not by him. However, an angel tells Joseph that the baby within Mary had been conceived by the Holy Spirit (Matt. 1:22–21). After his birth in the stable, when Jesus is presented at the temple, Simeon and Anna praise God and identify Jesus as the Savior and Redeemer of Israel.

About twenty-seven years later, John begins to preach a baptism of repentance for the forgiveness of sins (Mark 1:4) at the River Jordan. This results in hundreds confessing their sins as they are baptized. John points forward to the king, who soon appears. "I baptize you with water for repentance. But after me (in time) will come one who is more powerful than I, whose sandals I am not fit to carry. He will baptize with the Holy Spirit and with fire" (Matt. 3:11 and parallels). John proclaims repentance in light of the coming reign of God.

When Jesus appears at the Jordan River to be baptized, John tries to deter him, but Jesus goes into the waters in identification with us sinners. As Jesus leaves the river, praying, he sees Heaven opening, giving visible access to God's throne room. He hears the Father's voice quoting the Scriptures to affirm Jesus as his Son: "You are my Son, whom I love; with you I am well pleased" (Luke 3:22). More importantly, Jesus and John see the Holy Spirit descend on Jesus like a fluttering dove and then remain on him. In fact, God had told John that this would be the sign by which he would recognize this expected greater one (John 1:31–33). We cannot say how many others knew what had happened, but John rejoices at the coming of the bridegroom for his bride, the Church, even as his popularity declines. John also identifies Jesus as the Lamb of God, who takes away the sins of the world. According to John 3:34, Jesus speaks the words of God, for God gives him the Spirit without any limitations.

Immediately after his baptism, Jesus, full of the Holy Spirit, is led by that same Spirit into the desert, where he fasts for forty days. He grows very weak in his humanity while facing three difficult temptations: to satisfy his own hunger, to do something spectacular to win the crowd, or to avoid the cross for earthly glory. Surprisingly, Jesus not only triumphs over the devil's temptations by using the Word of God but returns to Galilee in the power of the Spirit (Luke 4:14). He amazes his listeners in Capernaum with his personal authority in teaching and by setting a demonized man free (Mark 1:21–28). He then travels to his hometown of Nazareth to tell the people there that his ministry fulfills Isaiah 61.

The power of God was coming from Jesus and healing all the sick he encounters, including a multitude near Tyre (Luke 6:17). According to Matthew 12, after challenging the religious leaders and healing a man with a shriveled hand, Jesus travels through the Galilean countryside and heals all the sick who find him but tells them not to reveal his identity. Matthew states that these actions and words fulfill the prophecy in Isaiah 42, quoted earlier, about the one upon whom God would place his spirit while expressing delight in him!

We may well ask, What was the source of Jesus' outstanding healing and authority? The religious leaders, especially the Pharisees (who opposed Jesus because he performed healings on the Sabbath, formed friendships with sinners and tax collectors, and was successful in his ministry), accused Jesus of setting people free from demons through Beelzebub, a chief demon. Here is one example: "Then they brought a demon-possessed man who was blind and mute, and Jesus healed him, so that he could both talk and see. All the people were astonished and said, 'Could this be the Son of

David?' But when the Pharisees heard this, they said, 'It is only by Beelzebub, the prince of demons, that this fellow drives out demons'" (Matt. 12:22–25).

Based on their monotheistic religion, Jewish religious leaders would have denied the existence and powers of multiple personal centers in the godhead which were doing the healing. They would rather attribute these healings to evil forces. Jesus immediately showed the illogic of their position. A seriously divided kingdom or family cannot stand. Therefore, if demons are being cast out by another demon, even if that demon is Satan, the kingdom of evil will collapse. But Jesus gives the true alternative: "But if I drive out demons by the Spirit of God, then the kingdom (reign) of God has come upon you" (Mark 12:28). According to Luke, Jesus explains what is really happening: "When a strong man, fully armed, guards his own house, his possessions are safe. But when someone stronger attacks and overpowers him, he takes away the armor in which the man trusted and divides up the spoils" (Luke 11:21–22). Jesus has been despoiling the kingdom of evil. Then Jesus warns these officials that to blaspheme against the Holy Spirit of God by attributing Jesus' works to evil is to commit an unpardonable sin. In regard to the Christian movement, Gamaliel later says that if such a movement were from man, it would fail, but if from God, even the Jewish council would not be able to stop it. Christians believed that God was indeed at work in Jesus and among them as they followed him.

One of the clearest Scriptures connecting the work of the Holy Spirit through Jesus and healing is found in Acts 10:38 within Peter's message to Cornelius, a God-fearing centurion, and his other Gentile friends. Peter tells them, "How God anointed Jesus of Nazareth with the Holy Spirit and power, and how he went around doing good |works| and healing all who were under the power of the devil, because God was with him." As Peter goes on to tell them about Jesus' death and resurrection, his hearers come to faith and the Holy Spirit sovereignly falls upon them. They are baptized and included in this new movement.

Jesus is anointed and empowered for a healing ministry. His ministry also freed people who were under the power and reign of evil in their lives. (This is not to specify what proportion of illnesses, infirmities, or diseases are caused by demons rather than by a host of other factors, which were unknown in the first century.) Though Jesus was a good deed-doer in the best sense, he was nevertheless killed, and then rose on the third day.

The passages discussed so far in this chapter indicate that the Holy Spirit of God had clearly been involved in the life and healing ministry of Jesus, as He will be in our lives. We cannot actually estimate the number of times Jesus' healings were accomplished through his own divine nature or through the Spirit. In some ways, Jesus may have humbled himself by not doing his mighty works except through the power of the Holy Spirit.

However, in his early encounters with demons that were oppressing or indwelling human beings, the demons defensively asserted that they knew who Jesus really was; namely, the "Holy one of God" (Mark 1:21). His usual tactic, while casting them out, was to silence or muzzle them, keeping them from prematurely identifying him as the Anointed One, the Son of the Living God. Jesus usually called himself 'the son of man' as God had addressed Ezekiel (Ezek 7:14) but points to Dan 7:13 at his trial before the Sanhedrin.

Overall, we believe that God was working powerfully in the preaching, teaching, healing, and deliverance ministries of Jesus the Christ, without any hindrances. Though they may have taken different roles at various times, the Father, Son, and Holy Spirit worked in perfect harmony to redeem and transform humankind and will create new Heavens and a new Earth. Is it possible for Christians to be caught up in such movements and ministries of God, resulting in a spreading Gospel wave, carried by Spirit-endowed believers?

The Holy Spirit and the Ministry of the Disciples

I am personally interested in finding out whether healings that are carried out by believers follow a pattern similar to that of healings carried out by Jesus, including those associated with the activity of the Holy Spirit. This is not to limit God's healing activity through Christians who might not identify themselves as Spirit-filled, or as God uses the healing pattern of James 5:14–16 with established elders. I will attempt to use the New Testament to answer these questions.

According to Mark, the earliest Gospel, Jesus sent the twelve apostles into ministry sometime before Peter's confession of faith at Caesarea Philippi and the transfiguration of Jesus, which is recounted near the midpoint of the Gospel account. The accounts of Jesus sending out the twelve apostles are found in Matthew 10, Mark 6, and Luke 9. Additionally, there is an account of Jesus sending out seventy-two individuals. When I was teaching physics, I always gave my students instructions before they began their experiments, hoping they would pay attention. Likewise, Jesus prepared his twelve apostles before sending them out in advance of his visiting many towns in Israel. Clearly, our relationship with God through his Son Jesus Christ, in truth and spirit, is the basis for any possible Christian ministry.

Before he gives either group practical instructions for the way they are to travel, minister, find accommodations, and deal with the reactions of townspeople, Jesus gives them authority to drive out unclean spirits (demons) and to heal diseases and sickness. Luke indicates that the twelve also received power for this ministry.) They are to go only to the lost sheep of Israel (Matt. 10:6), preach the good news of the kingdom (reign) of God and call people to repentance as they heal the sick, cleanse lepers, drive out demons, and even raise the dead. They are to go out as Jesus' commissioned representatives or ambassadors, then do the things that Jesus had been doing since his baptism. They go in pairs, without baggage, without money to purchase their own lodging or meals. They rely on the goodwill hospitality of townspeople. While obeying Jesus, they discover that God actually works through them in wonderful ways. Jesus' own authority, or right to minister, had somehow been transmitted to them, and God's power is evident as people are healed or set free. This takes place despite their incomplete understanding of who Jesus is or of God's plan that his Son would die on the cross for their and our sins. One would betray Jesus and then commit suicide, another would deny Jesus, and the rest would flee before being surprised by the Resurrection. Jesus had not yet breathed on them, telling them to "Receive the Holy Spirit" (John 20:22). They had not yet experienced the baptism with the Holy Spirit at Pentecost or the subsequent infillings. Nevertheless, their ministry is successful, and they report to Jesus what they had done (Luke 9:12).

Somewhat later, Jesus appoints seventy-two other people to be sent out (*apostled*, sent with a mission) two by two as his advance agents to every place and town where he is preparing to go (Luke 10:1). Jesus states that the harvest had been abundant but that the workers are few. He tells them to ask the lord of the harvest to send out workers, then Jesus makes his hearers part of the answer to their own prayers. They are to travel light, accept the first offer of hospitality, proclaim peace (shalom) to the house, and stay there. They are to proclaim the near presence of God's reign and to heal the sick. If they are not welcomed, they are to wipe the dust from their sandals as a testimony against those who do not welcome them and to warn the unreceptive again of the proximity of God's kingdom, which requires a response. Rejecting his workers and representatives is equivalent to rejecting Jesus himself.

I am intrigued by the fact that these workers are completely unknown to us. Were they part of a larger group of disciples who had been following Jesus since John the Baptist's imprisonment, or were they individuals who had been healed recently? Were members of the various religious parties or local officials among them? Were they all unmarried men, or could there have been married couples among them?

When the seventy-two return with joy, they tell Jesus that even the demons had submitted to them in Jesus' name. The name of Jesus did and still does carry significant authority when used by Christians. Jesus states that he has given them authority to trample on snakes and scorpions in the wilderness and to overcome the power of their spiritual enemies (see Ephesians 6), and nothing will harm them. Indeed, he sees Satan falling like lightning during their mission. Yet, they should rejoice more over the fact that their names have been written in Heaven, in the book of salvation, than about their successes. Jesus, full of joy in the Holy Spirit, rejoices that God has gladly revealed these things to spiritual babes, or young children, while hiding them from the wise and learned of his day. The Father has committed everything to his Son, so that we cannot know God unless the Son reveals him to us! The disciples, through these missions, begin to realize that they might actually be able to do the same works of healing and deliverance that are the hallmark of Jesus' ministry. Indeed, according to the Gospel of John, Jesus tells his disciples, "I tell you the truth, anyone who has faith in me will do what I have been doing. He will do even greater things than these, because I am going to the Father. And I will do whatever you ask in my name, so that the Son may bring glory to the Father" (John 14:12–13).

Yet, despite their early successes in preaching and healing, Jesus' disciples misunderstand the reality of Jesus' purpose in coming to die for the sins of the world, and they fail badly when he is arrested, tortured, and killed. They are slow to believe in his resurrection. They are unprepared to preach boldly or to fulfill their new callings without the earthly presence of their master and friend.

They need a new counselor, comforter, advocate, helper, and teacher resident within them. This Holy Spirit and his anointing are evident in the life and ministry of Jesus, but before his death, Jesus tells them: "Unless I go away, the Counselor will not come to you; but if I go, I will send him to you" (John 16:7). Instead of the Spirit being within a few leaders in the history of Israel, God wants his Spirit to be actively involved in the life of every member of his new people, the Church, the Body of Christ. Before his ascension, Jesus tells his followers to wait in the city of Jerusalem, for they will soon be baptized with the Holy Spirit and receive the personal power of God for mission and ministry throughout the world.

On the fiftieth day from his resurrection, coinciding with the Jewish festival of First Fruits, when the disciples are not only waiting in the upper room used for Jesus' last supper but are also spiritually united, they hear and feel a violent wind blowing through the building, see what seems to be fire separating into little flames over each believer, and are simultaneously filled with the Holy Spirit. His presence is manifested as the Galilean disciples begin speaking in the dialects and languages of the gathered crowd, whose members come from many nations. When someone suggests that these disciples are drunk, Peter explains that it is not only too early in the day to be drinking but, in fact, the Galileans' condition is a fulfillment of Joel 2:28–32, which prophecies that God will pour his Spirit on all people in the last days, resulting in prophecies, dreams, and visions. Many become believers that day, forming the nucleus of a new community described in Acts 2:42–48. When Peter and John see the man who had been lame from birth at the temple gate, they tell him they have no money and command him "In the name of Jesus Christ of Nazareth, walk" (Acts 3:6). The man's entrance into the temple courts causes such a reaction that Peter takes the opportunity to boldly preach about Jesus and his resurrection. Alarmed officials bring Peter and John before the Sanhedrin, which wants to find out "By what power or name did you do this?" (Acts 23). Luke tells us that Peter is filled with the Holy Spirit as he confidently answers this question. These disciples are clearly different after Pentecost! When the council members "see the courage of Peter and John and realized that they were unschooled, ordinary men, they were astonished and took note that these men had been with Jesus. We should recognize that the patterns of ministry that the apostles and other disciples had learned during their approximately three years with the Lord, as well as their whole direction, outlook, and views about God and his relationship with humankind, had been transformed. They have certainly learned much by watching, hearing, interacting, and participating with Jesus, but now they are empowered by the Spirit. In a short time, the apostles are performing miraculous signs and wonders among God's people near the temple (Acts 5:12). Even Peter's shadow heals the sick. When a group of Spirit-filled "deacons" are chosen, Stephen and Philip do great wonders and signs. Opposition, from a group of Jews outside Palestine infuriated by Stephen's message, leads to his early martyrdom.

We can see the same pattern repeated as God not only expands the Church geographically but also sovereignly includes Samaritans and Gentiles among those who call Jesus Lord. When the Church is scattered after Stephen's death, Phillip visits the Samaritans. He preaches about the kingdom and about Jesus, and then he heals the sick and sets demoniacs free, leading many to believe and then receive water baptism. When the apostles hear about this early fulfillment of Jesus' words, which are recorded in Acts 1:8, Peter and John visit them. "When they arrived, they prayed for them that they might receive the Holy Spirit, because the Holy Spirit had not yet come upon any of them; they had simply been baptized into the name of the Lord Jesus. Then Peter and John placed their hands on them, and they received the Holy Spirit" (Acts 8:15–16). It is likely that the presence and power of the Spirit have been manifested through various gifts. Later, when Peter is staying in Joppa with Simon the Tanner, he experiences a vision that teaches him to never call any person unclean. He is then told to go with the men who were just arriving to take him to Cornelius, a Roman centurion! When Peter begins to preach to these Gentiles, he tells them that God does not show favoritism and that Jesus had been anointed by the Holy Spirit, then healed people and set them free of the devil. God sovereignly interrupts Peter's sermon by baptizing the group in the Holy Spirit with various manifestations of the Spirit, including speaking in tongues. The Jewish believers, with Peter, are amazed that even Gentiles, like us, had received the Holy Spirit. These new believers receive water baptism in the name of Jesus after God's action. The elders of the Jerusalem Church have difficulty accepting this new reality but move toward acceptance by the conclusion of the Jerusalem council (Acts 15). Through God's sovereign action, a Jewish sect became a worldwide religion.

Saul, persecuting the Church after Stephen's martyrdom, is stopped and blinded on the road to Damascus. He is then shocked to discover that the one he had been fighting against was God's Son and his rightful Lord. Only after seeing a vision and being reassured does Ananias lay his hands on Saul, healing and transforming him and ending his physical and spiritual blindness. Saul is filled with the Holy Spirit and is then baptized with water. He immediately begins to preach the Gospel that he had opposed in Damascus. He spends a considerable time reaching a new understanding of his own Jewish background and this new reality before becoming Jesus' chief missionary to the Gentiles.

The book of Acts continues to record healings and deliverances that are similar to the work of Jesus yet individually different. Paul tells a man in Lystra, who had been lame from birth, to get up—and he does! This results in Paul and Barnabas almost being worshiped, until Jewish opponents arrive. In other cities, a fortune-telling slave girl is set free, two people are raised from the dead, and a shipwrecked apostle heals every sick person on an island after he himself had been bitten by a viper yet did not swell up or die.

I believe that one crucial reason for the power of the Holy Spirit, along with the good gifts that he distributes freely in our lives, is ministry. The Holy Spirit also baptizes us into the Body of Christ, gives us assurance of salvation, sets us apart, reminds us of Jesus' words, and leads us into all truth. We are not sinless, we are often wounded, with several limitations, but God's Holy Spirit of truth can enable us to so preach so that people are converted and to pray that people are set free and made whole, as the Body of Christ is built up. God wants all Christians to use their talents and gifts for God's glory.

I do not believe that Christians are able to live the Christian life on their own steam. The normal Christian life is a life of walking, empowerment, guidance, and provision by the Holy Spirit, with God's generous gifts being used and his fruits growing within to bless others. The healings that happen as we lay on hands and pray are accomplished by God using his "cracked pots." We must always keep in mind the personal but mysterious nature of the Holy Spirit, who operates in perfect union with God the Father and his only Son, Jesus Christ, for our salvation and transformation.

A List of Scriptures About the Holy Spirit in the Christian Life

1. "If you then, though you are evil, know how to give good gifts to your children, how much more will your Father in Heaven give the Holy Spirit to those who ask him!"(Luke 11:13)

2. "[Jesus answered,] I tell you the truth, no one can enter the kingdom of God unless he is born of water and the Spirit. Flesh gives birth to flesh, but the Spirit gives birth to spirit. The wind blows wherever it pleases. You hear its sound, but you cannot tell where it comes from or where it is going. So it is with everyone born of the Spirit." (John 3:5–6:8)

3. "But the Counselor, the Holy Spirit, whom the Father will send in my name, will teach you all things and remind you of everything I have said to you." (John 14:26)

4. "And with that he breathed on them and said, 'Receive the Holy Spirit.'" (John 20:22)

5. "For John baptized with water, but in a few days you will be baptized with the Holy Spirit. You will receive power when the Holy Spirit comes on you; and you will be my witnesses . . ." (Acts 1:5, 8)

6. "The disciples were filled with joy and with the Holy Spirit." (Acts 13:52)

7. "And hope does not disappoint us, because God has poured out his love into our hearts by the Holy Spirit, whom he has given us." (Rom. 5:5)

8. "The mind of sinful man is death, but the mind controlled by the Spirit is life and peace. . . . The Spirit himself testifies with our spirit that we are God's children." (Rom. 8:6, 16)

9. "Do you not know that your body is a temple of the Holy Spirit, who is in you, whom you have received from God? You are not your own." (1 Cor. 6:19)

10. "Now to each one the manifestation of the Spirit is given for the common good. To one there is given through the Spirit the message of wisdom, to another the message of knowledge by means of the same Spirit, to another faith by the same Spirit, to another gifts of healing by that one Spirit, to another miraculous powers, to another prophecy, to another distinguishing between spirits, to another speaking in different kinds of tongues, and to still another the interpretation of tongues. All these are the work of one and the same

Spirit, and he gives them to each one, just as he determines."
(1Cor. 12:7–11)

11. "So I say, live by the Spirit, and you will not gratify the
desires of the sinful nature. . . . The fruit of the Spirit is
love, joy, peace, patience, kindness, goodness, faithfulness,
gentleness, and self-control." (Gal. 5:16, 22)

12. "Do not get drunk on wine, which leads to debauchery.
Instead, be filled with the Spirit." (Eph. 5:18)

13. "The Spirit and the bride say, Come! . . . Whoever is thirsty,
let him come; and whoever wishes, and let him take the free
gift of the water of life." (Rev. 22:17)

Chapter 4

The Role of Faith in Healing

To what extent was belief, faith, or trust in Jesus of Nazareth a prerequisite for receiving healing from Jesus in the context of the Gospels, or through the ministry of the Apostles and other believers as recorded in the Book of Acts? Whose faith is correlated with a person's receiving healing: the faith of the sick or wounded person, the faith of his or her friends, or that of the person engaged in ministry to the person in need? Are there such requirements for faith that few may expect healing, or are we encouraged by Jesus and others to exercise faith as small as a mustard seed in the expectation of God's working in our lives? I will endeavor to base my results on the twenty-six individual accounts of healing in the Gospels and the nine individual accounts of healing or resuscitation in the book of Acts, plus the information that can be glean from the more general group healings. In Table 1 (found in chapter 1), I show that in individual Gospel accounts, Jesus either reacts to the expressed or implicit faith of the person in need or to the friends of that person, or he encourages someone's faith in eleven out of twenty-six healing events. The Gospel accounts of these group-healing encounters do not specifically mention faith, but they do indicate that individuals came to Jesus or their friends brought them to Jesus for healing. The healing accounts in Acts provide only one explicit reference to faith. I will now proceed through the individual accounts in the order listed in the initial International Order of St. Luke the Physician (OSL) study and Table 1.

In Mark, the earliest action-packed Gospel (without infancy narratives or large teaching blocks), a man suffering from leprosy (or some other skin disease) comes to Jesus, falls on his knees, and says: "If you are willing, you can make me clean (Mark 1:40)." This statement expresses the man's confidence in Jesus' ability to cleanse him as well as his recognition of Jesus' own freedom to decide whether to heal him. His statement mirrors our own primary questions: Can God heal me? Is God willing to heal me now, or later? In response to the leper, Jesus is filled with compassion, reaches out and touches the man, and says that he is willing to heal him. Immediately, as Mark says, the man's leprosy is cured. Now, the former leper is told to obey the Mosaic laws by going to the priest to certify his cleansing and to make the required sacrifices, which he does. However, he can't keep his cleansing a secret, so he spreads the news across town. In Matthew's compact parallel account, which follows the Sermon on the Mount, the leper calls Jesus Lord, and there is no mention of his telling other people about his cleansing. Luke, the physician, notes that the man had been covered with leprosy. We learn in Luke, however, that after being healed the man received the same orders as those reported in Mark, and we are told that the news spread so widely that crowds came to hear Jesus and to be healed.

There are two somewhat different accounts (Matt. 8:5–13, Luke 7:1–10) of the paralyzed and dying servant of a centurion being healed from a distance. The accounts may have been passed down through multiple traditions. In Luke, the centurion sends a group of Jewish elders to Jesus to ask him to heal the servant. They tell Jesus of the centurion's love for Israel and his work in building their synagogue, evidence that he deserves help. As Jesus approaches the centurion's home, the centurion sends his friends to tell Jesus that he is not worthy of having Jesus under his roof. He then expresses his faith in a way we will discuss. We may note the favorable way centurions are mentioned elsewhere in Luke-Acts. Matthew simply drops all references to interactions with elders or friends, and focuses on the essential dialog. However, he also includes Jesus' prediction that people would come from all directions and nations to feast with the patriarchs, while the proper subjects of the kingdom (reign) of God, the Jews, would be thrown out into outer darkness, due possibly to their not believing or trusting in Jesus.

In these accounts, the centurion asks Jesus not to enter his house. As a friend of the Jewish people, he was probably aware that if Jesus were to come onto his property he (Jesus) would be rendered ritually unclean or defiled. With real humility, the centurion also recognizes his essential unworthiness or inability to receive Jesus, and he does not wish to trouble Jesus with further journey. By calling Jesus Lord (kurios), the centurion may be indicating his recognition of Jesus' divinity.

Then follows the statement that reveals the centurion's faith: "Just say the word (Logos[7]) and my servant will be healed (cured)." The centurion then explains the basis for his confidence that a word from Jesus will result in healing. The centurion, an officer over approximately eighty soldiers, is himself under the authority of legates, tribunes, and prefects in the Roman army. He also has soldiers and servants under him, whom he can successfully command. Disobedience or rebellion within the ranks could even result in execution. When Jesus had first spoken in a synagogue, his listeners recognized his teaching authority and his act of casting a demon out of a man. Here, the centurion recognizes Jesus' authoritative ability to say the word, express the command, and his servant would be healed.

Jesus responds with astonishment and, I think, considerable joy: "I tell you the truth (amen)! I have not found anyone in Israel with such faith" (Matt. 8:10). In the Gospel according to Matthew (which emphasizes the limitation of the mission of Jesus and his disciples to the lost sheep of Israel, and repeatedly shows that Old Testament Scriptures had been fulfilled), Jesus points to the centurion's faith and a future worldwide spread of the Gospel. We also read of Jesus' command to the centurion and his declaration: "Go! It will be done just as you believed it would" (Matt. 8:13). The man goes home and is not surprised to find that his servant has been healed. After a short stop at Peter's home, where his mother-in-law is healed and people gather after the Sabbath is over for healing Then Jesus and his disciples return to Capernaum where "so many gathered that there was no room left, not even outside the door as he preached the word to them (Mark 2:2).

The healing of the paralytic in Capernaum illustrates the faith of the people who bring sick, weak, and demonized persons to the great physician, even at great difficulty to themselves. This event is significant enough that all three synoptic Gospels tell the story. Mark tells us that Jesus had been speaking the word to the crowd gathered at the house, while Luke begins by noting the presence of possibly hostile Pharisees and teachers of the law and the reality of the healing power of the Lord in their midst. Matthew chooses not to tell us about the efforts of the four mat bearers.

Already, Jesus has become popular enough that the house itself and the area outside its open front door and courtyard are jammed with people who are eager to listen and receive God's help. Four men who brought a paralytic man have serious difficulty getting him into the house, much less close to Jesus. However, they climb the exterior stairs to the flat roof, pull apart the clay tiles set across the roof beams, and manage to lower the paralytic man safely into the middle of the crowd, right in front of Jesus! They spare no effort in making sure that their neighbor and friend has an opportunity to be healed. They are even willing to act like robbers, going over the wall to get their friend into the kingdom (Matt. 11:12).

According to all three evangelists, Jesus "saw their faith" (Matt. 9:2, Mark 2:5, Luke 5:20) just as Paul later saw that another paralytic individual (in Lystra) had faith to be healed. Others—including the owners of the house that had been torn apart by the paralytic man's friends—probably reacted negatively to the disruption, falling debris, and sudden light. Jesus pays attention to the faith of the four friends and to the paralytic's real condition. Whether it had been the paralytic man's idea or that of his friends, the paralyzed man had enough faith to be brought to Jesus.

What comes out of Jesus' mouth surprises everyone: "Son, take heart, your sins are forgiven!" (Matt. 9:2). (Jesus says the same thing later to a woman who had lived a sinful life but had boldly entered a Pharisee's house to give Jesus a costly, loving present; Luke 7:47–8.).

Immediately, some of the scribes and Pharisees in the crowd react negatively in their minds, and their lips begin to move. They begin to say to themselves that Jesus is speaking against God, blaspheming him, because only God can forgive sins. (Their negativity probably changed the spiritual atmosphere.) Jesus hears their thoughts and challenges them: "Why do you entertain evil thoughts in your hearts? Why are you thinking these things? Which is easier: to say, 'Your sins are forgiven,' or to say, 'Get up and walk?'" Even if the man realized that his guilt was gone, no one else did. But when Jesus tells him to walk, the man experiences a new and obvious freedom and ability to rise, move, and walk in obedience to Jesus. The amazed, praising crowd recognize Jesus' authority to forgive sins and to set people free. We do not know whether the man's paralysis had been caused by a psychological reaction to extreme guilt, if it had been a judgment from God, or if it had been caused by a real, physical fall. But we do know that his need, his request, and the actions of four men resulted in his being made whole!

Two healing stories in the synoptic Gospels form a doublet: the raising of the synagogue president's daughter and the healing of a hemorrhaging woman (Matt. 9:18–26, Mark 5:22–43, Luke 8:40–56) with the second one inside the first. Luke, a physician himself, is kinder toward the failure of physicians to heal the woman than Mark.

In Matthew, Jairus (the ruler or president of the synagogue in Capernaum where Jesus' Galilean base for ministry had been located) goes to Jesus with an urgent request for help. He does this even though Jesus' authority and popularity, his fellowship with sinners, and his actions in performing healing works on the Sabbath are beginning to produce negative reactions among Jewish leaders. Jairus may have recognized that only Jesus could do anything to help him. So Jairus moves through the crowd, sees Jesus, falls at his feet in supplication, and begs Jesus to come to his house because his only child, his 12-year-old daughter (Luke) is dying. (Mark and Matthew include an additional discussion of Jesus putting his hands on the girl, so that she would be healed and live.) Jesus rises and follows Jairus but is interrupted by another desperate person. According to Mark and Luke, some people came from Jairus' house to tell him that his daughter is already dead. They then ask, Why bother the teacher anymore? As far as they are concerned, there is nothing more to be done except to bury the child and mourn her loss. But Jesus ignores them and tells Jairus, "Don't be afraid; just believe, and she will be healed (saved)." Jesus encourages him to not give up hope but to believe that his beloved daughter will be all right.

When Jesus and Jairus arrive at the house, a crowd of wailing mourners with accompanying flute players has already gathered, and emotions are running high. Jesus has the nerve to tell some of the mourners to either stop wailing or leave, because the girl is not dead but sleeping. They laugh at him bitterly because they know that the girl has died, that she is not breathing and has had no heartbeat for some minutes. Jesus enters the room where the girl's body is lying; he is accompanied only by his inner three disciples and the girl's parents. According to Mark, Jesus takes the girl's hand and says in Aramaic, "*Talitha koum!*" (meaning "Little girl, I say to you, get up!"). And the girl did! Luke describes the girl's spirit returning to her body in much the same way that many people today have described near-death experience. Jesus tells the girl's astonished parents to give her something to eat and warns them not to tell anyone what has taken place. Clearly, the girl's father had faith in Jesus' ability to heal, but he needed help to continue believing after the child had died.

In the middle of this account is a story about a woman who had been bleeding for twelve years. During this long period, she was considered as unclean as a leper, forbidden to touch people, unable to enter a synagogue or, especially, the court of women in God's holy temple. To reach Jesus, she had to keep her condition and identity a secret. "Doctor" Luke comments that "no one could heal her" (Luke 8:42). Mark (Mark 5:26–27) is much sharper: "She had suffered a great deal under the care of many doctors and she had spent all she had, yet instead of getting better she grew worse!" (Matthew doesn't mention the physicians at all.) Yes, we can do much more today; but the costs may be impossibly high. The woman's case also might have seemed hopeless, with people blaming her condition on her sinfulness. Centuries ago, Job was blamed for the disasters which fell upon him.

Nevertheless, the woman moves purposely through the crowd, behind Jesus, trying to touch his clothing by reaching between his disciples. The disciples are only aware of the crowd bumping into them as they try to protect Jesus. Later Mark learned from the disciples that the woman had been saying to herself: *If I just touch his clothes, his cloak, I will be healed!* Later, many people would touch Jesus' clothing and be healed or set free and the same was true of people who touched the apostle Paul's sweat rags while he made tents in Ephesus. But this woman is a pioneer. Somehow, her faith, her belief, allows her to act, and that action is met with positive results when she touches Jesus' garments.

Mark uses one of his favorite words ("Immediately") to describe the cessation of the woman's bleeding ("the fountain dried up"), and Luke mentions her feeling or knowing that she had been freed from her lengthy suffering ("scourge"). As she stands there or begins to move away, Jesus notices her! The crowds had been following Jesus and pressing, almost crushing, him—yet Jesus asks, "Who touched my clothes?" (Mark 5:30). Everyone in the crowd denies touching Jesus' clothing, and the disciples protest that the people are just crowding against him. Yet Jesus knows that someone has made personal contact with him, contact that had resulted in power flowing from him. Jesus looks around until the woman comes to him, falls at his feet, and tells him the whole truth about her healing. All three evangelists (Matthew, Mark and Luke) agree that Jesus told the woman that her faith had healed her. In this case, Jesus doesn't need to encourage the woman's faith, which had motivated her to take what might have been her only opportunity to be healed. Jesus calls her "daughter"—then tells her to be freed from her suffering and to go in peace. All three accounts use the verb "*sōzō*," which also means "saved," for the woman's healing and wholeness. This woman's faith and courage, which allowed her to overcome a serious and embarrassing condition, resulted in her being healed and accepted—and to return to society.

In Matthew 9:27–31 is a unique account of Jesus healing two blind men in Capernaum, which is somewhat similar to the account of Jesus healing two blind men in Jericho at the end of his ministry. in that both accounts say that the blind men cried to the Lord using the messianic title "Son of David." In the story, two blind men follow Jesus as best they can while crying out loudly, "Have mercy on us, Son of David" When Jesus goes indoors, they go to him and he asks them, "Do you believe that I am able to do this?" (Matt. 9:26–27). He neither specifies the action he is to perform nor asks them what they need, but he gives them an opportunity to express their faith that he can do what they want. They say, "Yes, certainly, Lord." Jesus then touches their eyes and says, "Let it be so or let it be done, according to your faith" (Matt 9:30). As the men open their eyes and begin to see, Jesus, breathing deeply, warns them sternly not to let anyone know about this miracle. Unfortunately, they can't be silent and instead spread the news all over Galilee and beyond! Their cry for mercy asks Jesus to act out of his compassion, sparing them from a fate they don't deserve. He gives them an easy question to answer because he does not want to turn them down.

As they go outside, a demonized man who is unable to speak is brought to Jesus. Jesus ejects the demon, and the man amazes the crowd that looks on by speaking clearly. Transporting someone into the presence of Jesus is often enough for that person to be healed, as was the case for the blind and mute demonized man (Matt. 12:22–23, Luke 11:14–15) who is brought by several people to Jesus and is cured. Spirits such as the one that had occupied and afflicted the man in this story are known to interfere with their victim's hearing; thankfully, through deliverance people can respond to the Gospel and other portions of the word of God. These demonic entities are probably more common today than we think.

The Gospel accounts do not indicate whether the man with the shriveled hand (Matt. 12:9–14, Mark 31–6, Luke 6:6–11) had any personal faith in Jesus or in his ability to heal. In fact, it seems apparent that this man was either planted by the religious authorities to challenge the healing work that Jesus had been performing on the Sabbath or was simply used by the religious authorities as an excuse to challenge Jesus about healing on the Sabbath. Jesus may have questioned the authorities before telling the man to stand up and stretch out his arm. In plain sight of all, the man's hand is completely restored, which motivates the Pharisees to get together to plot against Jesus. In some cases today, when a healing leader carries out a healing demonstration in agreement with God's will, he or she is backed by the Lord. In the same way, Luke's unique account of a woman who had been crippled for eighteen years (Luke 13:10–17) says nothing about positive faith. In this account, Jesus calls the woman forward and tells her that she has been set free from her infirmity. When he lays hands on her, she quickly straightens up with praises on her lips. The woman's infirmity had been, in fact, the result of Satan binding or tying her up in a very uncomfortable position.

On another Sabbath, Jesus is eating at an important Pharisee's home while others were watching him very carefully. By coincidence, a man with dropsy or edema is among the Pharisee's guests. In time, Jesus asks the dinner guests whether it is lawful to heal on the Sabbath and, receiving no answer, he grabs the afflicted man, heals him, and sends him home. He then gives his own argument for healing the man. We do not know whether the man had expressed any desire for healing or faith in Jesus.

Now, in Mark 7:24–30 and in Matthew 15: 22–28 we encounter a remarkably feisty Canaanite or Syro-Phoenician woman who approaches Jesus on behalf of her daughter, who has been badly demonized or is suffering with an unclean spirit. This encounter takes place in Gentile territory, in the vicinity of the Mediterranean Sea, close to Tyre. The woman enters the house where Jesus and his disciples are resting, falls at his feet, cries out, asks Jesus for mercy, and then tells him about her daughter's condition and begs him to drive the demon out. At first, Jesus says nothing while the disciples urge him to send the woman away so that they would not have to listen to her. His reply in Mark is less sharp than that recorded in Matthew, which includes his saying that he has been sent only to the lost sheep of Israel. Mark writes: "'First let the children eat all they want,' he told her, 'for it is not right to take the children's bread and toss it to their dogs'" (Mark 7:27). In other words, Jews were God's children, while Gentiles were "dogs" more like wild mastiffs than pampered pets. However, the woman comes right back, saying, "But even the dogs under the table eat the children's crumbs!" Neither the limitation in Jesus' mission nor the irritated disciples, nor even Jesus' rather sharp challenge would deter her. She would accept even healing crumbs if only her daughter were healed. According to Mark, Jesus says: "For such a reply, you may go! The demon has left your daughter." Mathew adds, "Woman, you have great faith! Your request is granted." Because the woman is able to find a way to meet Jesus' challenge, her daughter is set free from a distance and her mother is able to go home to find her daughter at peace. I don't think that the disciples would have done anything on their own to help this woman and her daughter. The woman behaved like the persistent widow before what seemed to be an unjust cynical judge, who turned out to be a merciful savior. This Canaanite woman ranks with the Centurion who had a dying servant as having expressed their notable faith in a creative way.

Using the Order of Saint Luke listing, we move to the blind man in Bethsaida, who requires two touches from Jesus. Having heard about Jesus in some way, some people bring this man to Jesus and beg him to touch the man. Instead, Jesus first takes the man outside the city, where he spits on the man's eyes, lays his hands on the man, and then asks him if he can see anything. The man reports seeing people like trees walking, which suggests that the man must have once been able to see. Jesus lays his hands on the man a second time, opening his eyes and restoring his sight. Jesus sends the man directly home rather than allowing him to travel through the village. Again, the Scriptures do not mention faith or trust, except to indicate that the man submitted to this unusual procedure. An earlier account of the deaf, almost mute man (Mark 7:32–37) follows a similar course.

Near the end of Jesus' ministry, as he travels along a sort of no-man's-land between Galilee and Samaria and is about to turn toward Jerusalem, he meets ten men who have leprosy. They properly remain at a distance from him as they raise their voices, saying, "Jesus, master, have mercy on us." Here, the verb "have" is an imperative. Jesus doesn't ask any questions but sends the men to the local Levitical priests, who can certify their conditions. Because they obey Jesus' command, all ten are cleansed before they reach their destination. However, one of the men, having seen that he has been healed, returns to Jesus, glorifying God loudly and then falling on his face before Jesus to thank him. Jesus says, "Were there not ten cleansed? Where are the other nine? . . . Was no one found to return and give God praise except this foreigner?" (Luke 17:17–18). Jesus then tells the man to get up and go because his faith has saved him (*sōzō*)—his faith has made him well. Each of the ten men had faith enough to cry out to Jesus and then obey him. Only the Samaritan, by his willingness to return to thank Jesus, received wholeness from the Lord.

Of all the accounts of the father who brought his epileptic, demonized son to Jesus, I find Mark's account most interesting because it reveals the state of the father and Jesus' encouragement. This encounter occurs shortly after Peter, James, and John witness the glory of the transfigured Jesus, along with the appearances of Moses and Elijah, on Mount Tabor. Soon enough, elation kept secret is followed by crowds, critics, and chaos. The people surge toward Jesus, who observes the other disciples and the law teachers arguing with each other. When Jesus asks them what they are arguing about, the father pipes up: "I brought you my son, who has a spirit that has robbed him of speech. Whenever it seizes him, it throws him to the ground. He foams at the mouth, gnashes his teeth, and becomes rigid. I asked your disciples to drive out the spirit, but they could not" (Mark 9:17). After speaking against an unbelieving, perverse generation and asking how long he would stay with them or put up with them, Jesus has the boy brought to him and, as often happened, the agitated spirit manifests its presence. Seeing this, Jesus asks how long the boy had been that way. . The father implores: "But if you can do anything, take pity on us." Jesus immediately challenges him, saying, "If you can? Everything is possible for him who believes!" The father rises to the opportunity, saying, "I do believe; help me overcome my unbelief, my lack of faith." That is sufficient for Jesus. He identifies the spirit that possesses the boy and commands it to leave and never return. After a final convulsion, the boy seems dead, but Jesus helps him up to begin a normal life. On another occasion, Jesus warns people about leaving their spiritual house empty, making it possible for an unclean spirit to bring other spirits and make the human's condition much worse. With this in mind, I urge people who are set free to receive an infilling of the Holy Spirit as well as inner-healing ministry for complete restoration.

When Jesus is alone with his disciples, they ask him why they could not drive the spirit out. They had previously been successful while on their mission to the lost people of Israel, but in this new situation, with critics watching, nothing had happened. Jesus replies that this (difficult) kind of demon can only be driven out by prayer. (Some manuscripts add fasting, which I see as very helpful.) In Matthew's shorter account of this incident, Jesus blames the disciples' failure on their tiny faith. Even faith the size of a mustard seed would enable the disciples to tell the mountain to move, and it would obey! We have a real advantage now, because of the victory, ascension, and glorification of Jesus Christ after his sacrificial death on the cross for us, which increases our faith. Many people today, especially those coming from false religions or the occult, need to be freed from demonic oppression, which prevents them from hearing and responding to the Gospel.

When Jesus identifies a man who had born blind (John 9:1–38), the disciples ask whether it was the blind man's own sin, or that of his parents, that had caused the man's blindness. Their assumption, also found in other Scriptures, is that the man's blindness is a curse, a punishment, or consequence of sin. We might wonder whether to pray for the healing of a person whose lifestyle has led to his or her suffering. Jesus refuses to blame the man for his affliction but instead indicates that the man had been blinded "so that the work of

God would be demonstrated in his life (John 9:3)." Before darkness falls, Jesus and his disciples must do the work of the Father who had sent Jesus. As long as he is in the world, he is the light of the world. Up to this moment, the blind man has played no role in the discussion. Then Jesus acts: he spits on the ground, makes mud from the spit and dirt, and applies the mud to the man's eyes. He then tells the man to go and wash in the pool, *Siloam*. Alone, or with help, the man reaches the pool, washes, and can see! (It may have taken him a while to learn how to sort out the new impressions entering his brain!)

Clearly, this is an outstanding, unusual miracle. Suddenly, this man's life is exciting and challenging. Some of his neighbors don't believe that he is the former blind man. Some ask how he had been healed, which he recounts more than once! When he is taken to the Pharisees, the Pharisees conclude that Jesus is a sinner because he healed the man on the Sabbath. They react by bringing in the formerly blind man's parents, who identify him but won't say who performed the man's healing. The Pharisees tell the man to give glory to God by telling the truth. He wisely tries not to say anything beyond what he knows by experience, and he defeats the Pharisees when he says that Jesus could not have performed this unique miracle if he were a sinner! They retort that the man had been soaked in sin at birth, and they throw him out.

Finally, Jesus comes to the now-healed man and asks him if he believes in the son of man. The man indicates his willingness to believe if Jesus would identify him. When Jesus says that he is the son of man, the man says, "I believe" and worships Jesus. Jesus has come into the world so that those who are blind will see, while those who think they see will become blind. This great healing miracle, according to the Father's plan, has turned a lonely man into one of the greatest witnesses to the Gospel, both by irrefutable evidence and by his words. Only the raising of Lazarus would exceed this miracle. God had planned this encounter long before it had taken place.

Now we come to the blind beggar, whom Mark identifies as Bartimaeus, the son of Timaeus. Jesus, with his disciples and an accompanying crowd, is leaving Jericho and moving resolutely toward Jerusalem, where he will be acclaimed as a peaceful king by the people, opposed by leaders, condemned, and then executed. When this blind beggar hears the noise of the crowd coming toward him, he asks someone what is happening (Luke 18:36). When he learns that Jesus is approaching, he shouts, "Jesus, Lord, Son of David, have mercy on me!" (Mark 10:46). The leaders of the entourage and others in the crowd rebuke him and tell him to be quiet; but Bartimaeus keeps on shouting. Had he already heard about the man born blind? What would we have done in his place? Despite his grim march toward what Jesus called his hour, his time of suffering and death, Jesus stops. Then, he calls Bartimaeus and orders that the beggar be brought to him. The crowd encourages Bartimaeus to take courage and stand up. With alacrity and energy, he throws down his cloak and his coins, and approaches Jesus. (Only Matthew includes a second blind man in his narrative.)

Then Jesus asks Bartimaeus, "What do you want me to do for you?" (Mark 10:51). Bartimaeus could have asked for less, but he seeks it all: "Lord, I want to see!" (Mark 10:52). Faith includes asking for the things we need and not allowing ourselves to be discouraged by the opinions and comments of other people. According to Matthew, "Jesus touched Bartimaeus' eyes and restores his sight" (Matt 20:34). Both Mark and Luke note Jesus' statement that the formerly blind man had been healed by his faith. Rather than going home, this man becomes Jesus' disciple and follows him into the great city of Jerusalem. (How he must have wept when he saw Jesus dying on the hill called Golgotha!)

When Lazarus lay dying in Bethany (John 11: 1–15), his sisters Martha and Mary send someone to tell Jesus that his friend, whom Jesus loves, is sick. Jesus tells his disciples that Lazarus' sickness will not end in death but will glorify God, and he deliberately remains where the messenger for two more days. Jesus' statement that Lazarus had fallen asleep (John 11: 11–15) was misunderstood until Jesus said plainly that Lazarus was dead but this delay in their traveling happened so they would believe. Fatalistically, Thomas urges the disciples to go and die with Lazarus. By the time they arrive in Bethany, Lazarus has been entombed for four days.

Martha and Mary say to Jesus, "If you had been here, my brother would not have died" (John 11:21), and onlookers ask why Jesus hadn't prevented Lazarus' death. The disciples' faith, combined with their earlier experiences, assured the disciples that if Jesus had been there in time, then laid hands upon him or rebuked the disease, Lazarus would have been healed. (I don't think they had considered the possibility of his healing Lazarus from a distance.)

However, Jesus has done nothing, leaving the sisters confused, grieving, angry, and losing hope. Martha says, "But I know that even now God will give you whatever you ask" (John 11:22). Jesus tells her that her brother will rise again, in agreement with the doctrine of the Pharisees, but Martha assumes that it will be at the end of this age. Jesus surprises her by saying, "I am the resurrection and the life" Believers in Jesus will live spiritually even if they die physically, and if they live and believe in him, they will never die. When Jesus asks Mary if she believes this, she simply identifies him as the Christ, the Son of God.

Having gone with Mary to the tomb, Jesus weeps, then tells the people there to remove the stone from in front of the tomb. Practical Martha protests that by this time, after the spirit of the man has left, there would be a stench, but Jesus tells his disciples and the others who are standing around the tomb that if they believe then they will see the glory of God. In prayer, Jesus expresses his confidence that God has heard him (an echo from the account of the man born blind) and will act decisively so that the people will trust in Jesus. At Jesus' command, Lazarus actually comes back to life and then slowly leaves the tomb, still wrapped in his grave clothes.

This amazing final miracle in the Gospel according to John triggers both immediate faith among the people who witness the event and fierce opposition among the religious authorities, who would rather sacrifice Jesus and Lazarus than have their positions and the nation destroyed. God used the faith of Martha and Mary, which had been stretched to the breaking point and encouraged by their master, to glorify Jesus, all the while moving him quickly toward his hour of suffering.

My final example of the role of faith in healing is the story of the crippled man in Lystra (Acts 14:8–12), the only account in Acts that couples faith with healing. According to Luke's narrative, as the apostle Paul is preaching in Lystra, a man who has been lame from birth and has never walked is listening to him. Paul sees that this man has the necessary faith to be healed, and he tells the man, "Stand up on your feet!" The man quickly jumps up and begins to walk! This miracle prompts the crowd to proclaim Paul and Barnabus gods and to prepare to offer sacrifices to the two men. We don't know whether Paul saw this man's readiness for healing in his face, in his posture, or in his movement. God may have given Paul a word of knowledge or discernment., When Paul gave the lame man the opportunity to rise and be healed he acted in faith.

Overall, faith is mentioned in eleven out of twenty-seven individual Gospel incidents, whether covered by one, two, or three Gospel writers and including varying details. Such faith is not attested in any accounts of group healings, other than those of the two blind men (Matthew) and the ten lepers, which are treated individually in this chapter. Paul provides an account of an individual having faith for healing, and Acts mentions faith in only one of its twelve stories of healing, deliverance, and people being raised from the dead. There are nine accounts of group healings that do not mention faith. So, in the majority of the Gospel accounts of healing or deliverance, the faith of those healed, or that of their friends, of Jesus, or of other ministers is not referenced.

In many of the incidents I've discussed in this chapter, the person Jesus heals shows strong faith (often against what to us would seem difficult odds, including the approaching death of a loved one, contrary crowds, and reactionary authorities). Jesus holds these individuals out as positive examples of faith and healing. When the paralyzed man is brought to Jesus by four house wreckers, Jesus notes the man's faith and that of his advocates, then forgives the man's sin and heals him.

Where faith seems shaky, weak, or even absent, Jesus often gives people a chance to say what they want, admit their doubts, and rise to the occasion by expressing what faith they do have. Some express their faith by acting as if they have indeed been healed, rather than waiting passively to be healed. Even the shaky faith of the father whose son had been possessed by a demon is enough for Jesus to set the man's son free.

In other cases, Jesus seems to simply act on the basis of his Father's will to demonstrate the power and glory of God. Once, in his hometown, where his neighbors had pegged him as the carpenter's son, Jesus could do little because they lacked faith. When the twelve apostles and the seventy unknowns go on their missions, they preach the good news (faith comes by hearing), cast out demons, and heal the sick with evident success, except in cases where they were actually rejected. Likewise, we cannot set or demand any level of faith that is necessary for healing to take place, even though we know the presence of faith is advantageous. In some cases, those who are prayed for need to accept the gifts God gives! From our limited information, it seems that Jesus healed everyone who approached him, whether on their own volition or with the help of others. Other Scriptures from the Old Testament and the New Testament Epistles demonstrate that faith provides the best environment for healing and deliverance. In a congregational healing service, the attendees, ministers of healing, and those who are in need of healing make a difference, but God's spirit moves and distributes his very good gifts as he wills! Usually, it is wrong to blame people for not being healed on a given occasion. Instead, we should encourage them to receive ministry again.

Supplemental Scriptures on Faith and Trust

1. "If you believe, you will receive whatever you ask for in prayer." (Matt. 21:22)

2. "Whoever believes in me, as the Scripture has said, streams of living water will flow from within him." (John 7:38)

3. "I tell you the truth, anyone who has faith in me will do what I have been doing. He will do even greater things than these, because I am going to the Father." (John 14:12)

4. "By faith in the name of Jesus, this man whom you see and know was made strong. It is Jesus' name and the faith that comes through him that has given this complete healing to him." (Acts 3:16)

5. "To open their eyes and turn them from darkness to light, and from the power of Satan to God, so that they may receive forgiveness of sins and a place among those who are sanctified by faith in me." (Acts 26:18)

6. "Consequently, faith comes by healing the message, and the message is heard through the word of Christ." (Rom. 10:17)

7. "We live by faith, not by sight." (2 Cor. 5:7)

8. "Now faith is being sure of what we hope for and certain of what we do not see." (Heb. 11:1)

9. "And without faith it is impossible to please God, because anyone who comes to him must believe that he exists and that he rewards those who earnestly seek him."(Heb. 11:6)

10. "But when he asks [for wisdom], he must believe and not doubt, because he who doubts is like a wave of the sea, blown and tossed by the wind." (James 1:6)

11. "The prayer offered in faith will make the sick person well;
the Lord will raise him up. If he has sinned he will be forgiven." (James 5:15)

Chapter 5

Reactions to Healing Events in the Gospels and the Book of Acts

Part 1 — Jesus

Given the various responses to contemporary healing ministries by those who belong to various Christian denominations, by those who practice various forms of traditional or alternative medicines, and by healers or shamans belonging to different religious systems, we should not be surprised by many of the reactions we find in the New Testament regarding the healing ministry of Jesus, the apostles, and other Christians during the first century C.E. Some may be disheartened by the way leaders of the Pharisees, a relatively small but well-regarded Jewish party, had so quickly united in opposition to Jesus' practice of healing on the Sabbath, which they incorrectly interpreted as a violation of the law (the Torah). The Pharisees had also been disturbed by Jesus' fellowship with sinners, his popularity, the tremendous success of his healings and deliverances, and his tendency to challenge the Pharisees. We will first consider the reactions of the following groups of people.

1. Individuals who had been healed, along with their relatives
2. Jesus' own disciples
3. Synagogue congregations, the crowds of people who witnessed the healing works of Jesus and/or the apostles
4. Religious authorities, including those belonging to the Pharisees, Sadducee, Zealots, Herodians, and Essenes of Quran

We will then look at the overall consequences of Jesus' teaching, preaching, and healing ministry, which lead to his arrest, torture, execution, and eventual resurrection. We will also consider the ongoing ministry of the apostles and others as recounted in the four gospels and Acts. In this process, we will look primarily at individual healings but also include group healings and their larger consequences. We will see that these healings, deliverances, and nature miracles, which are hard to deny or discount, were then and remain challenging to those who want to disbelieve or who maintain an alternate world view, such as a belief in deism or naturalism. I will continue to use the event order set out in the OSL initial study manual. Again, healing events were recounted by one, two, or three Gospel writers, with minor variations with respect to their traditions and the guidance they received from the Holy Spirit. We cannot say that the Gospels are in chronological order, but we may be able to discern some trends in attitudes, or hardening of categories, as we progress from Jesus' own baptism toward his crucifixion the cross.

Reactions of Healed Individuals and Their Relatives

Table 4
Reactions of People Who Were Healed and of Their Relatives

Healed Individual	Description of the Event
Official's son	He becomes a believer after hearing that his son's fever has disappeared.
Peter's mother-in-law	When her fever disappears, she gets up and begins to serve her guests.
Leper	According to Mark, the leper does not immediately obey Jesus by going to the priest but instead talks freely about his cleansing, which prompts great crowds to follow Jesus. Luke doesn't say that the leper told everyone about the healing, but everybody found out.
Lame man at Bethsaida	While obeying Jesus by getting up, picking up his mat, and going home, the man is healed. When confronted for carrying the mat on the Sabbath, he cannot identify Jesus but says he had been ordered to do so. When Jesus warns the man to stop sinning, the man reveals to the Jews who had healed him.
Gadarene demoniac(s)	In the Markan account, after the demoniac is set free he begs Jesus to let him go with him, but Jesus orders the man to go home to his family and tell them what the Lord had done for him. Presumably, the man obeyed.
Woman with hemorrhage	In two of the accounts (Mark, Luke) Jesus' question moves the woman to fall at his feet and tell him and the people around her how she had been healed by touching Jesus (testimony).
Raising of the ruler's daughter	In the Lucan account, the girl's parents' react with astonishment when Jesus heals their daughter.

Healed Individual	Description of the Event
Two blind men (Matt.)	After giving the men sight, Jesus warns them not to let anyone know what has happened, but they ignore the warning and spread the news over the region.
Man born blind (John 9)	The man is healed when he goes to the pool of Siloam, then washes off the mud that Jesus had put on his eyes and then returns home. This is the greatest, most extensive positive reaction to personal healing in the New Testament. The man's neighbors ask if he is the man who had been born blind. He says that he is and then describes his healing. When the Pharisees ask him a second time about his healing, he describes it. The man's parents testify that he had been blind but can now see—but they would not say that it had been Jesus who healed their son. This man calls Jesus a prophet and then demonstrates that Jesus is a righteous man, not a sinner, even though he heals on the Sabbath. Given the opportunity to meet and see Jesus, the Son of man, the man worships Jesus.
Ten lepers (Luke)	All ten obey Jesus by going to the priests. After all ten are healed, one of them, a Samaritan, goes back to Jesus, praising God loudly, then falls down at his feet to worship him.
Blind man/men in Jericho	In two of the accounts, the formerly blind man regains his sight and immediately follows Jesus on the road to Jerusalem. Luke adds that the man praises God.

From the information in Table 5, we may conclude that the primary response of the people who had been healed by Jesus was to tell their stories to others, even if Jesus had told them not to say anything. I've had the same reaction when I have received or witnessed healings. I do not endorse William Wrede's theory that Jesus never claimed to be the Messiah but then Mark added the secrecy motif on his own;[8] but I can see how Jesus' warnings to be quiet may have caused people to do exactly the opposite of what he asked. It is our duty and privilege to testify or witness to others about the good things that the Lord Jesus has done for us.

At least one set of parents also testifies that their son had been born blind but is now able to see. In a few cases, such as the raising of Lazarus, the healing itself makes such an impact that the news spreads widely. Secondary responses to the healings include friends and family of the healed individual following Jesus as disciples, praising God, and worshiping Jesus. Such responses enhance the popularity of, and interest in, the ministry of Jesus and his disciples.

The Disciples' Response to the Healing Ministry of Their Master

Few recorded reactions of the disciples after a completed healing or deliverance by their rabbi and teacher are included in the Gospel accounts. The disciples' reactions may have been consistent with those of the crowd, which we will cover later in this chapter.

According to Matthew, when the Canaanite or Syro-Phoenician woman begs Jesus to set her daughter free, the disciples want Jesus to make her leave (Matt. 15:23). In fact, at times, they even seem anxious to protect Jesus from children, needy hungry people, and danger. We do not know what they said or did after she was sent home.

However, after the accounts of the disciples' successful mission, the confession of Peter at Caesarea Philippi, and the transfiguration of Christ, which was observed by the inner three, we find the lengthy account of the man with a seriously demonized son, whom the other disciples could not set free. After Jesus encourages the boy's father to have faith, and then heals the youngster, the disciples ask Jesus privately why they had failed in their healing efforts. Jesus explains that the main problem was their not having enough faith. He says that if they had faith as small as a tiny mustard seed, they could tell a mountain to move and it would do as they commanded. Indeed, he says, nothing would be impossible for them (Matthew and Mark). He also indicates that the kind of difficult demon that had possessed the boy cannot be ejected without prayer (some manuscripts include fasting). The disciples may have still been smarting from Jesus' public rebuke aimed toward a difficult, unbelieving generation.

In the case of the man born blind (John 9), the disciples want to attribute the man's condition to his personal sin before birth or to the sins of his parents, but Jesus sees the true purpose of the man's condition—to be a revelation of the glory of God's work when he is given sight, demonstrating that Jesus is indeed the light of the world. On a few occasions, the twelve apostles express their own views about the causes of illness, are concerned about their failure to heal, and try to protect Jesus, but we see little in terms of their expressing surprise, growing more committed to Jesus, or becoming more faithful. The people comprising the larger group of seventy-two unknowns are surprised and excited about the success of their ministries and deliverances when they return from their mission trips.

Reactions of Synagogue Attendees and Crowds to Healing

In this section I will present an extensive and interesting set of reactions that are documented in the Gospels. Will there be a definite change as we go forward in time with knowledge about Jesus and his growing ministry, and of religious parties' increasing opposition to Jesus? We will again operate inductively by considering a list of reactions and statements about Jesus and his ministry. Sometimes the enthusiastic reactions of the crowd may have been restrained by the presence of authorities who oppose this new ministry.

Demonized man in synagogue is delivered (Mark and Luke). In this early record of Jesus preaching in the synagogue at Capernaum, his Galilean base, the people are first amazed because Jesus preached with authority rather than citing previous rulings or traditions the way a lawyer would. When an unclean spirit within a man cries out defensively, Jesus silences him and then casts him out. In response, the amazement of the people rises to a new pitch and some say, "What is this teaching? With authority and power he gives orders to evil spirits and they come out (Luke) and obey him (Mark)." The news about Jesus spreads throughout Galilee.

Paralyzed man is cured and his friends react (Matthew, Mark, and Luke). After the paralyzed man is lowered into the room by his friends and Jesus encourages him by declaring his sins forgiven (much to the alarm of the authorities), Jesus declares the authority of the Son of Man, then tells the man to walk, which he does. The people are once again amazed, filled with **awe**, and **praise God**, saying that this healing is remarkable or has before been seen.

Widow of Nain's son is raised from death (Luke). Jesus enters Nain in the company of a crowd and sees the only son of a widow being carried away in a coffin. Moved by compassion, Jesus tells the widow not to cry, touches the coffin to stop its progress, and commands the young man lying in the coffin to get up. The young man does as Jesus tells him and starts to talk; and Jesus returns the boy to his surprised mother. The people are filled with awe (*phobos*[9]), and then praise God by saying, "A great prophet has appeared among us! God has come to help his people!" (Luke 7:16). Now the news about Jesus spreads throughout Judea.

Gadarene demonized man is set free (Matthew, Mark, and Luke). This is a special case in that Jesus and his disciples are in predominantly Gentile territory, including one of the ten Greek cities

(Decapolis), where people are herding pigs, which Jews considers unclean. After Jesus sets the man free from a legion of demons, which are sent into the herd of pigs, which promptly drown in the lake nearby. the herders hurry into town to tell everyone what has taken place. When the people, out of curiosity, go to see the drowned pigs and the healed, dressed man, they become afraid (*phobos*). Then those who had seen what had taken place, ask or plead with Jesus to leave their region. He and his followers do as they are asked. The townspeople's reaction is similar to that of the frightened disciples after Jesus calmed the storm!

Synagogue ruler's daughter is raised from the dead (Matthew, Mark, and Luke). This is a pre-raising reaction from a crowd of people who are already mourning a little girl's death when Jesus arrives "too late" and sees the wailing, mourning crowd. According to Mark, Jesus asks, "Why all this commotion and wailing?" When he tells the people to go away because the child is asleep, not dead, they laugh at him because they know better. He puts them out, goes into the room along with the girl's parents and three of his disciples, and then tells the child to get up—and she does. The crowd leaves, but the news spreads throughout the region even though the parents were quiet!

Demonized mute person is set free (Matthew). After Jesus heals two blind men; a demonized mute man is brought to Jesus. When the demon is driven out of the man, the man begins to speak. This crowd says, "Nothing like this had ever been seen in Israel." Jesus' ministry is unique. (The Pharisees say that Jesus drives out demons by the prince of demons.)

Deaf, almost mute man is healed (Mark). In the Decapolis (ten towns) area, people bring a deaf, almost mute man to Jesus and beg him to place his hand on the man's ears. Instead, Jesus takes the man aside, puts his fingers into the man's ears, spits, and says, "Be opened." When the man is healed, Jesus orders the people not to say anything, but they disobey. They are so **amazed** that they report that Jesus had *done everything well, even causing the deaf to hear and the mute to speak, working miracles.*

Man's demonized, epileptic son is healed (Matthew, Mark, and Luke). Only Luke records the reaction of the crowd to Jesus rebuking the spirit and healing the boy, and that reaction is **amazement** at the greatness of God, along with **marveling** at Jesus' works.

Man born blind is given sight (John). After the man washes and can then see, he goes home. Some of his neighbors ask if he is the same man (mildly positive), while others say that he only looks like the same man (negative). He has to tell them that he is the man who had been born blind, forcing his neighbors to consider the possibility that a man born blind can now see. His neighbors had not observed the miracle, only its effect.

Blind, mute, possessed man is healed (Matthew, Mark, and Luke). Jesus heals the man (Matt.) by driving out the mute demon (Luke). In Mark, the **astonished, amazed** people ask, "Could this be the Son of David?"(that is, Is Jesus the Messiah or Christ?) However, others claim that Jesus is operating by demonic power or they test him by asking for a miraculous sign from Heaven.

Woman crippled by spirit for eighteen years walks again (Luke). Though the Synagogue rulers object when Jesus heals the woman on the Sabbath. and Jesus responds to the objections, the people are delighted with the wonderful things Jesus has been doing and his victory over his humiliated opponents.

Raising of Lazarus from the dead (John). Before God acts, some of the Jews comment on Jesus' love for Lazarus, but others ask, "Couldn't he have kept this man from dying?" After this outstanding and crucial miracle, many of the Jews who had come to mourn with Martha and Mary put their faith in Jesus. Others, however, report what has happened to the Pharisees, triggering their final preparations to eliminate Jesus.

I had expected that there would be an escalation of reactions as Jesus' ministry began in Galilee, moved to Judea, then to Perea, and back toward Jerusalem. However, that did not happen. People consistently reacted with amazement, surprise, even delight to Jesus' miracles because there was none of the rapid, widespread communication that is normal for us today. I did examine a map that showed the locations where Jesus' healings took place, but I could not perceive a simple pattern. I do find that the views about Jesus' role and identity were just becoming more definite as he moved toward Jerusalem and his final week: Phrases or titles heard include Prophet, God among us, greatness of God, Son of David (just before Palm

Sunday). Though the people did not fully understand who Jesus was, they reacted positively by asking questions, showing wonder, acclaiming him and pointing to his true identity, as the severity of the conditions cured by Jesus increased, like a fireworks program.

Reactions of Religious Leaders to the Ministry of Jesus

We will list the reactions of synagogue leaders, local members of the Pharisees in Galilee or Judea, recognized teachers of the law, a rare member of the Sadducees, and high officials from Jerusalem. We will study their arguments in more detail in a separate chapter. We cannot explore the many challenges, discussions, and arguments over issues not related to healing. I do see Jesus' ministry of healing and deliverance, largely among the ordinary people of the land, some marginalized by their diseases and resultant poverty, to be a significant factor in his being condemned, then put to death.

- *Paralyzed man with friends' pre-healing reaction (Matthew, Mark, and Luke).* After the man is let down through the roof and Jesus notes their faith, Jesus says to the paralyzed man, "Take heart, son, your sins are forgiven." In this case and in that of the invalid at Bethesda, there seems to be some relation- ship between the invalid's previous sins and current weakness. However, the local Galilean and travelling Judean Pharisees and teachers of the law are listening to what Jesus is saying.

As soon as Jesus tells the paralyze man that his sins are for-given, they begin thinking to themselves (Mark), "Why does this fellow talk like that? He's blaspheming! Who can forgive sins but God alone?" Jesus immediately challenges them, by asking whether it is harder to say that someone is forgiven or to tell them to get up and walk. Even when he does the latter The officials are not convinced.

- *Lame man at Bethsaida (John).* After the lame man obeys Jesus' commands to get up, pick up his mat, and walk on the Sabbath, some Jews [probably officials] tell him, "The law forbids you to carry your mat." When he says that the man who healed him told him to do so, they want to know this man's name. Surprisingly, Jesus finds the man and tells him to stop sinning or something worse might happen to him. The former invalid then informs the Jews that it was Jesus who healed him, so the offended Jews persecute him.

- *Man with a shriveled hand (Matthew, Mark, and Luke).* This individual may have been placed in the synagogue con-gregation so that Jesus would heal him and then face their accusations. Matthew's tradition is slightly different in that the officials ask Jesus first whether it is lawful to heal on the Sabbath, then Jesus presents his argument and has the man stretch out his arm, which is instantly healed. In Mark and Luke, Jesus just challenges these leaders by asking questions that they refuse to answer, and then Jesus has the man extend his hand for healing. Jesus is angry. After the healing, they are furious and plot among themselves and with the Herodians to kill Jesus.

- *Demonized mute person (Matthew).* Immediately after two blind men are healed, a demonized man who had been mute is brought to Jesus, who drives the demon out, and the man is able to speak. However, after the amazed crowd says that this healing is unique, some Pharisees say, "It is by the prince (ruler) of demons that he drives out demons." They are not able to deny the reality of the healings, but they attribute them to an evil power. Jesus' shows they are wrong after healing the demonized man who was blind and mute (Matt. 12:22–29,Mark 3:20–27, and Luke 11:14–20).

- *Man born blind (John 9).* After this notable miracle occurs, the formerly blind man testifies to his neighbors and to the Pharisees, giving details and making some assertions about Jesus. (We will look at the argument in more detail later.) Because the healing takes place on the Sabbath, some Pharisees say that Jesus is not from God, that he is a sinner. Others ask how a sinner can do such miraculous signs (*semeia*). Some do not believe that the man had been blind in the first place, and they call on his parents in to testify. Again, the man is brought in and "the Jews" tell him to "give glory to God" by telling the truth. The Pharisees claim to be disciples of Moses, to whom God spoke. They say that they know nothing about Jesus or his origin. But the healed man argues that, given the unique miracle that he has performed, Jesus must be from God. The Pharisees then claim that the healed man has been soaked in sin his since birth, and they throw him out. They will not believe, so they attack the messenger.

- *Blind, mute, and possessed man (Matthew, Mark, and Luke).* As the severity of the illnesses or disabilities increases, followed by dramatic healings, the more the negative reactions of the religious leaders grow. After the man is healed and the people ask if Jesus can be the expected son of David, the Pharisees claim that it is "by Beelzebub, the prince of demons that this fellow casts out demons." Jesus points out that divided kingdoms collapse. But if he drives out demons by the Spirit of God (Matt.) or by the finger of God (Mark), then the kingdom or reign of God has come upon them, with the strong man being tied up and his possessions taken away. Jesus refutes their negative theories.

- *Woman crippled by spirit for eighteen years (Luke).* When Jesus tells the woman that she is set free from her infirmity and lays his hand on her; she straightens up and praises God. But the synagogue ruler is indignant and tells the woman and Jesus that there are six days in the week for work, so Jesus should perform his healings then, not on the Sabbath. Jesus' reply humiliates the official and delights the crowd.

- *The man with dropsy (Luke).* At the house of an important Pharisee on the Sabbath, with law experts and other Pharisees in attendance, Jesus is under scrutiny, with the sick man sitting in front of him. Jesus asks his audience directly whether it is lawful to heal on the Sabbath but the onlookers refuse to answer. Jesus heals the man, sends him home, and argues that the people who witnessed the event would do the same thing.

- *The raising of Lazarus (John).* When the Pharisees and Sadducees learn about this incredible miracle, the chief priests call a meeting of the Sanhedrin, the supreme legal body in Judaism. The Pharisees and Sadducees say, "What are we accomplishing? Here is this man performing many miraculous signs. If we let him go on like this, everyone will believe in him, and then the Romans will come and take away both our place and our nation" (John 11:48). Then Caiaphas, the high priest, prophesies, "It is better for you that one man dies for the people than that the whole nation perishes" (John 11:50). From that day, they actively plot to take Jesus' life. By 71 C.E., about forty years after Jesus' death and resurrection, radical Jewish leaders and people had violently rebelled against Rome and the city of Jerusalem, including Herod's temple lay in ruins!

We might consider these reactions as few or unimportant, but many of them are attested to by all three synoptic Gospels and taken together they represent a significant portion of the Gospels during the period from the onset of Jesus' ministry at his baptism to his final arrival in Jerusalem. As Jesus deliberately continues with his preaching, teaching, storytelling, and healing ministries, accepting the love and acclaim of the people who believe in him, he knows what will happen to him. Those who oppose him will have their day but not the victory.

When Jesus raises Lazarus, who had been in the grave for four days, this sets into motion the final plan that culminates in Jesus' death. In summary, we see that the authorities who do come to observe Jesus' ministry not only object to his teachings and claims but oppose his performing healings on the Sabbath, and they begin to say that the source of Jesus' power is demonic, which amounts to blaspheming the Holy Spirit. A few leaders, like Nicodemus, privately express their support for Jesus. We find no direct reactions during Jesus' healing ministry by the Herodians, Essenes, or Zealots.

When we examine the various group healings, they yield little additional information about reactions of authorities. However, these healings were probably important contributors to Jesus' rising popularity. Here is a list of group healings from the OSL introductory manual:

List of Group Healings[10]

1. At Simon Peter's house: Matt. 8:16–18, Mark 1:32–34, Luke 4:40–41

2. After leper is healed: Luke 5:15–16

3. Near Capernaum: Matt. 12:15–16, Mark 3:7–12, Luke 6: 17–19

4. Following John the Baptist's inquiry: Matt. 11: 2–6, Luke 7:18–23

5. Before feeding a crowd of five thousand: Matt. 14: 13–14, Luke 9:11

6. At Gennesart: Matt. 14: 34–36, Mark 6:53–56

7. Before feeding a crowd of four thousand: Matt. 15:29–31

8. Beyond the Jordan (Perea): Matt. 19: 1–2

9. In the temple: Matt. 21:14

10. At Nazareth: Matt. 13:53–58, Mark 6: 1–6

11. General statements about Jesus as healer

    a. All kinds of sickness: Matt. 4:23–25

    b. Every sickness and disease: Matt. 9:35–36

    c. All who touched him: Mark 6:56

    d. All who were oppressed: Acts 10:36–38

In the second section of this chapter, we do the same thing for the apostles and other Christians who went out in mission to preach

God's word and heal the sick, as recorded in the Gospels and book of Acts.

Part 2 — Disciples

In the Gospels, after observing Jesus for considerable time, the twelve apostles are sent out on a mission with fairly strict limitations, including not speaking to Gentiles. They are to proclaim the kingdom or reign of God, heal the sick, cleanse lepers, and cast out demons. They are to give as freely as they receive. For their work they are given authority and power to act as Jesus' ambassadors. How do people react to this ministry? Are they successful? What are the results of their ministry?

- *Mission of the twelve (Matt. 10:1–8, Mark 6:7–12, and Luke 9:1–7, 30).* Matthew gives no report of the apostles' success or their personal reactions to their short-term mission. In Mark 6:12–13 we find that they preach that people should repent, drive out many demons, and anoint many sick people with oil and heal them. Beyond this, King Herod hears about these activities, for Jesus' name was becoming well-known—but Herod thinks that John the Baptist has risen from the dead after having been decapitated by Herod. In Mark 6:30, the disciples report to Jesus about their teachings and actions. According to Luke 9:6, they "Set out and went from village to

village preaching the Gospel and healing people everywhere."
We have no particular reactions from the people who were
healed and set free, nor any reactions from religious leaders
and critics.

• *Mission of the seventy-two (Luke).* Because the harvest had
been great and the workers few, Jesus sends an additional
seventy-two disciples out on mission to heal the sick and tell
people that the reign of God is near them. We know nothing
about these workers. When they return, they are excited and
joyful because even the demons had submitted to them *in Jesus'
name.* We have no reactions from people who were changed or
any comments from the authorities. However, Jesus certainly
responds by saying that he saw Satan (the adversary) fall
from Heaven to Earth after Jesus had given the 72 disciples
authority to trample over evil. These disciples should rejoice
more in the fact that their names are written in God's book of
life than in their successes. Filled with the Spirit, Jesus exults
because the Father has hidden such things from the wise and
learned, but has revealed them to babes.

After Jesus' death and resurrection, the mission of all Christians
is to make disciples of all nations, baptizing them and teaching them
to obey everything that Jesus has commanded them. This certainly
includes healing. Late manuscripts of Mark 16:16–18 state: "These
signs will accompany those who believe: In my name they will drive

out demons, speak in new tongues. . . . place their hands on sick people and they will get well." As recorded in John 14, Jesus promises that those who have faith in Jesus will not only do the things he had been doing but even greater things, because he was going to the Father (John 14:12–13).

When we consider individual healing events in Acts, we must remember that we are dealing with several different cultures and with people who may be Hellenistic Jews, God fearers, or polytheistic pagans with little knowledge of Judaism. Such reactions have a common component but should vary with their respective cultures. Usually, during missionary trips, the apostle Paul starts with a Jewish base within a synagogue, builds a nucleus of believers, and then moves out to evangelize all, with accompanying signs of God's presence and power including spiritual gifts and healings.

- *The lame man at the temple is healed (Acts 3:1–16).* The first healing in the book of Acts is dynamic, attention getting, with several reactions and results soon after the Day of Pentecost. It is similar to the healing by Jesus at the pool of Bethesda and Paul's later healing at Lystra. When Peter and John see the man, he asks them for money but is given something far better. Peter commands him to get up and walk in the name of Jesus, then helps him up as his feet and ankles instantly became strong. For the first time in his life, the man enters the temple walking, leaping, and praising God. This obvious healing produces wonder and amazement among the people who recognize him! This attracts a sizable crowd around the apostles and the healed man. Peter asks the people why they are surprised and stare at the apostles as if it had been their own power (*dunamis*) or godliness that had healed him. Peter states that the God of Israel has glorified his servant Jesus, whom the Jews, including their leaders had disowned and murdered. They had killed the author of life, but God raised him from the dead. *"By faith in the name of Jesus, this man was made strong and . . . given this complete healing as you all can see."* Then the priests and Sadducees, who ran the temple, come up with the captain of the guard, who is disturbed because the apostles are teaching about Jesus and the resurrection. Although the guards seize Peter and John and put them in jail, many who heard Peter's message believe. When the Sanhedrin Council meets, they interrogate the apostles about the power and name by which the lame man had evidently been healed. Filled with the Holy Spirit, Peter testifies that it was by the name of Jesus, whom they had crucified but whom God had raised, that the man had been healed.*(Acts 4:8–12)*. The council cannot deny the healing, but they command the apostles not to teach in the name of Jesus. In the process of this confrontation, many people join the Christians.

- *Deacons Appointed by the apostles, scattered by persecution, Philip preaches in Samaria (Acts 8:6–17).* When Philip preaches the word of God among the Samaritans, his message is accompanied by miraculous signs, including the expulsion of noisy evil spirits and the healing of many paralyzed and crippled people. Many joyful men and women, including a messed-up magician named Simon, believe in Jesus and are baptized in water, and are then filled with the Holy Spirit after Peter and John arrive and lay their hands on the converts. As the Church moves out to include Samaritans, Christians begin to fulfill Jesus' command to make disciples of all nations (Matt. 28:19).

• *God uses Ananias to heal Saul (Acts 9:10–22).* As Saul travels north to Damascus in Syria to persecute Christians there, Jesus stops him, speaks to him, and leaves him temporarily blinded. Then, in a vision, God calls Ananias, an ordinary believer, to visit Saul and place his hands on him. Ananias protests but then obeys. He finds the righ*t house, places his hands on Saul, and then tells him that he has come so that Saul can see again and be filled w*ith the Holy Spirit. After "scales" fall from Saul's eyes, he is immediately baptized in water, takes some food, and is strengthened. Saul then visits the wary, nervous disciples and then begins to preach in the synagogues that Jesus is the Son of God! This alone is a remarkable result of his encountering Jesus, experiencing salvation, and healing. The people who hear him are astonished and find it difficult to square this new reality with Saul's former hatred of Christians.

Paul becomes stronger in the Spirit and argues with and angers his opponents, until he has to escape them by being *lowered* from the city walls in a basket! Later, his message is accompanied by signs and wonders too!

- *Aeneas, the paralyzed man at Lydda, is healed (Acts 9:32–34).* While remaining in Judea, Peter visits Lydda and encounters a paralyzed man who had been confined to his bed for eight years. After Peter declares that Jesus is healing him and then commands the man to get up and take care of his mat, Aeneas does get up. Knowledge of his restoration quickly spreads through Lydda and Sharon so that the people there turn to the Lord.

- *Tabitha is raised from death in Joppa (Acts 9:36–40).* When a beloved disciple named Tabitha dies, her body is prepared and placed in an upstairs room. Her friends send men to nearby Joppa for Peter and urge him to come quickly. Upon Peter's arrival, the distraught widows shows him the clothing Tabitha had made. Imitating Jesus, Peter puts everyone out of the room where Tabitha lay, then kneels down, prays, and commands her to get up. Indeed, she opens her eyes, sits up, and is helped to her feet. After Peter presents her to the members alive, the *news spreads* rapidly, so that many believe in the Lord.

- *Man crippled from birth is healed in Lystra (Acts 14:8–19).* The apostle Paul is now in southern Galatia (modern Turkey), preaching in the town of Lystra, where he would later join Timothy in ministry. As the crippled man listens to Paul, the apostle sees, perceives, or discerns that the man has the necessary faith to be healed. When Paul says, "Stand up on your feet!" the man jumps up and begins to walk. Then, the crowd cries out in their own language that the gods, namely Zeus and Hermes, had come down. They think that their town had been destroyed before because they hadn't welcomed Zeus. Hurriedly, the priest of Zeus brings animals for sacrifices to their "divine" visitors. When Barnabas and Paul figure out what is happening, they rip their robes at this blasphemy and then urge the crowd to turn from these false gods to the true God, the source of everything. The disappointed crowd is turned against Paul by angry Jews arriving from Antioch, and he is soon stoned almost to death and dragged outside the city. So the crowd that had acclaimed them tried to destroy them. This had also happened to Jesus.

- *Slave girl with a spirit in Philippi (Acts 16:16–37).* In this ancient Greek city of Philippi with a strong Roman colony, where few Jews live, Paul preaches to Lydia and others at the riverside and makes some converts. Then, Paul encounters a slave girl with a spirit by which she predicts the future and makes money for her masters. She gives the apostles free publicity by shouting that they were "servants of the most high God, who were telling people the way to be saved." After several days of this, Paul tells the spirit, "In the name of Jesus Christ I command you to come out of her." The spirit leaves right away, so that the girl can no longer predict anything. Her owners seize Paul and Silas, take them to the marketplace (agora), where they face the magistrates and are accused of being Jews who are advocating customs unlawful for Romans to accept or practice. The authorities have them stripped, beaten, thrown into jail, and kept very securely! Despite their pains, the Christian leaders praise God in their chains, and then are interrupted by an earthquake that sets everyone free. The distraught jailer, who is about to commit suicide because he thinks the prisoners have escaped, then becomes a believer along with his entire family. In the morning, Paul, a Roman citizen himself, demands that the officials show them out of the city. In a few years, the new Church at Philippi becomes one of Paul's favorites!

- *Miracles through Paul in Ephesus; group healings (Eph. 19:11–20).* In the great city of Ephesus, known for its shrine to the goddess Diana, Paul's preaching and tent making are accompanied by miracles. Even his sweat rags and aprons heal illnesses and drive out demons. Some Jews, including the seven sons of Sceva, try to imitate Paul's ministry by adding Jesus' powerful name and mentioning Paul when commanding demons to leave someone. In one case the demons say, "Jesus I know, and I have heard about Paul, but who are you?" The demonized person rips the Jews' clothes off and beats them up, and they run away in fear. They had no right to use the name of Jesus. As the news spreads, the results include great reverence for Jesus' name with people renouncing magical practices then burning their scrolls covered with incantations! The Gospel spreads quickly and begins to affect the selling of idols, almost resulting in a riot among the silversmiths.

- *Eutychus falls, dies, and is restored in Troas (Acts 20:7–12).* When Paul returns on another missionary trip to a region near Ephesus, he preaches a very long sermon on the Lord's Day. Eutychus falls asleep and then falls out of a window and is picked up, seemingly dead. But Paul throws his arms around Eutychus, squeezes him, and says that he is alive. Paul breaks bread with believers there (Eucharist) and preaches until morning. Eutychus's family and other church members **are comforted** that he has been restored to them.

- *Father of Publius on Malta and others are healed (Acts 28:7–10).* Paul is on his way to Rome for judgment and eventual execution, but is shipwrecked on the island of Malta. Paul has already been protected from a deadly snake bite as he gathers firewood. Soon Paul sees Publius's father, who is sick with dysentery and fever. Paul goes to him, prays, lays his hands on him, and heals him. Then, because the news gets out, other sick people on the island go to Paul and are healed. This account is similar to the healing of Peter's mother-in-law of a fever, followed by the neighbors gathering. Luke has not recorded any reactions to this ministry.

Conclusions

The healing ministries of Jesus, his original disciples, and other Christians played a significant, life-changing part in the spread of the good news. Responses of the individuals who were healed and the crowds who witnessed these healings were largely positive and included expressions of amazement, praise to God, and honor to those involved in the healing ministry. However, the reactions of religious authorities were and still are strongly influenced by their earlier training and their desire to protect or enhance their own turf and to maintain their influence.

There is little evidence that Jesus was regarded in Israel in the first-century B.C.E. as a Hellenistic magician, wonder-worker, or Greek physician who followed the patterns or methods associated with Hippocrates and healing centers such as the one at Epidaurus.[11]

The conventional first century Jewish theory about health and sickness associates God's blessings, such as prosperity and health, with obedience to God, and associates misfortunes, such as sickness, with disobedience. This applies first to the people of God, then to individuals. The laws of sowing and reaping were assumed to hold true. In harmony with a deistic, mainly transcendent, view of God, ordinary people would not expect Yahweh to be actively involved in their lives. However, through Jesus' coming to dwell with us in humility, his demonstration of God's love and healing, his taking upon himself the penalty of our sins, and his sending forth the Holy Spirit, the new era of the Church with healing was birthed.

Christian healing ministries continued strongly through the fifth century as persecuted Christians showed forth the love, compassion, and power of their Lord in both hostile and supportive environments. In *The Healing Reawakening*, Francis MacNutt shows how this important ministry then declined within the institutional, powerful, political Church, despite revivals.[12]

Chapter 6

Three Major Issues Concerning Jesus and Religious Leaders

We have listed and considered the various reactions to Jesus' ministry of healing by those who he had healed, their relatives, Jesus' disciples, crowds, and religious authorities. Now we will look at the complaints from authorities and Jesus' responses to those complaints in terms of three issues: healing on the Sabbath, forgiveness of sins, and the source of Jesus' power. On average per Gospel, the Pharisees are mentioned twenty-one times, the Sadducees two times, law experts two times, and Herodians 0.8 times.

Issue 1—Healing on the Sabbath

Early in Mark (1:29–34), after attending synagogue in Capernaum on the Sabbath, preaching, and authoritatively casting out a demon, Jesus goes to Peter's house and heals Peter's mother-in-law of a fever. No officials objected to this early ministry. Mark notes that when the townspeople hear about Jesus, they go to Peter's house in the evening, after the first visible stars have signaled the end of the Sabbath. (In fact, none of the group-healing scenes in the Gospels are reported as having occurred on the Sabbath, which lasts from sundown on Friday to sundown on Saturday.)

In the lengthy account of the lame man at Bethesda (John 5:1–18), who is healed on the Sabbath, Jesus commands the man, "Get up! Pick up your mat and walk." When the religious authorities see the man, they tell him that the law forbids carrying one's mat on the Sabbath, citing, for example, Jeremiah 17:21, which states: "Be careful not to carry a load on the Sabbath or bring it through the gates of the city." This was a rather obvious violation of the Sabbath not requiring one to know the complicated oral law of the experts. When the healed man indicates that the person who had healed him had also commanded him to carry the mat, the authorities ask him who this fellow was, but the man has no idea because Jesus had slipped away.

Surprisingly, Jesus returns to the man later, at the temple, and tells him to stop sinning, or something worse than his previous disability might happen. In so doing, Jesus reveals his true identity, and the man returns to the authorities and identifies the healer as Jesus! This results in Jesus being persecuted, but note Jesus' statement: "My Father is always at his work to this very day, and I, too, am working" (John 5:17). Jesus' own actions and words both challenge the officials and put Jesus in jeopardy. In this case, as in the account of Jesus forgiving the paralyzed man, Jesus seems to stand above and exempt himself from the authorities' rules. Presuming that Jesus spoke the truth, then we must think about our categories and the reality that Jesus identifies himself with God the Father, who is always working, and that he is also the Lord of the Sabbath.

By the end of the first century when the Gospel according to John became available, the Church was largely comprised of Gentiles, who had moved away from legalistic concerns about the detailed observances of the law.

In the case of the man with the shriveled hand (Matt. 12:9, Mark3:1, Luke 6:6), Jesus sees the man, knows what is going on, and asks the Pharisees and law experts an important question (Mark, Luke): "Is it lawful on the Sabbath to do well or to do evil, to save life or [to] kill?" Jesus wants them to concede that it is lawful and right to do well, in particular, to save (*sōzō*) a life on the Sabbath. In fact, the rules at that time permitted the limited use of medicines, the setting of bones, and the rescue of people on the Sabbath. But in this account, the officials do not say that doing well (possibly including healing chronic conditions or disabilities) is lawful. Jesus' question gives the authorities an opportunity to see things differently. Jesus is angry but under control when he heals the man, while the officials react with fury.

Mark also includes from his early sources the tradition that the authorities had asked Jesus the more specific question of whether it is lawful to heal on the Sabbath, with the intention of getting information to accuse him. Using his own question, Jesus gives an example, before stating that it is lawful to heal on the Sabbath: "If any of you has a sheep and it falls into a pit on the Sabbath, will you not take hold of it and lift it out?" (Matt. 12:11–12). Even if some Sabbath rules seemed to forbid this work, the vast majority of people would rescue the sheep. Jesus then states, "How much more valuable is a man than a sheep? If we would rescue a sheep, even a neighbor's, would we not rescue a human being, created in the image of God?" This is the argument from lesser to greater. His conclusion is that it is lawful to do well on the Sabbath; then he heals the man and sends him off. Note also that the man stretches out his arm and is restored, without anyone being able to prove that Jesus had actually done anything! As an article in the *Dictionary of Jesus and the Gospel*[13] states: "[T]he Markan Jesus insists that God can hardly be offended or his will transgressed by the doing of good and the restoring of health on the Sabbath (regardless, apparently, of whether the deed can be construed as 'work')" Afterward, Jesus leaves the synagogue and heals other people.

In another passage (John 7:21–24), not directly connected which his healing works, Jesus refers to the circumcision of all male babies on the eighth day, even if that day falls on the Sabbath: "Now if a child can be circumcised on the Sabbath so that the law of Moses may not be broken, why are you angry with me for healing the whole man on the Sabbath?" This surgical work was not performed to save a life but to mark the boy with the sign of the covenant according to a higher law. According to Rodney Whitacre, Jesus is using a "how much more" argument to support his healing the whole person on the Sabbath, and Whitacre quotes Rabbi Eliezer, who said, "If one supersedes the Sabbath on account of one of his members, should he not supersede the Sabbath for his whole body if in danger of death?"[14]

In the longest healing account, which includes the most extensive argument between some of the Pharisees and the man born blind but now sees, we realize the extent to which people can refuse to see, believe in, or admit the truth about Jesus, despite the evidence right before them. A man convinced against his will is of the same opinion still. Before the healed man encounters the religious authorities, Jesus states that the man's blindness and cure "happened so that the work of God might be displayed in the world. While I am in the world, I am the light of the world" (John 9:3, 9).

Before the Pharisees speak with the formerly blind man, the neighbors try to make up their minds whether the man is the same person they had known. This gives the man the opportunity to tell his neighbors how Jesus had miraculously healed him. Of course, the man was healed on the Sabbath, so he is soon taken to the religious authorities to face their questions, theories, and conclusions.

When the Pharisees ask the man how Jesus had healed him, the man describes how Jesus put mud, which he had made with his spittle, on the man's eyes, and how after the man had washed (in the pool of Siloam) he could see! That is his basic testimony. What are they going to do about it? Well, one group jumps to the conclusion that Jesus is "not from God" because spitting, making mud, and applying it, by their rules, are actions that amount to working on the Sabbath. Therefore, they conclude, Jesus did not keep the Sabbath. But others ask how a "sinner" could do such miraculous signs! They ask the man what he would say about Jesus, because Jesus had opened his eyes, and the man replies that Jesus is a prophet, one who speaks for God. This was the primary view among the ordinary people.

The Pharisees then call the man's parents in to testify because the Pharisees "still did not believe that the man had been blind and had received his sight" (John 9:18). The man's parents are afraid of the officials because they know that anyone who publicly acknowledged Jesus as the Christ, the anointed one of God, would be thrown out of the synagogue. When the man's parents are asked if the man is their son and whether he had been blind but is now able to see, they state that he is their son, who had been born blind, but that they "did not know how he could see now, or who had opened his eyes" (John 9:21). Having no firsthand knowledge except their son's statements, they take the easier way, and tell the authorities to allow their son to speak for himself because he is of age.

Therefore, the officials question the man a second time, calling him to "give glory to God" by telling the truth because they, the majority subgroup, know that Jesus is a sinner. But the man sticks to what he knows. He doesn't know whether Jesus is a sinner, but he knows that he had been blind but can now see! When the officials want to go over the healing process again, he sarcastically asks them if they want to become Jesus' disciples. They retort that he is Jesus' disciple, but they are disciples of Moses, to whom God spoke. They have no idea where this new person had come from.

Now, the man sallies forth and states how remarkable it is that the officials don't know where Jesus had come from (not Nazareth of Galilee, which they despised; and Jesus wouldn't tell them), yet Jesus had opened the man's eyes, which had been closed from his birth. He continues: "God does not listen to sinners. He listens to the godly man who does his will. Nobody has ever heard of opening the eyes of a man born blind. If this man were not from God, he could do nothing." (John 9:33). I believe it must have been God who gave this man a remarkable reply, as he did Peter, saying that Jesus was the Christ, the Son of God. Both the man and the officials who questioned him probably assumed that good things happen to good people, but the opposite to bad people. Then, the Pharisees resort to an ad hominem attack by telling the man that he had been steeped in sin at birth, for he had been born blind, and they continue, "How dare you lecture us!" (John 9:34). After the man is thrown out, Jesus gives him an opportunity to indicate his desire to believe in the Son of Man and commit his life to Jesus in trust and worship. In a real sense, the man can now see both physically and spiritually, while those who had always possessed physical sight were adamantly blind to the reality that Jesus was the miracle-working messiah among them. This is the most interesting and lengthy argument, which resulted in their ejecting the former blind man rather than admit that they were wrong. Do such miracles prove that Jesus is good despite his apparent violation of the Sabbath laws?

Now we come to the account of the woman who had been crippled, bent over, by the influence of an unclean spirit for eighteen long years. Jesus encounters her and the synagogue ruler on the Sabbath (Luke 13:10–17). As soon as he sees the woman, he calls her to the front and declares that she is free of her infirmity. Then he puts his hands on her, and she straightens up and begins to praise God. However, the synagogue ruler protests that there are six days for work, and the people should come to the synagogue on one of those six days, not on the Sabbath. His anger is actually directed toward Jesus, but he speaks to the people. Of course, the people could have come on another day, but they had assembled on the Sabbath, and Jesus may have only been available for a divine appointment on that one day.

Jesus calls this official and others hypocrites and actors because, at home, they untie their animals on the Sabbath and lead them to water! They don't practice what they preach. Arguing from the lesser to the greater, he asks, should not a daughter of Abraham, a Jewish woman whom Satan had kept bound, be set free of her bonds on the Sabbath? If the officials would set an animal free, why would they protest when a woman was set free? He reasons that this type of healing, which involves the silent ejection of a demon and setting someone free, can be justified on the Sabbath. In response, Jesus' enemies feel ashamed and humiliated, while his followers are able to benefit from the wonderful things that Jesus had been doing! Later, Jesus gives the apostles the authority to bind evil or release people and the power of the Holy Spirit, in agreement with God's actions in Heaven.

In another unique event, recorded by Luke (Luke 14:1–6), Jesus is invited to the house of a prominent Pharisee for a meal. A man suffering from dropsy or edema had been strategically seated near our master, and all eyes focused on Jesus. Jesus asks the Pharisee and his dinner guests whether it is lawful or permitted to heal on the Sabbath. They probably know that there are special rules that permit saving a life on the Sabbath, but they say nothing and refuse to answer his question in the affirmative, lest they give blanket approval. Jesus heals the man and sends him away. Jesus initiates the healing with the Father's approval in the power of the Holy Spirit, but some guests only see a law breaker.

Again, Jesus argues from the lesser to the greater, contending that if it is permissible to rescue an animal from drowning on the Sabbath, then surely it is lawful to save a boy who has fallen into a well. They would rescue him quickly. Therefore a man who is waterlogged should be healed. The dinner guests have nothing to say, because they sense that Jesus is right. Both edema and falling in a well could be life-threatening. Centuries before, a servant saved Jeremiah from perishing in a dry cistern (Jer. 38:6–8).

In these examples, one can think of Jesus as doing some type of work on the Sabbath, even though he only touches someone, gives a command to a person or spirit, or declares an individual healed. However, through the first century, there are no accepted elaborations of the law (Torah tōrāh) covering such actions. I could argue that the Holy Spirit performed the actual healings, even as he does today, and touches others with his extended hands in healing. I could say that Jesus was only doing what the Father was doing or, certainly, I could give him an exception from limitations that other human beings labor under, because he is the Son of God. In addition, I could recall how Jesus said that he is the Lord of the Sabbath, and how he quoted examples in which king David, the forerunner of the Messiah, did things that were lawful only for a priest, and Jesus is considered by the author of Hebrews to be a new type of priest after the unique pattern of Melchizedek (Gen.14:18), rather than Aaron. In fact, Levitical priests functioned in the holy temple on the Sabbath. That temple and priesthood was terminated by the Romans.

I do not believe that Jesus actually violated the Sabbath law as instituted by God, even though he did not always follow the extensive set of rules formulated by the later Pharisees. The officials could have ruled that healing on the Sabbath, even when it did not involve saving a life, was lawful, but this would have removed one of their greatest reasons for opposing Jesus at the point of his greatest popularity.

In preparing for this paragraph, I read two articles by Herold Weiss about the Sabbath in the Gospels[15, 16] and a very helpful book by Yong-Eui Yang,[17] which traces the development of Sabbath regulations from the Pentateuch through the historical books, the Apocrypha, and the intertestamental period, to the views of the Qumran community and rabbis during and beyond the time of Jesus. The Sabbath observances are related to the completed creation work of Yahweh and his covenantal relationship with his separated, redeemed people. As one moves through time toward the first century, especially near the end of that century, one finds a great increase in the rules regulating work on the Sabbath. Even when being attacked by the Greeks during the period of the Maccabees, the Jews at first did not defend themselves on the Sabbath, but they eventually did so, gaining and maintaining their freedom until the Roman Empire took Palestine. One of these laws (there were thirty-nine in all) addressed the bearing of burdens on the Sabbath made it unlawful to carry just five garden seeds on the Sabbath. Rabbis, but not members of the Qumran community, permitted the assisting of an animal giving birth and removing offspring from a pit. The rabbis did allow physicians to save lives and circumcise Jewish boys on the eighth day, and the daily temple sacrifices took precedence over the Sabbath. In other words, work that could be carried out before or after the Sabbath did not override the Sabbath. The stricter school of Shammai forbade charity, or alms, and prayers for the sick on the Sabbath. Such complex forests of rules made it difficult for ordinary people to strictly keep the Sabbath. In these studies I did not find one specific rule prior to the healing work of Jesus that forbade healing on the Sabbath.

Additional Historical Comments

1. Though in general healings on the Sabbath were not permitted; they were allowed if the disease were definitely or possibly life threatening. Jesus tends to soften the commandment against healing for the sake of life, which goes beyond self-defense or saving animals.[18]

2. Some argued that if the law allowed circumcision on the Sabbath then the healing of the whole human body should also be permitted. In other words, a person in danger of death could be healed on the Sabbath. In an acute case, Rabbis allowed the healing of a damaged eye but not the healing of a chronic eye problem.[19] However, when Jesus had healed the man born blind, he had also done work in mixing dirt and spittle to make mud.[20]

Issue 2—Pronouncing Forgiveness

In the healing of the paralytic, reported by all three synoptic Gospels (Matt. 9:1–7, Mark 2:1–12, Luke 5:12–25) with some variation in length and emphasis, Jesus notices the faith of the paralyzed man's four friends, then immediately calls the man son, and tells him to take courage and that his sins are forgiven. This statement produces an immediate reaction from the Pharisees and law experts! For the first time, the word *blasphemy* was being said under their breaths about this fellow. To blaspheme God was either to speak against him with irreverence or to revile him, or to say or do things that belong only to God. Then, they continued, "Who can forgive sins but God alone?"

When we sin, either deliberately or with some degree of ignorance, in thought, word, or deed, we are always sinning against God; but we may be sinning against other people and ourselves as well. With God's help we can forgive those who have sinned against us; but what about God? Among the people of Israel, unintentional sins would be forgiven after an innocent animal was sacrificed or sent out into the wilderness bearing the sins that had been committed. Many classes of deliberate sins against God, if substantiated by two witnesses, could promptly result in death by stoning. Even among God's new people, sin has negative consequences and we need God's forgiveness and help as we turn from sin!

When King David sinned by committing adultery with Bathsheba and killing her husband, Uriah, the prophet Nathan identified David as the culprit. David then said to Nathan, "I have sinned against the LORD" Nathan replied, "The LORD has taken away your sin. You are not going to die" (2 Sam. 12: 13–14). So a prophet could speak for God and say that a person's sin had been removed because that person had heard the Word of the Lord. But the scribes didn't believe that Jesus was a prophet, and certainly did not believe that he was the messiah, or the Son of Man pictured in Daniel coming on the clouds with tremendous authority and power. Therefore, Jesus had no right or power to tell the paralyzed man that his sins had been forgiven.

Jesus challenges their thoughts then asks them: "Which is easier to say, 'Your sins are forgiven,' or to say, 'Get up and walk'?"(Matt 9:5). Obviously, it is the latter, because no one looking at the person could determine whether his or her sins had been forgiven. But if I say, "Get up and walk" and the person tries but cannot move, it is obvious that someone has failed. To prove his point, Jesus tells the man to get up, take his mat, and go home, which he does. Jesus' assertion that the Son of Man has authority (*exousia*) to forgive sins is demonstrated by his ability to do something even more difficult. We can only speculate about other issues, such as the relationship between the paralyzed man's past sins and his weakened condition. There are connections between wrong thinking, sin, disease, forgiveness, and healing. In Psalm 103:3 we hear: "God forgives all your sins and heals all your diseases." In Psalm 11:4 we read: "Have mercy on me; heal me, for I have sinned against you." Then God says, "Return faithless people; I will cure you of your backsliding" (Jer. 3:22).

In Luke 7 we have the account of a woman characterized as a sinner by all the righteous, who comes to the place where Jesus is reclining as a guest and bends down, weeping, to anoint his feet with costly perfume. Using the parable of two men, one who owed little and the other much, Jesus notes how the person who is forgiven much loves his creditor more. Jesus identifies this woman as such a person. He tells her that her sins are forgiven, her faith has saved her, and she can go in peace. The other guests, including the law experts, ask, "Who is this, who even forgives sins?" (Luke 7:49).

Because of her encounter with Jesus, this sinner goes home forgiven and whole, and perhaps in better spiritual condition than the skeptical law experts. It would not be long until Jesus, by his atoning death on the cross, provides for the abundant forgiveness, justification, and redemption of all those who truly come to him by faith — whether they are respectable or notorious sinners! This would be followed by the destruction of the holy temple in Jerusalem and the termination of the Levitical sacrificial system, which was no longer necessary.

Issue 3—The Source of Jesus' Power

As Jesus continues to teach, heal, work miracles, and set people free, it becomes very difficult for the Pharisees and law experts to deny the reality of such works or signs. Consequently, they question Jesus' origins, point to his violating their traditions and his fellowship with sinners, and begin to attribute his casting out of demons to the work of a major demonic prince, Beelzebub. In the ancient Ugarit culture of what is now Syria, "Ba'al" is the name given to one of the culture's many deities but was eventually became identified as the Canaanite fertility or storm God, which some Jews mocked as the Lord of the flies, the garbage dump, and the plague. In Jesus' day, this was a name for one of Satan's chief agents in the first two heavenly regions (Eph. 6:12).

In the unique account of the healing of a man who had been demonized and rendered mute (Matt. 9:32–34), the amazed onlookers note the uniqueness of this healing in Israel. But the Pharisees say that Jesus cast out demons by the prince of demons. On this occasion, Jesus' reaction isn't recorded.

In the International Order of St. Luke manual, three accounts (Matt. 12:22–29, Mark 3:20–27, and Luke 11:14–26) describe Jesus' reaction to accusations about the source of his power. Mark's account follows lakeside group healings and deliverances that silence the spirits when they try to identify Jesus as the Son of God. Jesus selects the twelve apostles and then tries to eat, but his family comes to take charge of him because he is "out of his mind" or beside himself, and then the Pharisees show up. Both Matthew and Luke record the healing of a demonized man who had been mute. According to Matthew 12:22, the people ask whether Jesus is the son of David or even the Messianic king. Only Luke notes that the Pharisees also ask Jesus for a sign. The Pharisees then claim that Jesus had driven out demons by Beelzebub, the prince of demons, and attribute his works to an evil source.

As usual, Jesus rebuffs this attack creatively. First, he tells the naysayers a story, showing that divided kingdoms, cities and households or families will not stand or survive, much less thrive. He also asks, "If I drive out demons by Beelzebub, by whom do your people (sons or disciples) drive them out?" Their lack of success, like that of the later sons of Sceva, might indicate that their source of power and their Pharisaic training was defective!

However, if Jesus had actually been driving out demons by the Spirit of God or the finger of God, attached to his strong arm, then the kingdom or reign of God was indeed coming upon them in power. His source of both power and authority was none other than God! By another story, Jesus describes what is actually happening: "When a strong man, fully armed, guards his own house, his possessions are safe. But when someone stronger attacks and overpowers him, he takes away the armor in which the man trusted and divides up the spoils" (Luke). Likewise, "No one can enter a strong man's house and carry off his possessions unless he first ties up the strong man" (Mark). Jesus is saying that freeing people from Satan's grip requires the help of someone stronger than they are, namely Jesus or possibly his disciples, who can bind the strong man removing his armor, then take his possessions from him. If Satan was struggling against himself, his rule would not survive. As Peter says, "God anointed Jesus of Nazareth with the Holy Spirit and power, and he went around doing good and healing all who were under the power of the devil because God was with him" (Acts 10:38). Jesus' opponents should also have realized how inconsistent it would be for someone who consistently does good to be motivated by an evil source, such as the one that produces the acts of the sinful nature as listed in Galatians 5!

Now, as we go further in Matthew and Mark, we find Jesus warning his hearers about the unpardonable sin. "Every sin and blasphemy will be forgiven men, but the blasphemy against the Spirit, will not be forgiven. Anyone who speaks against the Holy Spirit will not be forgiven, either in this age or in the age to come" (Matt. 12:31–32). "Whoever blasphemes against the Holy Spirit will never be forgiven; he is guilty of an eternal sin" (Mark 3:29). He says this because some Jewish authorities had been saying that Jesus was possessed by an evil spirit (Mark 3:29–30). In fact, they had been sinning against the Holy Spirit by attributing Jesus' good works to an evil spirit. Throughout the past twenty centuries leaders have sometimes done the same thing when new movements have arisen.

As Jesus pointed out, it is difficult for old wineskins to tolerate or contain new wine (Mark 2:22)

Jewish leaders from Galilee, then from Judea, including Jerusalem, objected to Jesus' practice of healing people on the Sabbath, thought his declaring forgiveness blasphemous, and attributed his healings and nature miracles to an evil source. They were probably jealous of his popularity, angry about his winning arguments, and fearful about being able to maintain their own status and perks. The Jewish leaders were never able to prove Jesus wrong until his arrest; then, in the Sanhedrin, they declared him a blasphemer and had him executed for admitting to being the Messiah and saying that they would see him coming on the clouds of Heaven in fulfillment of Daniel 7:13–14. His execution was not the end of him; but the beginning of something wonderfully new.

Chapter 7

Deliverance

My own personal background includes a scientific education resulting in a doctorate in physics with specialization in theoretical nuclear structure, plus further work in nuclear reactions. These studies and the accompanying worldviews did not often consider the possibility that God might have designed and created the universe which was so fascinating for researchers to explore with significant success.

However, I was also growing up in the Episcopal Church and was early given C. S. Lewis' adult science fiction trilogy, and then his nonfiction works explaining and defending the Christian faith. While teaching at Penn State–Fayette Campus in Uniontown, PA, I was moving toward Christian faith and commitment in 1973, then was filled with the Holy Spirit in 1974. As I became involved in Church activities, reading the scriptures, participating in small groups, I also accepted a call to the ministry, took courses, was ordained in 1986, and led a small parish as vicar for 21 years. Though somewhat of an idealist, I already knew about my own sinful nature and failures, saw how world systems could wreak havoc, and considered the possibility of there being angels and demons. But one Sunday morning after preaching about putting on the armor of God from Ephesians 6, I encountered a startling reaction in a woman whom I had given Communion and was anointing with oil. She was oppressed by evil. Then, after a board meeting, another woman came seeking deliverance, not a handout. I was also surprised to find out that witchcraft existed in our county. I remembered the movie about an exorcist in 1973 and did not want to move in that direction.

The Holy Scriptures, ancient traditions, and our use of reason point toward the existence of real evil, found within proud, rebellious angelic beings, in the fallen nature of human beings and in the corrupt world systems that surround us. Our world is often characterized by increasing disorder, competition, disease, weakness, and death rather than life, peace, and joy. Things might well seem hopeless, were it not for God's revelation, healing, and redemption. Evil will lose in the end.

I also realized that a large number of medical conditions brought on by bacteria, viruses, chemicals, pollen, and the presence of other human beings may well do us in, depending on our immune systems, the state of our souls (thinking, emotions, and wills), and the way we treat or mistreat ourselves. I have also noticed how certain conditions of which I am prone just seem to happen before and after a healing conference, an important message that I am preparing, or a house blessing! In fact, studying or writing on the subject of deliverance may itself be dangerous.

We must consider the possibility that the person for whom we are praying may not only have a physical or mental ailment, bear emotional wounds from past events, or lack a personal relationship with God through Jesus Christ but may also suffer from temptation, external or internal oppression from the enemy, even virtual control or possession. Often, we need to ask God, "How should we pray?"

In the Hebrew Scriptures, Satan or the devil appears in the guise of a wise serpent that successfully tempts Eve and Adam to doubt God's goodness and his word in prohibiting their eating from the tree of the self-knowledge of good and evil in Eden. Later, this adversary incites the Lord to take everything away from Job, and then inflicts Job with painful sores and unkind friends, to get him to curse God and die. Satan pushes King David to take a census of Israel, leading to serious plague and uses foreign wives to make wise Solomon act like a fool. According to Zechariah 3:1, the Lord rebuked Satan while pointing to Joshua the high priest and describing him as a stick snatched from the fire. Mark briefly mentions, but Matthew and Luke (Matt. 4:1–11, Luke 4:2–13) give, the three temptations of Jesus in the wilderness after his baptism by John. When Officials accuse Jesus of casting out demons, Jesus argues that if Satan is casting out, or opposing Satan, then his kingdom was coming to an end. Jesus is functioning as the stronger one who binds the strong man, then despoils him of his possessions, or people. When Peter opposes Jesus' plan to die for our sins, Jesus calls him Satan because he is thinking about the things of man, not of God. During the last week of Jesus' life on Earth, Judas agrees to betray Jesus to the authorities, and Satan enters him at the last Supper. Satan had permission to sift Simon Peter like wheat, but Jesus had already prayed that Peter's faith would not fail after he had denied his master three times. Speaking to the Gentiles, Peter (Acts 10:38) describes Jesus' mission as healing all who were under the power of the devil. Ananias and Sapphira are taken over by Satan when they sell their property and lie about it to the apostles. They die on the spot!

Paul (in Acts 26:18) describes the Gospel as turning people from darkness to light and from the power of Satan to the power of God. Paul promises that the God of peace would soon crush Satan under believers' feet (Rom. 16:20). By his death, Jesus has already destroyed the one who holds the power of death over human beings. Generally, the devil and his forces lie, attack, tempt, accuse, and condemn believers.

Jesus sacrificially loved human beings while consistently opposing evil wherever he found it. Jesus refused to yield to temptations coming from Satan, the crowd, or his disciples; faced sudden fierce squalls on the Sea of Galilee, and contended with the hostile mob pushing him into the hands of the Sanhedrin, then the procurator of Rome, and then mocking him as he hung dying on the cross.

He was tempted in every situation as we are (Heb. 4:15), yet he is without sin.

That Christians need to resist temptation, speak the truth in love, and rely on the Lord during persecution is made clear by this selection of Scriptures.

- "And lead us not into temptation, but deliver us from the evil one." (Matt. 6:13)
- "Watch and pray so that you will not fall into temptation. The spirit is willing, but the body is weak." (Matt. 26:41)
- "Do not deprive each other (conjugal rights) except by mutual consent and for a time, so that Satan will not tempt you" (1 Cor. 7:5).
- "No temptation has seized you except what is common to man. And God is faithful; he will not let you be tempted beyond what you can bear. But when you are empted, he will also provide a way out so that you can stand up under it" (1 Cor. 10:13).
- "I have forgiven . . . in order that Satan might not outwit us. For we are not unaware of his schemes." (2 Cor. 2:10–11)
- "Satan himself masquerades as an angel of light [as good]." (2 Cor. 11:14)
- "For we wanted to come to you . . . but Satan stopped us." (1 Thess. 2:18)

- "Your enemy the devil prowls around like a roaring lion looking for someone to devour." (1 Pet. 5:8)
- "The coming of the lawless one will be in accordance with the work of Satan displayed in all kinds of counterfeit miracles, signs and wonders." (2 Thess. 2:9)

We should draw near to God and then resist the devil, using the word of God as Jesus did. God promises us a way out without giving in to sin.

Associated with their evil leader, Satan, are many unclean spirits or demons. Doing a rough calculation based on the number of angels, with one-third having fallen with Satan, their number could be as high as 200 million, presuming no reproduction. Looking briefly at the Hebrew Scriptures we find that humans who worship false gods or idols are really sacrificing to demons. Paul (1 Cor. 10:21) says that we cannot drink the cup of the Lord Jesus and the cup of demons by also participating in their rites. In 1 Timothy 4:1 the spirit of God says that in later times people will abandon the faith and follow deceiving spirits and things taught by demons.

Our scriptural basis for the origin and early fall of Lucifer from the Heaven of God's throne, taking with him something like one-third of the original number of angels created by God before humans, is relatively limited. Consider Isaiah 14:12: "How you have fallen from Heaven, O morning star, son of the dawn! You have been cast down to the earth, you who once laid low the nations! You said in your heart, 'I will ascend to Heaven; I will raise my throne above the stars of God; I will sit enthroned on the mount of assembly, on the utmost heights of the sacred mountain. I will ascend above the tops of the clouds; I will make myself like the Most High.'" Lucifer's pride and self-elevation lead to his tragic downfall and transformation into the adversary (Satan). Even Jesus speaks of him as the prince of this world, as one who has authority over the people of this world—until rendered helpless under Jesus' control.

People may become the slaves of evil through early traumas, following inherited sinful tendencies, unrepentant sin, and participation in the occult. When Jesus sent the twelve and the seventy-two on mission, he specifically gave them delegated authority over unclean spirits. Because I needed encouragement to move cautiously into the area of deliverance, I was told that I too had that authority. Such a ministry is still needed today, even among Church members. After receiving prayer, I was set free from a spirit of religion and a spirit of resentment, resulting in more personal freedom.

When Jesus first speaks in the synagogue at Capernaum, not only are the people in the audience surprised by the note of authority in his teaching, they also observe the way he deals with an unclean spirit within a man that was reacting to Jesus' presence (Mark 1:21–28, Luke 4:31–37). Luke says that the man had a spirit, a demon, that was unclean, that took him over. The demon asked what Jesus wanted with "them" and then tried to stop Jesus by threatening to reveal his identity. Jesus sternly told the spirit to be quiet and leave the man. While briefly shrieking, then throwing the man down, the demon had to obey and left. This confrontation is a great confirmation of Jesus' personal authority and identity.

Then follows an extreme case of demoniac(s) among the tombs northeast of the Sea of Galilee (Matt. 8:28–34, Mark 5:1–20, and Luke 8:26–39). Matthew gives the condensed version. The naked, unkempt, demoniac is so violent, so powerful that no one can keep him chained up or even pass by him without being attacked. As Jesus and his disciples land on the shore near the wild man, he begins to run toward them, but crumples and falls on his knees before Jesus. If C. S. Lewis' picture in the *Screwtape Letters* is accurate,[21] the demons inside this man could see the blinding light of Jesus and were already weakening as Jesus lost no time in commanding the evil spirit(s) to leave the man! As in the earlier account, they defensively cry, "What do you want with us, Son of God? Have you come to torture us before the appointed time?" And: "Swear to God that you won't torture me!" Even in this extreme situation, Jesus is winning.

When Jesus asks the one speaking his name, he says, "My name is Legion, for we are many"(Mark 5:9). A Roman legion might have about six thousand soldiers. They beg Jesus not to send them out of the geographical region, or worse, into the Abyss (described in Revelation 9:2). For us to seek information from demons, including their names, without our having the gift of discernment, might lead to our being lied to or reacting in fear about the numbers against us.

One contemporary book, Strongman's His Name identifies strong spirits associated with their traits: divination, jealousy, lying, perversion, pride, whoredoms, infirmity, bondage, fear, error, seduction, and death and pictures several spirits functioning together around or within a demonized person.[22]

Apparently, demons like having someone or something to inhabit and control. When the demons beg Jesus to let them enter a large herd of pigs, Jesus gives them permission. When the demons suddenly inhabit the animals, they go berserk and rush like stampeding buffalo down a steep bank into a lake, where they all perish, leaving the demons homeless. The frightened pig herders run into town and tell everyone what had happened.

Despite having been possessed by a legion of demons, the former demoniac is soon seated calmly, in his right mind and wearing clothing probably given to him by the startled disciples. Despite his earlier wildness and super strength, this man is able to approach Jesus and be set free. When the locals arrive and see the man in a perfectly normal state, they are quite frightened by the power of God in Jesus (just as the disciples had been after Jesus had quieted the storm on the nearby sea) and they ask Jesus to leave their region. These Gentiles may have had the reverential fear of God instilled in them.

Then, the former demoniac asks to be permitted to follow Jesus as a disciple. With compassion and love, Jesus tells the man to go home to his family and tell them how the Lord had shown him mercy.

Once again the news spread rapidly over the region of the ten Greek cities (Decapolis) We may conclude that neither great storms nor powerfully possessed human beings could overcome the authority and power of Christ.

According to Matthew, after Jesus has healed two blind men, a mute demonized man is brought to him. If that person were brought to us, we might not know the cause of his disabilities without a gift of discernment or asking other people. After Jesus drives out the demon, the man begins speaking and the crowd claims that this type of healing had never before been seen in Israel (Matt. 9:32–34).

Then we come to the Syro-Phoenician woman who found Jesus in the pagan seacoast region of Tyre and Sidon. (Her feisty faith, which overcame Jesus' statement that the bread of healing is for children, not dogs, is discussed in chapter 4.) Her request of Jesus, whom she calls Lord and of whom she asks for mercy, is for her absent daughter. She asks Jesus to set her daughter free. When Jesus responds to her bold reply, he says: "Woman, you have great faith! Your request is granted! The demon has gone." When the happy woman goes home, she finds her daughter resting in bed. Again, Jesus' declaration was synchronized with the reality of God's action. Once more, Jesus accomplishes a deliverance with seeming ease.

In the case of the boy who was both demonized and epileptic, or moonstruck, we have also considered the faith of the father, who appeals to Jesus to do something if he can, after Jesus' disciples had already failed to set the boy free. This deliverance occurs shortly after three other disciples had seen the transfiguration of Jesus on the mountain and heard God's voice in a cloud. (We have moved from the mountaintop of revelation, to the valley of seeming chaos and despair.)

According to the descriptions in all three Synoptics, the boy had often been in danger of dying as he went into various seizures, falling helplessly onto the ground, into the water, or into a nearby fire with foaming mouth, rigidity, gnashing teeth, and convulsions. While many people may have experienced seizures due to traumatic brain damage, like mine, his was due to a spiritual attack.

Once Jesus finds out how long the boy's condition had lasted and tells the father that all things were possible, Jesus has the boy brought to him, and while the demon has the boy in another convulsion, Jesus rebukes the demon, commands it to come out, and (after identifying it as a deaf and mute spirit) orders it never to enter the boy again. Toward the end of the incident, the boy lies on the ground, looking like a corpse, but Jesus takes him by the hand and lifts him to his feet. The boy is healed and free of this nasty demon. When the disciples are alone with Jesus, they ask him why they had failed to heal the boy. Jesus says that the demon could not be forced to leave the boy except by prayer, and he notes their prior lack of faith. (Some manuscripts add fasting to prayer as a necessity.) Prior to the deliverance, when the boy's father tells Jesus about the disciples' failure, Jesus speaks clearly about an unbelieving and perverse generation, then he asks with some frustration, "How long shall I stay with you? How long will I put up with you!?" In the midst of several negative environmental factors, Jesus sets this boy free. (Unless I have to deal immediately with a demon, I prefer to team with people who have various spiritual gifts and prepare with confession, prayer, putting on the armor of God, and fasting before attempting to set free a demonized adult or child. The Christian who will be prayed for should prepare likewise or have wounds from their past healed with forgiveness.)

In Matthew 12:22–29 and Luke 11:14–25 we find an account of a man afflicted with blindness, weakness, and inability to speak, a condition imposed on him by a demon. Rarely does God's word provide any indication of how such demons gain access and then take control of people. Jesus drives the demon out, which allows the man to be healed and to speak. Only in this case does the crowd asks whether Jesus might be the Son of David or the Messiah. The Pharisees' counterclaim was that Jesus had been casting out demons by Beelzebub, the prince of demons. In the Lucan account, Jesus describes the situation in which an evil spirit leaves a man and then wanders in desert places without finding any rest, eventually deciding to return to the house (the person) he had left. Finding the place cleaned up but empty, the demon finds seven spirits that are more evil than he, and they all invade that same house. Inhabited by eight demons with various evil characteristics, the man is in far worse shape than he had been before being rid of the first demon. When an individual is set free and the house cleansed, it is critical that the person to be born again and then filled with the Holy Spirit so that the demons will not be able to get back in!

Now we come to the final unique account in the Gospel according to Luke of a woman who had been crippled and bent over by a spirit for eighteen long years of sitting in a synagogue on the Sabbath. That morning, Jesus had been teaching but had decided to take action despite the controversy it might cause. He calls the woman forward and tells her, "Woman, you are set free (loosed) from your infirmity." He then puts his hands on the woman and she immediately straightens up and praises God. The synagogue ruler says indignantly that there are six other days in the week during which the woman can have been healed. But Jesus says that if each of his hearers would untie his ox or donkey on the Sabbath to give it water, should not this daughter of Abraham, whom Satan had kept bound for eighteen years, be set free on the Sabbath? (I would suggest that the house of the Lord, the sanctified place where we worship and praise God, is an ideal place for setting people free. Indeed, praising and worshiping God in preparation and receiving communion around God's table is an excellent way to strengthen the team while weakening the enemy. Using holy water and salt or anointing with oil has a definite effect! Our overall focus should not be on any unclean spirit in our midst, but on Jesus and his powerful work of redemption and deliverance on the cross, which has won the essential victory. Truly, every knee will bow and every tongue will confess that Jesus IS Lord, to the glory of God!)

These individual accounts, as well as the summaries of Jesus' healings in group settings, demonstrate that Jesus had been uniformly successful in setting people free from evil, unclean spirits. Such deliverances occurred in a variety of places where Israel had once existed as a unified state but had been overrun by foreign empires. Most were places where the true God and various false Gods had been worshiped or honored. Some of the people who had been delivered were definitely part of God's first people, the Jews.

You may look at what happened when crowds gathered to be healed and set free after Peter's mother-in-law had been healed, at Jesus' teaching from the boat, at Jesus' ministry at Capernaum, and at his ministry while John the Baptist's disciples made their inquiry. Sizable numbers were set free from demonic influence, oppression, or control. Today, the oppressed crowds might include those addicted to various substances or behaviors.

Now we consider the ministry of Jesus' disciples and other early Christian leaders. I have already summarized their ministries in the next chapter on healing patterns. In imitation of their master, the twelve and the seventy-two not only preached the good news in a simple way and healed the sick but also cast demons out of other people. Their only notable failure was the demonized boy discussed earlier in this chapter.

In the book of Acts, we read how Deacon Phillip, traveling to Samaria during the first persecution under Saul's leadership, began his ministry with miraculous signs, with paralytics and other crippled persons being healed, and with evil spirits leaving many people with loud shrieks. Such works of God produced great joy in the city and even impressed Simon, the showman, who was baptized along with the others then received the Holy Spirit with them at the hands of the apostles. (Unfortunately, Simon wanted to purchase God's power for his own use!)

When Saul was converted on the road to Damascus, blinded, then healed and filled with the Holy Spirit, he spent some time alone, then ministered and preached in Damascus and Antioch before setting out on his first missionary trip with Barnabas. From that time he was renamed Paul. While sharing their faith with Sergius Paulus, a proconsul on the island of Crete, Saul and Barnabas had a powerful encounter with a Jewish sorcerer named Bar-Jesus, who opposed their message. Paul had told the man that he was a child of the devil and an enemy of everything that was right. Paul said that the hand of the Lord was against the man and the man would be unable to see for a while. The defeated man could only with difficulty find his way out of the building in his own darkness.

In Philippi, Paul makes converts, including Lydia, down by the riverside. Later, when he is preaching downtown, he gets free publicity from a slave girl who also acts as a channel for a fortune-telling, deceptive spirit. (Such involvement in occult activities is condemned in the Old Testament!) The girl cries out often, saying that Paul and Barnabas are servants of the most high God and that they are telling people the way to be saved (Acts 16:17). After several days, Paul turns around, looks at her, and commands the spirit to leave her in the name of Jesus, which it does. It did. Then her statements about people and predictions failed. The angry owners had the missionaries beaten and thrown in jail. Even their sufferings led to the out spread of the Gospel and the growth of the church, because the jailer and his family came to faith. When Paul told the authorities that he was a Roman citizen, he was quietly and quickly escorted out of town.

When some Jewish exorcists tried to use the name of Jesus to deliver a powerful demonized man, the spirit knew Jesus and had heard about Paul, but did not recognize them and beat them until they ran away naked. They had no right to use Jesus' name because they did not belong to him. According to accounts from the second through fourth centuries of the Christian era, ordinary believers were routinely casting out demons and healing the sick. In Italy today, for example, there are dozens of official clergy exorcists in the Roman Catholic Church.

In this chapter, we have seen that unclean spirits can disrupt a person's senses, his or her thinking and ability to communicate. They can cause some to act in a bizarre, violent, or crazy manner, very unlike their usual state. With sufficient control, demons can speak through humans and submerge their personalities. Some of these phenomena can also be caused by medical events, chemical changes, genetic anomalies, drugs, and human conditioning! In early Christian centuries, candidates for baptism were anointed and leaders prayed for them to be set free from demonic powers as they also renounced the world, the flesh, and the devil. There are sincere Christians who need to be set free from oppression. Some illnesses have a demonic component or cause; but I do not know the percentage. Other illnesses may be the result of disobedience and its consequences. Experience and gifts of discernment are very helpful in deciding which ministry should be pursued and whether to refer persons out. Jesus is still setting people free through the Church, his body.

In addition to dealing with our fallen, fleshly nature, we should also be prepared for outside temptations, lies, and accusations as we engage in a full healing ministry. Let us:

- "Put on the whole armor of God daily." (Eph. 6:10–13)
- "Study to show ourselves approved . . . rightly dividing the word of truth." (2Tim. 2:15)
- "Submit yourselves therefore to God. Resist the devil, and he will flee from you." (James 4:7)
- "Cast off the works of darkness and let us put on the armor of light. Let us walk honestly . . . and put on the Lord Jesus Christ, and make not provision for the flesh to fulfill the lusts thereof." (Rom. 13:12–14)

- "Be sober, be vigilant; because your adversary the devil, as a roaring lion, walks about, seeking whom he may devour: whom resist steadfast in the faith." (1 Pet. 5:8–9)

Today there are many books dealing with the problem of evil, overcoming temptations, and setting people free from demonic oppression. Deliverance was and is a valid ministry for Christians who do have both authority and power to deal with unclean spirits. However, we are to primarily focus on God as we study his word, praise and thank him, worship him in Spirit and truth, and allow him to sanctify us through and through.

I would suggest using one of the biblical or contemporary models in ministry as a starting point, while realizing that during ministry the presence of one or more unclean spirits may become manifest or be revealed by a gift of discernment. Don't rely on a demon for information. The ministry team may bind the spirit and set up an appointment for deliverance ministry, refer the person to a godly, sound minister in this area, or go ahead with the healing. Significant numbers of Christians are struggling alone with sin, addictions, and despair while much of the Church denies both the possibility of evil incursion and the power of God to set captives free. If we are out of our depth, unable to help someone, we should say so!

Selected Additional Scriptures on Deliverance in a Broad Sense

- Moses answered the people, "Do not be afraid. Stand firm and you will see the deliverance the LORD will bring you today. The Egyptians you see today you will never see again." (Ex. 14:13)

- "The LORD will deliver them to you, and you must do to them all that I have commanded you. Be strong and courageous. Do not be afraid or terrified because of them, for the LORD your God goes with you; he will never leave you nor forsake you." (Deut. 31: 5)

- "Then the LORD said to Joshua, 'Do not be afraid; do not be discouraged. Take the whole army with you, and go up and attack Ai. For I have delivered into your hands the king of Ai.'" (Josh. 8:1)

- "Then Hannah prayed and said: 'My heart rejoices in the LORD; in the LORD my horn is lifted high. My mouth boasts over my enemies, for I delight in your deliverance.'" (1Sam. 2:1)

- "The LORD who delivered me from the paw of the lion and the paw of the bear will deliver me from the hand of this Philistine." (1Sam. 17: 37)

- "Rather, worship the LORD your God; it is he who will deliver you from the hand of all your enemies." (2 Kings 17: 39)

- "You will not have to fight this battle. Take up your positions; stand firm and see the deliverance the LORD will give you, O Judah." (2Chron. 20:17)

- "In you our fathers put their trust; they trusted and you delivered them. . . . He trusts in the LORD; let the LORD rescue him. Let him deliver him, since he delights in him." (Ps. 22:4)

- "Rescue me and deliver me in your righteousness; turn your ear to me and save me. Be my rock of refuge." (Ps. 71:2)

- "At that time Michael, the great prince who protects your people, will arise. There will be a time of distress such as has not happened from the beginning of nations until then. But at that time your people—everyone whose name is found written in the book—will be delivered." (Dan. 12:1)

- "And lead us not into temptation, but deliver us from the evil one" (Matt. 6:13).

- "For I know that through your prayers and the help given by the Spirit of Jesus Christ, what has happened to me will turn out for my deliverance." (Phil.1:19)

Chapter 8

Healing and the Reign of Christ

I have already shown that healings and deliverances were major, integral, and vital components of Jesus' overall proclamation and demonstration of the Gospel, the life-changing good news, which was beginning to transform individuals, groups, and society, almost forcing his enemies to take harsh action against him. I want to look at his major theme of the kingdom or reign of God in the lives of individuals as the overall pattern in which we can situate his healing ministry as well as his proclamation of a new, radical, word of God, which calls us to very different lives. Many authors of healing books consider the changes that happen in our lives as we are brought to faith in Jesus the Christ, turn away from our sins and wrong attitudes, and then follow Jesus to as the most crucial spiritual healing. This acceptance of Jesus results in a new relationship with God, through our Savior, Lord, and Healer. This new birth has the potentiality of changing everything; but we often settle back into old familiar patterns of feelings, thoughts, and behaviors, rather than seeking further transformation.

In the New International Version (NIV) Gospel passages there are 114 verses that use the word "kingdom," while the rest of the New Testament has only 35. We can find 82 verses with the phrase "kingdom of Heaven" or "kingdom of God" in the Gospels. Matthew prefers the former phrase to avoid taking the Lord's name in vain. In the four Gospels, the word "reign" is used only twice, and Jesus does not speak about his ruling other people. What is this kingdom about which John the Baptist and Jesus speak so often? We will begin by considering several scriptures about the kingdom, including a variety of parables—stories or pictures about this emerging new reality among us.

After beginning with a genealogy of Jesus Christ, the descendant of Abraham and King David, showing that Jesus was of the kingly line of Judah, and then calling Jesus the Christ, or Messiah, the author of the Gospel according to Matthew notes Jesus' birth in Bethlehem, the city of David, and then presents the only account of Magi coming from the East, due to the appearance of a new star in the constellation of Pisces. According to their beliefs that star announced the arrival of a new king in the land of Israel, whom the Magi wished to worship. Their appearance before Herod the Great, vassal King under Rome, and their failure to report back, lead to Herod's attempt to kill all boys under the age of two living in

Bethlehem, the city where Micah had predicted the new king would be born (Mic. 5:2). Joseph, Mary, and Jesus escape Herod's wrath by fleeing to Egypt, then returning to Israel and settling in Nazareth.

About 30 years later, a strange prophet named John appears in the wilderness by the Jordan River, telling everyone, "Repent, for the kingdom of Heaven is near" (Matt. 3:1). Matthew identifies John as the voice in the wilderness of Isaiah 40:3, and Jesus later says that John is the forerunner, come in the power and spirit of Elijah. John labels the crowds and the religious leaders as vipers, and then warns them that they must produce fruit in keeping with true repentance, because the axe is already being laid at the root of their trees. Large numbers of people are baptized in the Jordan River as a sign of their repentance, while John points to the greater one coming, whose baptism will be with the Spirit and with fire, then result in the future separation of productive wheat and useless chaff. As soon as Jesus is baptized, spirit filled, and tempted, he preaches the same basic message, urging repentance because of the approach and nearness of the kingdom or reign of God (Matt. 4:17, Mark 1:15). Jesus also urges everyone to trust fully in the good news that he is proclaiming. In his hometown synagogue at Nazareth, Jesus tells his listeners that Isaiah 61 is even then being fulfilled! We too must change our minds and attitudes in the light of the impending kingdom of God. Right now we are at the crisis point of decision and commitment.

Near the end of his earthly life, Jesus rides into the city of Jerusalem, declaring himself to be the peaceful king of Israel, fulfilling Zechariah 9, as the disciples and the fickle crowds call him the Son of David (the Messiah). This prophetic action is followed by his cleansing the temple, experiencing focused opposition by the established high priestly families under Rome, and, finally, being rejected, mocked, and executed.

God's new reign had come in a radical counter-cultural way, totally unrecognized by the leaders but predicted by God's holy word and taught by Jesus. Scholars have argued for decades about the kingdom of God: whether it was present during the life of Jesus, or purely in the future, as during his prophesied millennial reign, or as inaugurated, having begun but not yet taking hold. Some writers picture Jesus as a failed revolutionary or as a wise man or guru who spoke timeless truths; but no theories are sufficient. Usually, we create a fictitious Jesus of our own imaginings.

According to a Web article by Kurt Struckmeyer,[23] many Christians think of the kingdom of God as his dynamic reign or rule in individual's hearts and minds, through his presence and words, a view that downplays Christ's overall direction of the Church as the Body of Christ. Luke 17:21 can be translated as "the kingdom of God is within you," or "among you." When looking at such scriptures, we need to check whether the pronouns are singular or plural in the original language. Americans think in more individualistic terms than did first century Jews.

Other people identify the kingdom of God with the Church, an organized society, where people recognize God's rule. But the broken, fragmented, sometimes warring groups and other failures of the Church make us leery of identifying any actual Church with God's kingdom. Others identify the kingdom with God's reign in a place or form of existence called Heaven. That can make God's reign seem future, illusory, or irrelevant. What about this world, its institutions, our environment, and outer space? What about visions of a recreated Earth and Heaven, resurrection, and the Church coming down? Isn't God's reign also here and now, among us?

Still others think of the kingdom of God as a country or territory on the Earth, where God reigns. But didn't Jesus admit that he is a king to Pilate, while saying that his kingdom is not of this world (John 18:36)? Wink thinks that the world (cosmos) is an evil existence, a form of domination through politics and economics, rather than geographical turf.[24] Jesus' values are the opposite of those of the world. We cannot avoid that conclusion when we read the whole Sermon on the Mount and then think of our performance. Other people view the reign of God as occurring in a separate, isolated, purified society, a mini–Utopia, where God hangs out with his special friends. Utopian communities, such as the Shaker community, Brook Farm, the Ephrata Cloister, the Harmony Society, and the Oneida Community, have been quite popular in North America. How long have they worked? Their ideals, strong leaders, and high hopes may only last until the human weakness of all become evident. Didn't Jesus tell a parable about letting the wheat and the tares grow together until the judgment?

Well, Mr. Struckmeyer has his own view: "The kingdom of God was Jesus' metaphor for his vision of the way things were meant to be. A vision is a realistic, credible, attractive future for an individual, group, or organization. The right vision is an idea so energizing that it jump-starts a new future by calling forth the skills, talents, and resources to make it happen. Then, it actually reshapes the present."[25] I liked this definition. Jesus doesn't actually define the meaning of the kingdom of God, but what does he say about it?

In Matthew 13:44–46 we find two brief parables: "The kingdom of Heaven is like treasure hidden in a field." When someone accidentally discovers the treasure in the field, he hides it again, then joyfully goes and sells everything he has in order to purchase the field. I thought of the costly robot and other equipment used to find Spanish treasure wrecks in the Caribbean. A merchant for pearls searches until he finds an exquisite, large, perfect pearl. Then he sells everything else in order to purchase that pearl. I looked all afternoon at the gem show in Tucson during February 2010, growing weary, but found nothing that was worth everything in my wallet. Jesus is saying that the kingdom of Heaven is very precious, worth even the loss of everything else — money, fame, and careers. Jesus urges us to seek first his kingdom, then everything else necessary will be given us as well (Matt. 6:33). He also realistically warns us that we cannot actually serve two masters. We will hate the one and love the other, or we will be devoted to one and despise the other. We cannot serve both God and mammon (money). Many of us actually have two or three idols, which we try to support, while pretending to serve the true God in church. Jesus often challenges us to follow him, even if it means taking up our cross then walking toward our own execution.

The kingdom of God is like a tiny mustard seed (Matt. 13:31). Some scholars argue whether it really is the smallest seed that people plant in the ground, in order to find fault with Jesus' parables. We are to simply listen to Jesus, let his words bring meaning to us, then respond. The mustard seed is very small, yet when it is planted it becomes a large garden plant, with treelike branches that can even shelter sizable birds! God's kingdom seems very insignificant at first, just affecting a few people, but after some months and years, it is able to shelter all sorts of people—even Gentiles! Jesus also speaks about yeast, often a sign of evil, which when placed in a large measure of flour or dough works (ferments) through the entire mass, causing it to swell up with holes, ready to be baked into bread. Even a small amount of the Gospel proclamation, or perhaps the infectious life of a Christian, acting as salt and light, can begin to affect a larger group of people.

Most of us know the story of the sower and the various kinds of soil (Matt. 13:1–9, 18–23) pretty well. Many in the original seaside crowd did not have the ears to hear or the eyes to see what Jesus was talking about. Even the disciples needed help to understand it. So we have what amounts to an allegory, which identifies each object in the story. The sower broadcast sows the word of God, which is the seed, making it land in various kinds of soil. The path represents the hard ground where everyone walks. The seeds lie on the surface, then are easily seen and snatched away by the birds. If we hear the message but don't understand it, Satan soon snatches it away, and it bears no fruit.

Some seeds fall on a rocky shelf with only a thin layer of soil, so the seeds cannot reach any depth. When watered, they soon sprout and quickly appear; but when the hot sun hits them, the tender new plants soon wither and die. A person can receive the word with joy, but because there is no depth, persecution or troubles terminate that life that has barely begun. Other seeds fall among hardy thorn plants, which grow quickly, expand, and block out the light. The seeds never produce mature, healthy plants. Nevertheless, some of the seeds fall on good ground, grow to maturity, and reproduce, multiplying thirty-, sixty-, or even a hundredfold. This represents people who hear, receive, and understand the word of God, then persevere and bring forth good results. That's where the emphasis of the parable lies. Despite all possible difficulties, God's reign does expand and bear good fruit as people respond to the good news.

In the parable of the wheat and the tares, even when good seed is sowed in good ground, the enemy, Satan, may sow tares, look-alike plants that will produce no grain, among the wheat, resulting in such frustration that a farmer is tempted to dig up the garden early and attempt to remove the tares, which would damage the wheat. At harvest time, the full grain can be removed and processed, while the leftover tares are bundled then burned (Matt. 13:24 –31). It is not wise to try to separate those in the kingdom from those who are not for the harvest. According to Mark 4, the farmer does not understand the processes by which plants grow and mature, but the plants do that on their own. When the plants are ready, the farmer puts his sickle to them, reaps, and enjoys the results anyway. Paul could truly say that he planted, Apollo and others watered, but God gave the growth!Similarly, the message of the Gospel, like a large net, lets down into the depths, which when raised will pull in all kinds of fish (Matt. 13:47–50). Some will be large, tasty, and sellable. Others will be too small, young, damaged, or harmful. At the harvest, they too can be sorted out and separated, with some thrown away. As God expands his reign through his son Jesus Christ, many people will be pulled in, and many will be attracted and seem to be part of the school of fish. Jesus warns, however: "Not everyone who says to me, 'Lord, Lord,' will enter the kingdom of Heaven, but only he who does the will of my Father who is in Heaven" (Matt. 7:21). Some will actually prophesy and drive out demons in Jesus' name, which are good things; yet, in the end, Jesus will state that he never knew them. It is possible for God to use people in ministry who still have serious character or moral flaws, as long as they are willing to be transformed or healed. Jesus won't break a bruised reed or snuff out a smoldering candlewick (Matt. 12:20), but he opposes the proud Pharisee and the self-satisfied young ruler.

If nonbelievers or cultural Christians attempt to use the Sermon on the Mount as a blueprint for life in this world (cosmos), they will realize their total inability to do what it says. As Jesus told Nicodemus, we need to be changed so radically that we can describe it as a new birth or a birth from above. A Christian veneer, often seen in Church, is not enough. We cannot even see the kingdom of God or enter it unless we are born again. Flesh can only give birth to flesh; but the Spirit gives birth to spirit, producing new life within us. Like the wind, the Holy Spirit gives us a new freedom to live differently. Unless we change and become like little children, trusting in Jesus, we will never enter the kingdom of Heaven (Matt. 18:3). This is the beginning of the new life, which also requires our further healing and change as we are cured of our waywardness, with a new heart or center within (Ezek. 18).

The Holy Spirit is the convicter, the encourager, the sanctifier, and the one who matures. Unfortunately, many of us go forward at an evangelistic service and are born again but later lose our first love for Jesus and stay in one place. We are languidly waiting for Jesus the bridegroom to appear, but some don't have the oil of the Spirit while the others who do fall asleep for a long time! This Gospel of the kingdom, the reign of Christ, must be preached in word and deed, with signs of God's presence and power, including healings to the whole world as a testimony, then the end will come (Matt. 24:14).

In humbling himself to become man, then dying on the cross for our sins, the true king became the suffering servant of all. The Son of Man did not come to be served but to serve and give his life as a ransom for many (Matt. 20:24). The disciple who wants to be first should become the slave of everyone else. Of course, Jesus is now raised from the dead, exalted to the right hand of God, above all other powers, authorities, and dominions, until all things are under his control. Yet, primarily, in his body, the Church, Jesus still humbly serves, heals, and refreshes other people. If we endure, we will reign with Christ as kings and priests, but now we win the victory by our faith, testimony, patience, and service to God and people in need, while building up the Church and God's kingdom.

In following Jesus Christ, walking with him and other disciples, we are not slavishly obeying the old law, especially the Pharisaic elaborations of every commandment, including the law of the Sabbath. For example, the rules about foods we can or cannot eat have been relativized by Jesus' comment that food cannot defile us or make us unclean. The words that come out of our mouths make us unclean (Matt 12:34, 15:11, 15:16). However, Jesus gave a strict interpretation of the commandments against adultery and murder by pointing to the sins of lust and sarcastic, hateful comments. In his *book What Jesus Demands from the World*,[26] John Piper lists, explains, and applies the commands of Jesus found in the Gospels. Many of these are humanly impossible without God's help! At his ascension, Jesus told his followers to make disciples, baptize them in the threefold name, and teach them to obey everything that he had commanded! If his followers truly love Jesus, they will obey what he has commanded, and he delivers on his promise to send another counselor, the Spirit, to be with them forever. Letting sin reign in our mortal bodies leads to death, and this applies to our giving way to fear, lust, unforgiveness, resentment, malice, self-pity, and despair. When we do sin then confess our sins, God is faithful and just to forgive our sins and cleanse us from all our unrighteousness (1 John 1:9).

In *Transforming the Inner Man*,[27] John and Paula Sandford echo God's frustration with the fruit from people's lives. Israel (Isa. 5:1–7) was planted in Canaan after the fertile ground was cleared, a watchtower and winepress built, and a hedge of protection put around. God expected a crop of good grapes, but the land yielded only bad fruit, bloodshed, and many cries of distress. Soon he would remove the hedge, break down the wall, and allow it to be trampled. Jesus described himself as the true vine, with his Father functioning as the gardener (John 15:1–16). Branches that bear no fruit will be cut off, like the fig tree that was given one extra year with special care. Branches that do bear fruit get pruned way back in the fall so that they will become more fruitful. Ouch! The only way we can be fruitful is to remain in Jesus, connected to him, so that the sap of the Holy Spirit can flow from Jesus to us. If we steadily remain in Jesus we will bear much fruit. Without Jesus, we can do nothing! Once, while walking outside after the retreat of heavy snows, I could see many branches broken off from the trees. They were doomed to dry out, wither, and die, then be thrown into the fire. Jude mentions men who are blemishes at love feasts, feeding only themselves, autumn trees without any fruit and uprooted, twice dead (Jude 11–13). However if we remain in Jesus, bearing much fruit, we can ask for whatever we want and it will be granted, because it will flow from our master. Land that drinks up the water but only produces destructive plants is in danger of being cursed. Since God is patient, we too need to be patient as we await some good results from the good seeds of the Gospel, which we have planted, watered, and mulched.

Consider the eternal life, which is a reality for Christians. By contrast, we are not to worry about food, drink, and clothing (Matt.6:25–27). Trying to save or protect our old life (*bios*) may result in our losing true life. Those who have lost many things, including their families, for Jesus' sake will receive much more and inherit eternal life (Matt. 19:29). The rich young ruler whom Jesus loved had obeyed the commandments but wouldn't lay aside his earthly treasure to follow Jesus. In Jesus is life (*zoe*), and that life is the light of men, shining in the darkness (John 1:4). God so loved the world that he gave his one and only son, that whoever believes in him shall not perish but have eternal life (John 3:16). Jesus is the bread of life, living water, and the cup of salvation. The Spirit gives life; the flesh counts for nothing (John 6:63). Jesus came that we might have life and have it to the full. He gives us eternal life so that we will never perish. As sin reigned in death, grace is now reigning through righteousness to bring eternal life (Rom. 5:18).

The Sandfords would say that any tree that produces bad fruit must have a bad root or bad source that needs to be located and removed. One example is the root of bitterness that defiles the whole person. James protests the inconsistency of a person who blesses God while cursing his fellow man. An apple tree doesn't produce thistles unless someone has grafted in another species that has thorns! The demands and acts (Gal. 5:19–21) of the sinful nature, which when followed lead to corruption and death, are contrary to the good fruit of the Spirit, namely love, joy, peace, patience, kindness, goodness, faithfulness, gentleness, and self-control (Gal. 5:22–23). James contrasts the earthly, unspiritual wisdom of the devil (James 3:14–16) with the wisdom from Heaven (James 3:17–18). The Christian should be manifesting the latter.

Near the beginning of the Epistle of James, the writer identifies the sources of our fights, quarrels, coveting, even killing as the ungodly desires within us. His corrective follows: "Submit yourselves, then to God. Resist the devil, and he will flee from you. Come near to God and he will come near to you. Wash your hands, you sinners, and purify your hearts, you double-minded . . . Humble yourselves before the Lord and he will lift you up" (James 4:7–10). We need the continuing work of God in our lives to be changed and purified. By our serving and helping one another using the talents, resources, and gifts that we have been given, we move toward maturity, consistency, and fruit bearing, to God's glory.

The reign of Christ in the world is currently expanding through the Gospel message being heard by the people of the world, with accompanying healings, signs, and wonders, and through the witness of personal transformation and emerging wholeness in the lives of Christians and the Church, with its subsequent impact, rather than by armed conquest and subjugation. Unfortunately, many Christians have begun with the new-birth experience and then stopped, rather than allowing God to do a complete remodeling job. Healing is integral to the reign of God in our lives.

Chapter 9

New Testament and Contemporary Healing Models

Model 1: Jesus' Disciples on Mission
(Matt. 10:1–42; Mark 3:14, 6:7–13; Luke 9:1–6, 9–10, 10:1–24)

W e have three synoptic accounts of the mission of the twelve apostles occurring before the midpoint of these narratives, after the disciples had "been in Christ's company, witnessing his miraculous works, hearing his doctrine about the kingdom, and learning how to pray and how to live."[28] In Luke we have an additional account of the mission of seventy-two other unnamed disciples. We don't know how the disciples felt as they moved out in mission, but we learn of their success and something of their excitement as they return, along with Jesus' own reaction and correction. Recall also the fact that the Holy Spirit was not within them, but only with them. Only Matthew mentions Jesus' instruction that the twelve apostles were only to go to the lost sheep of Israel, not to Samaritans or Gentiles.

The first three accounts state that Jesus gave the twelve apostles authority, which is the right to act as his representatives over evil spirits or demons in order to drive them out, but only Luke notes that they were given power (*dunamis*), which is the ability to complete this work. Without our actually being Jesus' disciples, with a legitimate right to use his supreme name, we probably will be defeated, as were the sons of Sceva! I had to read several books and be encouraged by an expert in deliverance before I was ready to use the power and authority that were already there. However, I certainly was not eager to participate even in low-level spiritual warfare; while learning obedience to Christ, my Savior and Lord.

The actual mission of the twelve apostles, according to Jesus, was to preach the message about the proximity of the kingdom or reign of God and to "Heal the sick, raise the dead, cleanse those who have leprosy, drive out demons. Freely you have received, freely give" (Matt. 10:6–8). Briefly, Luke says that the apostles were to preach the kingdom of God and to heal the sick (Luke 9:2). The Gospel should always be proclaimed both in words and in deeds or signs. Even though Jesus had been involved regularly in such a ministry, I am fairly certain that this was a very challenging assignment for his disciples. One contemporary training method begins with one person ministering and another watching, and then the balance gradually shifts as the second person begins to help in the ministering, then takes the lead, and eventually does it all.

Jesus also gave the apostles basic instructions for their traveling, staying, and responding to positive or negative reactions. They were to travel quite light, without money or extra clothing, for the worker was worth his keep (Matt. 10:9), and to stay at the first deserving house where they were welcomed, not seeking better arrangements but letting their peace (shālōm) come upon the house. If they were neither welcomed nor listened to, they were to shake the dust from their sandals as a testimony against the people or town, which would soon face judgment. Matthew adds a significant passage about future persecutions as Jesus warns his disciples to be both wise as serpents and innocent as doves. The apostles would be treated in the same way as their teacher and master, but anyone who gave them even a cup of water because they were disciples would be rewarded.

Matthew doesn't actually say what the twelve disciples did, but Mark indicates that they went out and preached that people should repent, drove out many demons, and anointed many sick people with oil and healed them. Luke just states that they returned to Jesus and reported what they had done. Matthew's unique mention of anointing is a precursor to the pattern of James 5 and later church practice.

In Luke 10, after the mission of the twelve, Peter's confession, and the transfiguration of Jesus, followed by the disciples' difficulty with a demonized child and Samaritan opposition, Jesus recruits a larger group of disciples by proclaiming: "The harvest is plentiful, but the workers are few. Ask the Lord of the harvest, therefore, to send out workers into his harvest field." Speedily and urgently, Jesus makes seventy-two of them part of the answer to their own prayers. He commands them to move out like lambs among potential wolves, carrying few possessions, not chattering on, until they greet their potential host with God's shalom, which will rest on worthy homes. They were to eat what was given to them, heal the sick, and tell them that God's reign was very near. If not welcomed, they were to ritually wipe off the dust from their feet in judgment. Listening to these disciples or rejecting them was the same as doing it to Jesus and the Father.

When they returned, the seventy-two unknowns were excited and joyful. They were surprised to find out that even demons submitted to them in Jesus' name. Paul said later: "At the Name of Jesus every knee should bow and every tongue should confess to the glory of God" as everything comes under Jesus' reign (Phil. 2:10). Jesus responds by saying that he has seen Satan, the adversary, taking a fall like lightning from the atmospheric Heaven. They had discovered that Jesus had indeed given them, such ordinary disciples, authority to tramp on harmful living creatures and to overcome the power of their real spiritual enemies without being stopped, as Paul demonstrated later on the island of Malta when a viper struck him! But instead of being elated about the unclean spirits being subject to them, these disciples should be rejoicing because their names were written in Heaven, in the book of life. Jesus, himself, rejoiced because God had revealed these things to babes, to little children, his disciples, not to those who were wise among men. In fact, the Son reveals the Father to us (Matt. 11:27).

These Jewish disciples of various ages, backgrounds, experiences, perhaps even gender, were surprised about the way that God had used them in ministry as his final group of representatives, preceding him as he moved toward Jerusalem and his final destiny. Can you imagine yourself being among them? Jesus Christ wants all of us to be ministers of Christ right where we are, but he envisions and expects the church to move outward in widening circles to have an impact on the entire world.

This first pattern of ministry, including both speaking and acting, is a bold one of expansion among people who might not know anything about the Christ, even today, in the mall, at sports events, or in family gatherings. It is pictured in Bill Johnson's book, *When Heaven Invades Earth.*[29] What would we do if we heard Jesus telling us to go and speak to a stranger? In most cases, ministry is learned by trying to do it with the help of others. Having an excellent disciple-trainer like Jesus, along with courage and fortitude, is necessary for launching out and winning others through preaching and by demonstrating the reality and power of the Good News.

In *Rediscovering Kingdom Healing,*[30] Mike Endicott has presented a straightforward form of this pattern featuring the proclamation of the good news, including the work of Christ on the cross to provide both forgiveness and healing, and our coming with expectant faith.

Model 2: Body Gifts of the Spirit
(1 Corinthians 12–14)

In addition to the wonderful gift of the Holy Spirit himself, who dwells within us, manifests his presence, produces in us the character of Christ and the fruit of the Spirit, but also provides spiritual gifts, which are new or enhanced spiritual abilities to build up and grow the Church, the Body of Christ as it engages in mission. Often, God appoints and gives leaders who build up the rest of the Church for works of ministry among themselves and to outsiders. According to Ephesians 4:11–12, "It was he who gave some to be apostles, some to be prophets, some to be evangelists, and some to be pastors and teachers, to prepare God's people for works of service, so that the Body of Christ may be built up, until we all reach unity in the faith and in the knowledge of the Son of God and become mature . . ." (see also 1 Corinthians 12:27).

In a well-known passage from 1 Corinthians 12, Paul addresses a congregation that employed spiritual gifts in a somewhat chaotic fashion, with an emphasis on tongues, which Paul usually places last in his lists. The apostle writes at length about such gifts within the dynamic model of the Church as the lively body and presence of Christ in the world. In so doing, he emphasizes both the diversity of gifts and the overarching unity of that Body, as directed by Christ the head.

"There are different kinds of gifts but the same Spirit, different kinds or varieties of service (deaconing) but the same Lord (Jesus) and various kinds of working, activities or energizing, but the same God works all of them in all the members" (1Cor. 12:4–6). To each person is given at least one manifestation of the Spirit for the common good. Paul then gives one list of the gifts of the Holy Spirit that are familiar to him: the word or message of wisdom, the word of knowledge, the gift of faith, the gifts of healings, miraculous powers, prophecy, discernment or distinguishing between spirits, speaking in various tongues, and the interpretation of tongues. These are distributed at various times to Christians according to the will of the Holy Spirit, enabling the Body of Christ to fully function in the world. Paul mentions gifts of healings and workers of miracles after leadership offices in a second list at 1 Corinthians 12:28. By asking the question "Do all have gifts of healing?" he reminds us that Christians do not all have the same gifts. In Romans 12: 1–9, Paul includes additional possibilities for giftedness after urging us to present ourselves to God as living sacrifices. These gifts include teaching, serving, encouraging, giving generously, showing mercy to people in need, leading, and administering. In recent years, Peter Wagner, a former professor at Fuller Theological Seminary, and others have expanded such gift lists to include 26 or more spiritual gifts, including intercession and martyrdom. In Exodus 35:30–34 there is also the wonderful gift of craftsmanship: the preparation of material objects for the glory of God.

From time to time, all Christians are to be witnesses, even without the gift of evangelism, to pray for the sick, without having a particular gift of healing, and to give, encourage, and help others. It is in the experimental use of spiritual gifts, with the help and encouragement of leaders, that ordinary Christians grow toward maturity and effectiveness. Being a Christian should not always be similar to being a spectator at a sports event!

By comparison with the wonderfully complex individual human body, largely unknown in the first century, the Church pictured by Paul in First Corinthians as the Body of Christ is conceptually and functionally simple but in actuality very dynamic and diverse. By the Holy Spirit, we were baptized into one Body, regardless of our being Jewish or Gentile, slave or free, even male or female, and all were given of the Spirit to drink (1Cor. 12:13), and all relate to Jesus the Christ as our physical organs relate to our minds and brains. He is in charge, issues commands, expects his body to respond, and deals with malfunctions, diseases, or disabilities within the members or subgroupings at every level. If we say that we don't belong to the body of Christ because we don't have the ability or gift we desire, and we thus cease to function, we are harming the body of Christ. If everyone had the same gift from the Spirit, we would be a strange organ, like a giant eyeball, not the body of Christ. Stressing one gift above all others as necessary, while downplaying or neglecting others, distorts and weakens the body of Christ. God is capable of bringing people with various gifts and abilities together as he wishes, to display the wonderful reality of Christians actually working together in harmony like a symphony or an acrobatic cheer-leading team. The encouragement of a man like Barnabas, friend of Paul, in the early Church was very helpful.

Since we are sinful and selfish, we tend to disrupt this ideal. Public speakers and those having the five leadership ministries may not need the same nurturing and honoring that a person with behind-the-scene helps, or the one having mercy, may require, but pride is a danger. God wants all members to be blessed as they minister with the resources and gifts they have been given, which are really necessary. To bury our single talent because of fear is to weaken the body and risk judgment. We know that when one part of our human body suffers, we suffer; but when that part becomes whole and strong, we rejoice and feel better. Unfortunately, in many ways, the contemporary body of Christ is divided, with many members not functioning or prospering, and communication from Jesus the head is blocked, distorted, or rejected, and his body, becomes weak, ineffective or even useless.

One Wednesday healing service with about six persons attending, St. Peter's Church in Uniontown, PA, began with Holy Communion, followed by laying on of hands at the altar rail. Each person participated by praying, sharing a Scripture, an impression, or an expression of faith, while others prayed quietly in tongues. Everything came together for healing without my trying to make it happen. As the visiting priest, I was the only ordained or commissioned official there. I had no desire to stifle the legitimate gifts that my friends were sharing with one another. Many years ago, I had been warned by the Lord not to get in the way of the things he wanted to do among us. Often during the first four centuries since the birth, death, and resurrection of Jesus, believers functioned in this way as God freely moved among them, inspiring them and using them to give someone else the good things which they had received.[31,32,33]

During prayer ministry for physical and inner healing, for deliverance, and for salvation, two or more people with varying gifts, experiences or talents can participate, forming a team. One person may gain knowledge from a picture, through feeling another person's pain, or through a single word that identifies the problem. Another person may be given a special gift of faith for a healing to come, or minister healing in a specialized way to those with back problems while not being able to do anything for a woman experiencing tremendous loss after a child has died. We often find this healing pattern among congregations that are part of the Pentecostal, charismatic, or third-wave movements of the Holy Spirit, but God has been working in this way at various times and places throughout the entire history of the Church.

There are significant numbers of Christians who have lived during the past several centuries who believed that most of the spiritual gifts mentioned above were temporary and actually came to an end by the time when the last apostle died and the Church had recognized only the books we have in our Bibles as the Holy Scriptures. This does not hinder God from healing people, but this pattern of ministry would not function. Some argue that the perfect has already come, so gifts such as tongues and knowledge have ceased. However, I believe that perfection has yet to come, with the appearance of our Lord Jesus Christ to wrap things up. We still see through a glass darkly but then one day face-to-face (1 Cor. 13). Jesus did not say that the Gospel would be accompanied by signs and wonders only in the first century or that we would do greater works only while the first apostles were still alive (John 14:12). The actual historical evidence supports the continuation of healing until anointing and the use of spiritual gifts were limited to clergy, with anointing for healing then being transformed into last rites for the dying. In an early version of *The City of God,* Saint Augustine argued that gifts of healing had ceased, but was forced by miracles in his own diocese to change his mind and rewrite the work.[34] Wherever the Holy Spirit freely empowers Christians, people are healed and transformed by his work. Today, this is a legitimate model.

Model 3: Elders in a Congregation
(James 5:13–18)

Although the Epistle of James (David's) addresses many questions about the dating, authorship, and audience,[35] we see another pattern for the healing ministry involving a group of elders (pres-byters) within a congregation that has a significant Jewish member-ship: elders were involved in Timothy's ordination (1 Tim. 4:14), they were to be respected and not dismissed without two or more witnesses (1 Tim 5:17–19), and Titus was to appoint elders in every town as the apostle directed (Titus 1:5). Such elders were to be "blameless, the husband of one wife and the parent of children who believe and are not open to the charge of being wild or disobedient (Titus 1:6)" In the pastoral letters of Paul there are other lists of requirements for overseers (bishops) and deacons. In Revelations, the twenty-four elders in Heaven may symbolically represent the twelve patriarchs and the twelve apostles.

In our passage from James 5, persons who are in trouble or suf-fering hardship are urged to pray. Those who are happy are told to sing songs or hymns of praise, and those who are weak or sick should call, summon, or invite the elders to take action). While such elders might simply be the wise, senior, experienced members of a congre-gation, they were increasingly selected, commissioned, or ordained by an apostle or his delegate. Even today, some Christians may not be healed until they actually obey this command from James. Such personal ministry by a godly group of elders may be more effective than intercessory prayer at a distance.

A person who needs help is to call a group of elders to pray over him and anoint him with (olive) oil in the name of the Lord Jesus. Although there are no records dating from the first century, records show that formulas or prayers were soon developed for setting apart oil for various healing purposes. Today, in Episcopal churches, oils for healing, as well as oil meant for individuals who are preparing to be baptized and chrism that is intended for use at baptism, are set apart for such uses by the bishop during Holy Week. Oil has a long history associated with healing and is connected with the Holy Spirit. Even during the early mission of the twelve (Mark 6), people were anointed with oil for healing after the good news of the imminent reign of God was announced.

The prayer offered in faith by the group of elders will make the sick person well, and the Lord will raise him up. Notice here that the word translated "make well or whole" is actually the verb *swzo*, which also refers to spiritual salvation. James's audience is encouraged to believe in the efficacy of their prayers of faith by the example of Elijah, who was essentially just like them. When Elijah prayed for the rain to stop, there was no rain in Israel for three and a half years, and rain did not arrive until he prayed that it do so. The prayer of a righteous individual *is* powerful and effective. It is amazing how God answers the prayers of people like you and me!

Before telling the paralyzed man to get up and walk, Jesus told the man that his sins were forgiven. He did the same for the woman who had been set free from her many sins and then reacted with abundant love toward the savior as she washed his feet. Some of our sicknesses and diseases are consequences of personal or family sins and disobedience. Of course, Jesus knew exactly what was taking place in the lives of people, including their lifestyles, rebellion, and the cries of their hearts.

Our receiving healing may be contingent on our willingness to confess our sins to one another (scary thought!), to renounce those sins, and to receive God's forgiveness. (For example, many people are healed when they actually forgive the people whom they have harbored grudges against for months, years, even decades.) Our subsequent obedience is then related to our emerging health in every dimension—spirit, soul, and body.

Although the passage in James just urges us to confess our sins to one another and pray for one another, the Church wisely provides an elder, priest, or pastor to listen to our confession, offer guidance, and say nothing afterwards. The pattern in James is somewhat broader, allowing other healing ministers to assure people of God's forgiveness. This pattern of ministry by elders may well be historically the last of the three patterns. It is closer to patterns of ministry by clergy during the first six Christian centuries.

All three of the patterns just discussed allow for the particular actions and words that are displayed in the Gospels of Matthew, Mark, Luke, and John and the book of Acts. We can ask questions, declare something true, express or respond to faith, pray, anoint, lay hands on people, or address the illness and any unclean spirits directly. In the process we discover how God desires to save and heal people, using every resource we present to him, to his glory and the benefit of many. Now, we will examine one contemporary pattern and practice to see if it could be considered a sound extension of the actions of God, our healer, found in the above patterns. We have considerable freedom to develop a new pattern, as long as it does not contradict the teaching of Scripture.

Model 4: A Contemporary Pattern for Ministry

This pattern is widely available on the World Wide Web and is a variant of the model developed by John Wimber in the context of the Vineyard movement and published in a workbook by Mike Evans.[36] Keep in mind that our patterns are only starting points that we should be free to drop or modify at the Lord's direction. (I have added some points from my earlier discussions of the things that Jesus said and did.) In some sense, our healing models are like any procedure we use to get something done, including launching a rocket or preparing, then baking a cake. The first time, I follow the steps very carefully. With practice and guidance, I begin to experiment, as my wife does in the kitchen. I am still learning how to use my second digital camera. With God's guidance and empowerment, this flexible healing model is fine.

1. **Interview the person whom you hope to minister.** Simply ask the individual what he would like prayer for or what she would like Jesus to do for her, then ask appropriate follow-up questions; but most of all, simply listen to gain some under-

standing of the problem. You do not need complex medical histories and the like.

2. **Invite the Holy Spirit to be present.** Audibly invite the Holy Spirit to be in charge, to guide you, and to minister through you. This will help you and the individual to whom you are ministering to realize that it is God who is doing the work.

3. **Pray and act as the Holy Spirit leads you.** If the person to whom you are ministering is fearful, you may first pray for God's peace. Then, you may start by addressing the person's request, or God may give you another place to start. Pray with your eyes open, to observe signs of God's working in the person, which will lead to your next step.

    a. Peter's plenitude of possibilities include:

        i.   Laying on of hands (with permission) to communicate love and to allow God's power to flow, which may result in heat or tingling

        ii. Anointing with holy oil for healing (If the church or denomination you belong to doesn't restrict this to clergy)

        iii. Petitioning God, declaring healing, or commanding the person, condition, or demons

        iv. Humbly sharing the gifts of faith and/or words of knowledge or wisdom, discernment, prophecy (pictures, words, or feelings), healings, or miracles as they come forth (If the person to whom you are ministering finds it acceptable, some team members may pray quietly in the Spirit. We freely share what we have received.)

b. As you are praying, you may ask the person how God is touching them or other questions prompted by God. These may indicate partial or complete healing.

4. **Bless the person to whom you are ministering.** This could be the type of blessing an ordained minister uses during worship, or it could be a simple, informal blessing such as "In the name of Jesus, I bless you with his peace, love, and forgiveness" or "May God bless you with a deeper experience of his presence and the fullness of his Spirit." The person may relax, experience a sense of peace or joy, and be healed.

5. **Post ministry follow-up.** Give helpful directions for any problems that may occur in the future, encouraging the individual not to accept negative thoughts or apparent return of the symptoms after they leave. If the person requires more healing prayer, affirm and encourage the individual and invite him or her to return. Do not tell somebody who has not experienced healing that the failure is the result of his or her sins or lack of faith. Significant follow-up is crucial after deliverance. After weekend healing missions where the speaker and the healing team have departed, someone from the congregation could use the registration list to contact the person.

Three Recommendations

1. Regularly read, study, memorize, and appropriately use the Holy Scriptures in ministry.

2. Stay with a sound theology that is consistent with the Scriptures, creeds, and other basic statements of the faith.

3. Do not import healing methods that come out of non–Christian religious backgrounds, even if those methods involve similar actions (e.g., Reiki, a form of energy healing that has been introduced into chapters of the International Order of St. Luke the Physician and other Christian organizations).

Overall Mission Patterns for Disciples and Ministers

1. "All authority in Heaven and on earth has been given to me. Therefore go and make disciples of all nations, baptizing them in the name of the Father and of the Son and of the Holy Spirit, and teaching them to obey everything I have commanded you. And surely I am with you always, to the very end of the age." (Matt. 28:18–20)

2. "After the Lord Jesus had spoken to them, he was taken up to Heaven and he sat at the right hand of God. Then the disciples went out and preached everywhere, and the Lord worked with them and confirmed his word by the signs that accompanied it." (Mark 16:20; see also verse 16)

3. "Again Jesus said, 'Peace be with you! As the Father has sent me, I am sending you.' And with that he breathed on them and said, 'Receive the Holy Spirit. If you forgive anyone his sins, they are forgiven; if you do not forgive them, they are not forgiven'." (Job 20:21–22)

4. "Do not leave Jerusalem, but wait for the gift my Father promised, . . . For John baptized with water, but in a few days you will be baptized with the Holy Spirit." (Acts 1:4–8)

5. "All of them were filled with the Holy Spirit and began to speak in other tongues as the Spirit enabled them." (Acts 2:4)

6. "Go into all the world and preach the good news to all creation. Whoever believes and is baptized will be saved, but whoever does not believe will be condemned. And these signs will accompany those who believe: In my name they will drive out demons; they will speak in new tongues; they will pick up snakes with their hands; and when they drink deadly poison, it will not hurt them at all; they will place their hands on sick people and they will get well." (Mark 16:15–18)

Chapter 10

Our Need for Inner Healing

T he New Testament clearly includes healing of physical diseases, infirmities, and disabilities; deliverance from demonic
oppression or even possession; as well as ways of handling temptations and the crucial restoration of our relationship with God
through the redemptive work of Christ, received by faith, which we
would call spiritual healing. Each has a doctrinal basis and practical
examples.

We also realize that our fallen, sinful nature, coupled with a
world of imperfect structures, under the influence of evil beings,
has not only impacted all relationships but has also harmed us in
numerous ways, through such experiences as abandonment, neglect,
and abuse. Various contemporary forms of inner healing, including
Theophostic prayer ministry, have freed and transformed the lives
of many people.

While attending a one-week course at Trinity School for Ministry, I experienced God's presence and love with tears as the leader read about and prayed through our first nine months in the womb. At a short Theophostic introduction, I discovered that I had believed the lie that I would always be alone. During an hour of soaking prayer in Boise, ID, I experienced God's Father love in a deeper way. On numerous occasions I have forgiven other people, God, and myself, then experienced greater freedom. I have also looked carefully at new healing methods before I adopt them and recommend them to other people.

Although we cannot find in the New Testament Scriptures a particular pattern for inner healing, we can observe relevant inter-actions between Jesus and other people. We also note throughout the whole Bible descriptions of a variety of conditions of the soul, the mind, and the heart. I will use a model of the human being as spirit, soul (mind, emotions, and will, with the will bridging into the spirit), and body. There are more than 800 Scriptures on the heart, which overlap with what we call our soul and spirit.

The Scriptures, especially the Psalms, present a variety of dif-ficult or harmful situations and human conditions with which we can identify. How can we be healed from their lingering effects? If my picture of the heavenly Father is distorted by my early experiences, how do I return to him and discover him to be like the father in the Lukan prodigal son story? If I have believed a lie about myself from childhood, how do I accept and then experience the truth that God wants to reveal to me? Forgiveness is important; but how do I do it? We'd like to run the race to Jesus as Paul did, but what sins, heavy weights, and burdens are hampering us?

Let's begin by simply considering some Scriptures from the Bible that are descriptive of our woundedness—and God's provision.

- "In bitterness of soul Hannah wept much and prayed to the Lord. . . . If God gave her a son, she vowed to give him to the Lord." (1 Sam. 1:10)
- Zedekiah "became stiff-necked and hardened his heart and would not turn to the Lord, the God of Israel." (2 Chron. 36:13)
- "Encourage one another daily, so that none of you may be hardened by sin's deceitfulness." (Heb. 3:13)
- "I will speak out in the anguish of my spirit, I will complain in the bitterness of my soul." (Job 7:11)
- "How long must I wrestle with my thoughts and every day have sorrow in my heart?" (Ps. 13:2)
- "He restores my soul. He guides me in paths of righteousness . . ." (Ps. 23:3)
- "Who may stand in his holy place? He who has clean hands and a pure heart, who does not lift up his soul to an idol or swear by what is false." (Ps. 24:3–4)
- "The Lord is close to the brokenhearted and saves those who are crushed in spirit." (Ps. 34:18)

- "My heart pounds, my strength fails me; even the light has gone from my eyes." (Ps. 38:10)

- "Why are you downcast, O my soul? Why so disturbed within me? Put your hope in God . . ." (Ps. 42:5)

- "The sacrifices of God are a broken spirit; a broken and contrite heart, O God, you will not despise." (Ps. 51:17)

- "When anxiety was great within me, your consolation brought joy to my soul." (Ps. 94:19)

- "My soul is weary with sorrow; strengthen me according to your word." (Ps. 119:28)

- "He heals the brokenhearted and binds up their wounds." (Ps. 147:3)

- Psalm 139

- "Hope deferred makes the heart sick, but a longing fulfilled is a tree of life." (Peter 13:12)

- "O my God, I am too ashamed and disgraced to lift up my face to you, my God because our sins are higher than our heads and our guilt has reached to the heavens." (Ezra 9:6)

- "I will give them an undivided heart and put a new spirit in them; I will remove from them their heart of stone and give them a heart of flesh." (Ezek. 11:19)

- "The Spirit of the Lord is on me, because he has anointed me to preach good news to the poor. He has sent me to proclaim freedom for the prisoners and recovery of sight for the blind, to release the oppressed." (Luke 4:18)

- "We demolish arguments and every pretension that sets itself up against the knowledge of God, and we take captive every thought to make it obedient to Christ." (2 Cor. 10:5)
- "At one time we too were foolish, disobedient, deceived and enslaved by all kinds of passions and pleasures." (Titus 3:3)
- "If we claim to be without sin, we deceive ourselves and the truth is not in us. If we confess our sins, he is faithful and just and will forgive us our sins and purify us from all unrighteousness." (1 Job 1:8)
- "He will wipe every tear from their eyes. There will be no more death or mourning or crying or pain, for the old order of things has passed away." (Rev. 21:4)

God Provides for Inner Healing

I believe that the love of God the Father, the grace and giving of our Lord Jesus Christ, and the personal power of the Holy Spirit are the real basis for every type of healing. I highlight these divine qualities knowing that there are many others! Not only is God aware of our inner conditions, including such things as an unbelieving or stony heart, our passive-aggressive rebelliousness, and our unforgiveness but he is capable of doing something about them! The question for many of us is whether we want to be healed and transformed? Other types of healing may have to wait for such inner healing.

In his earthly life of thirty years, but supremely on the cross, Jesus experienced every category of negative, intense, harmful experience. As Hebrews 4:13 states: "For we do not have a high priest who is unable to sympathize with our weaknesses, but we have one who has been tempted in every way, just as we are—yet was without sin. Let us then approach the throne of grace with confidence, so that we may receive mercy and find grace to help us in our time of need." His atoning sacrificial death as the Lamb of God provides for the forgiveness of our sins and our reception of such love, that we may actually forgive others and be set free from bitterness, resentment, and malice. He not only bore our sins, including those leading to addictions, on the tree, he also bore our shame, iniquities, loneliness, and alienation. Once again, such Scriptures as Isaiah 53: 3–12 and Psalm 22 give graphic testimony about what would happen to the suffering servant of Yahweh. Indeed, Jesus proclaimed such a mission from Isaiah 61:1–2 in the synagogue at Nazareth (Luke 4:18–21). As our great high priest and chief overseer of our souls, he always lives to intercede for us. Nevertheless, God's ways, thoughts, and priorities are often different than ours.

For non–Christians to be thwarted by circumstances when they attempt to run from God or to live in luxury without regard for other human beings, resulting in their desperate call to God for help is good. A woman who has gone through many sicknesses or trials, yet consistently becomes better rather than bitter may be greatly used in a nursing home. If I were to ask God to heal my arthritis while I am filled with envy and jealousy, I may find Jesus lovingly pointing out the real problem, even telling me a story.

When Jesus sent his disciples into town, then spoke to the outcast Samaritan woman at the well in Sychar at high noon, she was very surprised. Unlike any other Jew, Jesus asked her for a drink! Then he enticed her by saying, "If you knew the gift of God and who is that asks you for a drink, you would have asked him and he would have given you *living water*." There was something better, which even she could have! She was still thinking about ordinary water, but she was moving closer to God. He spoke of this living water as a well bubbling up to eternal life, and she asked for it. Then, he asked her to call her husband. When she admitted that she did not have one, he revealed to her his knowledge that she had had five husbands in the past and was then living with someone else. After calling him a prophet, she tried to move away from her own condition to a religious question about the proper place for worship. He didn't shame her or force her to go back, but said that Samaritans worshiped a God they didn't know as the Jews did, but soon those who please God would worship God in Spirit and in truth rather than focusing on a particular site. When she responded by saying that the Messiah (Christ), the anointed one of God, would explain all things, Jesus actually revealed himself to her as the Messiah. She ran into town to urge everyone to see the man who had told her everything she had ever done. This resulted in a major conversion of the townspeople. Jesus was not only a great fisher of men and women, he had revealed his knowledge of her surface need and her true underlying need for acceptance and a joyful relationship with God. During this conversation, she had been forgiven and raised up.

In an account (John 8:1–11) not found in many early manuscripts, Jesus was tested early in the morning in the temple courts, as some Pharisees and law experts dragged in a woman caught in the act of adultery, while letting the man go free. The Pharisees reminded Jesus about the Law of Moses, which prescribed execution by stoning, and then challenged him to say something. If he were tolerant, he could be accused of teaching law breaking. If he told the Pharisees to stone the woman, the people would view Jesus as unloving, even cruel. (One can also imagine the woman's extreme fear at that moment.)

Jesus seemed to ignore the Pharisees as he bent down and then wrote something in the dirt. When the Pharisees continued to badger Jesus, he replied, "If any one of you is without sin let him be the first to throw a stone at her." Then he wrote some more. Some commentators have wondered whether he was recording the Pharisees' sins in the dirt. As each man thought about his own past conduct, he walked away empty handed, with the older burdened men going first. Jesus then stood up and asked the woman where the Pharisees had gone and whether any had condemned her. She said none had, and then Jesus told her that he did not condemn her either. But he finished by telling her clearly to leave her life of sin! Jesus wasn't tolerant about sin! He didn't try to alter the Holy Scriptures. But she was forgiven, accepted, and given a new chance to live. She was probably as grateful as the woman who had poured precious ointment over Jesus' feet and wet them with her tears. For people who feel unloved and rejected, the experience of God's agape love and forgiveness is wonderful.

Simon Peter was the brash, outspoken leader of the apostles and one of the inner three; but he was far from perfect. Once, by revelation from God, he received and spoke the truth that Jesus was the Messiah! Shortly afterward, Peter was rebuked as Satan because he rejected Jesus' chosen path of suffering and death. At the Last Supper, Peter said he was willing even to die for his master, but he was told that by the next morning he would deny knowing Jesus three times! Satan would be allowed to sift the disciple like wheat (Luke 22:31), but Jesus had prayed that Peter's faith would not fail. On the day of resurrection, Jesus told the women to tell the disciples and Peter that he was going ahead of them to Galilee (Mark 16:7).

Then, one morning, the disciples were fishing in that sea. A voice from shore called out to them, asking if they had caught any fish. When they replied no, he told them to throw their nets on the right side, and they caught so many fish that their boat began to sink. This was almost a repeat of an earlier miraculous catch when Peter had asked Jesus to depart from him because he was a sinful man. This time, John said it was the Lord who had spoken, and Peter put on his clothes, then jumped out of the boat and swam to Jesus. (I might have hung back out of shame and guilt.)

215

After breakfast, Jesus asked Peter the same basic question and gave the same basic command three times while lowering the bar for Peter, so that he would be restored. (See the pattern shown in Table 5.)

Table 5
Peter's Restitution

Jesus' Question	Peter's Answer	Jesus' Response
Do you truly love me (agape) more than these?	Yes, Lord, you know that I love (*phileo*) you.	Feed my lambs.
Do you truly (agape) love me?	Yes, Lord, you know that I love (*phileo*) you.	Take care of my sheep.
Do you love (*phileo*) me?	Lord, you know all things; you know that I love you.	Feed my sheep.

Afterward, Jesus tells Peter with a double amen that when he reached old age, he would be taken where he didn't want to go, pointing toward his future crucifixion. Peter did bravely die for his master upside down, glorifying God! The application of truth with love by Jesus began the process of Peter's healing from pride and his terrible failure. Often, healing of our souls involves pain and suffering in the process, which many people avoid; yet it leads to true joy and effectiveness.

1. Before praying with strangers for inner healing, I may ask them if they are Christian believers. If they say they are not, I urge them to accept Jesus Christ as their Savior and Lord and to begin following him. Although the Holy Spirit can work on unbelievers from the outside, convincing them that they not only have committed sins against God and others but that is their nature, that Christ alone is righteous, and that there is a judgment to come. In fact, they need a new beginning inside, with God's presence, grace, and power within them for the remodeling God wants to do.

2. Christians also have a much better chance of maintaining their healing if the Holy Spirit is continually working behind the scenes. Any demonic opposition or oppression can also be taken care of without having the demons return with fresh reinforcements. If Christians communicate with God in the Spirit, perhaps by using the gift of tongues, the enemy may not be able to decipher their speech.

Issue 1 — Forgiveness

When Christians recall difficult or harmful experiences in the past that are still exerting a negative influence on their lives or keeping them from moving forward with Christ as disciples, witnesses, and ministers, they often need to forgive and be forgiven.

When we sin against God, we already know that we must regularly confess our specific sins to God in order to be forgiven and to be cleansed from all unrighteousness (1 Job 1:9). That's why many churches include confessions with an absolution in their weekly services. This restores our fellowship with God. Some of us may need help in accepting the reality of God forgiving us and then really forgive ourselves! If we are repeatedly attacking ourselves over some past sin, we may need help in dealing with someone else in our past and experiencing God's wonderful way of not remembering our sins against us. Of course, the devil is the accuser of the brethren; but there is no condemnation in Christ Jesus.

However, there are people we have significantly harmed, often those closest to us. How many people will not speak to us? Jesus tells us, "If you are offering your gift at the altar and there remember that your brother has something against you, leave your gift there. First go and be reconciled to your brother, then come and offer your gift" (Matt. 5:23–24). That would involve asking for and, hopefully, receiving forgiveness before it comes to the point where an adversary is taking us to court! We need wisdom as to how to do this. Twelve-step groups urge us to make amends, except where it is likely to cause further damage. As with much of the Sermon on the Mount, Jesus is telling us to do a difficult but right thing, like loving our enemies. Doing it promptly is much better than waiting twenty years!

When Peter asked how many times in a day he should forgive his brother, the apostle suggested a generous limit of seven times, but Jesus expanded it to seventy-seven or seventy-seven times seven times, not to set a numerical limit but to say there was none (Matt. 18:22). Jesus also provided a procedure for a Christian to go to another Christian who has wronged him or the Church in order to deal with the issue (Matt. 18:15–17) and restore the relationship. It involves going to the person alone, before telling anyone else, speaking about the fault, and then giving an opportunity for the person to listen, turn, and admit they were wrong. If this happens, that's the end of it. If necessary, two or three witnesses could be brought, or the church could be told, and as a last resort, the person treated as a non–Christian. Unfortunately, we usually gossip about the person first and things go rapidly downhill.

Inner healing involves dealing with things that have happened to us, triggering emotions, wrong beliefs, defensiveness, and other reactions, such as building walls, seeking approval, and distancing. They are often like beach balls being held underwater but very much in play. Jesus asks us to do a very difficult thing—to forgive unilaterally. When we actually obey him, we experience freedom and joy. Jesus modeled it on the cross when he said: "Father, forgive them, for they do not know what they are doing" (Luke 23:34).

When the disciples asked Jesus to teach them to pray, he gave them a model prayer that included the words "Forgive us our debts as we also have forgiven our debtors" and the comment afterward,

"If you forgive men when they sin against you, your heavenly Father will also forgive you. But if you do not forgive men their sins, your Father will not forgive your sins" (Matt. 6:12–15). According to Mark 11, after saying that someone with faith could tell a tree to bury itself in the sea, Jesus also commented, "And when you stand praying, if you hold anything against anyone, forgive him, so that your Father in Heaven may forgive you your sins" (Mark 11:25). In some sense, our fellowship with God and our being able to experience the reality of forgiveness from God can be blocked as long as we refuse to forgive others. Do not judge or you too will be judged—in the same way! This is particularly true of our unforgiveness and bitter root judgments against our parents!

After Peter's question about the number of times he must forgive, Jesus told a story about two servants (Matt. 18:23—35) of the same king. When the king settled accounts, he found out that one servant owed him something like $10 million. As the king ordered that the servant and his family be sold into slavery, the man knelt and begged for more time to repay, which was impossible. Amazingly, the king took pity on him, decided to cancel the entire sum, and let the man go free! However, when the man saw another servant, who owed him something like $4,000 dollars, who made a similar plea, the first servant threw the debtor into jail until he could pay the entire amount. The servants talked, and the master heard. He said that this wicked servant, whose huge debt had been cancelled, should have had mercy on the other man. In anger the king turned the first debtor over to the jailers to be tormented until he paid the entire amount! Have you ever noticed that when we are unforgiving, resentful, vengeful, and bitter, we are the ones who pay? Think about the number of times that you have sinned against God both before and after becoming a Christian. In my case, a quarter-million estimate might be too low. Through the work of Christ, they have all been forgiven. Why are we going after a fellow servant of Christ who owes us $500? Forgive and be set free; it's healing. Blessed is the person, whose transgressions are forgiven, whose sins are covered! Here is something from *The Bondage Breaker* by Neil Anderson.[37]

1. Forgiveness is not forgetting.
2. Forgiveness is a choice, a decision of the will.
3. Forgiveness is agreeing to live with the consequences of another person's sin.
4. Do not wait for the other person to ask for your forgiveness.
5. Forgive from your heart.
6. Forgiveness is deciding not to hold someone's sin against them anymore.

   Suggestion: Ask God to bring to your mind the people you need to forgive. List them as they come to you. Then add yourself at the bottom, and thoughts against God at the top.

See also Steps to Forgiveness in *Learning to Do What Jesus Did* by Mike Evans.

Issue 2—Truth Versus Lies, and Light Versus Darkness

Watching our thirty four-month-old grandson provides me the opportunity to observe the wonderful ability humans have to grow, learn, know, and trust. He likes throwing the light switch and seeing what happens. He is learning that his mom and dad are dependable and loving, before knowing the words or developing abstract learning. But some of the things children and adults learn through pleasant or painful experiences, the words they hear and the world-views they gradually develop or accept, may be partially or totally false. We can also believe something intellectually while acting according to a different reality. Romans 10:9 states, "If you confess with your mouth, 'Jesus is Lord,' and believe in your heart that God raised him from the dead, you will be saved. For it is with your heart that you believe and are justified, and it is with your mouth that you confess and are saved" (Rom. 10:10). The holy Scriptures contain all things necessary for salvation, but we may need to hear and receive them personally in our wounded hearts.

Jesus, who is the way, the truth, and the life (John 14:6), promised his disciples, "You will know the truth, and the truth will set you free." He also promised them that the Spirit of truth would indwell them, testify about Jesus, and guide them into all truth. The sword of the Spirit pierces to divide soul and spirit and discerns the thoughts of the heart (Heb. 4:12). When Jesus spoke he told his disciples the truth, including challenging individuals by identifying their real problems! We find the phrase, "I tell you the truth," which includes one or more amens, seventy-eight times in the Gospels. Among believers, words of knowledge and wisdom and discernment may be ways of identifying what the person really needs for healing, but we should share them humbly. There also are different types of ground into which the seed of God's word may fall then be productive or not. God desires to find truth, not lies, within us and teaches us wisdom in the inmost place (Ps. 51:6). True agape love, the love of God for us, "does not delight in evil but rejoices with the truth." (1 Cor. 13:6) Unfortunately, human beings have often exchanged the truth of God for a lie and have worshiped and served created things, such as power, sex, money, and ecstasy, rather than the Creator (Rom. 1:25). We should remember that there is nothing hidden that will not be disclosed (Luke 8:17). I prefer that such things be dealt with now by the Lord in healing and forgiveness.

We may also consider the theme of light and darkness. When Jesus came into the world, a great light began to shine on the people of old Israel, who had been living in darkness (Matt. 4:16). This was a light of revelation. When people saw and heard Jesus, they were also seeing and hearing the Father. Three disciples experienced the blazing light of Jesus' inner being on the mountain in the company of Moses and Elijah. This light and truth is capable of banishing the darkness within many people. Unfortunately, many people loved darkness and attempted to put out the light that pained them and hampered their evil deeds (John 3:19). When we follow Jesus, he gives us the light of life, so we do not need to stumble and fall. A brilliant light from Heaven, coupled with the voice of our Lord, turned Paul from zealous persecutor to effective, fervent apostle. Christians are a chosen people, a royal priesthood, called out of our darkness into the wonderful light of Christ (1 Pet. 2:9). We need the light and truth of Christ within to deal with unbelief, lies, and strongholds within us.

According to Proverbs 20:27, "The lamp of the Lord searches the spirit of a man; it searches out his inmost being." And Chronicles says, "The LORD searches every heart and understands every motive behind their thoughts (1 Chron. 28:9). God certainly knows our inner being, as Psalm 139 demonstrates, including the time when we were being formed in our mother's womb. "He who searches our hearts knows the mind of the Spirit, because the Spirit intercedes for the saints in accordance with God's will" (Rom. 8:27).

Since we have the word of God both spoken and written, which the Holy Spirit may illumine for us as a special rhema word about what Jesus said, and since he has a myriad of ways by which he can and does communicate personally with us, including through nature, writings, and the words of those praying for us, it seems evident that God can search out our inner being; identifying weaknesses, woundedness, defenses, and lies, from the past or present; then deal with them by his perfect application of the truth he brings and in the process love us into new life. In other words, inner healing is definitely possible. However, without our dependence on the Lord, we might impose our own ideas or directions about what happened, or even import another spirit.

I believe that past events are unchangeable, but our initial responses to them, including our emotional reactions and beliefs are not. I don't have any problem believing that God is always present throughout our whole life, whether we know it or not. If he wishes, God can demonstrate his presence with us or interact with us as we now experience the past event. His healing work, often unknown to the human minister, will certainly have some effect on our future! But I have no desire to tell people what they are seeing or what Jesus is doing. Wait quietly on the Lord with the person!

Issue 3—Father Problems and Judgments

Though human beings were created male and female in the image of God, the fall and its disastrous consequences seen realistically in the Holy Scriptures have led to a tendency to view God as being like our limited parents and other important authority figures in our lives. Our religious or secular upbringing and education present us with various models for reality which may or may not include God and his interactions with nature and human beings.

Even the holy Bible presents a series of developmental revelations about the nature of God. If God has created us in his image, we have often returned the favor. A tremendous mystery is associated with God, as Rudolf Otto once stated.[38] We cannot force God to reveal himself; yet he has done so in various ways so that we might actually know and even love him. Only the Spirit of God, like wisdom personified in Proverbs 3 can plumb the depths of God.

Shortly after I had been born prematurely in 1943, then almost died, my father was inducted into the army. On my first birthday he landed in England to fight in the Ardennes and Germany. He barely escaped being captured, and then became very sick with frostbite and pneumonia. He was part of the Silent but Great Generation. His life was affected by war and the Great Depression, and so was mine. I did not bond well with him at first. Dad didn't play much and wasn't very encouraging. If angry he would withdraw in silence and he was worried about having enough. I definitely have some of his characteristics. About two years ago, my sister sent me some old papers, among which I found an old A6 letter from the war, in which dad expressed his love for mom and for me. That touched me. Since I have become involved in the healing ministry, much of my own healing has occurred as I have experienced the amazing love of God in several different ways. The charismatic movement with its emphasis on experiencing God, made a difference. Going on a three day weekend experience as a pilgrim, with talks by lay persons, many surprises and much fun, which among Anglicans is called Cursillo, became for me an experience of God's love mediated through men. That in turn has changed the way I read the Hebrew Scriptures and think about God.

My worldview, like those of first-century Jews, has been formed by my upbringing, involvement in the Church, and education experiences. Two recent books by Ronald Nash[39] and James Sire[41] are helpful in considering contemporary worldviews. Studies of first century Mediterranean and specifically Palestinian cultures would also be helpful. During the time of our American Revolution, enlightenment viewpoints and deism emphasized regular natural physical processes rather than divine interventions. Our early experiences of fathers and mothers, along with our reception of various worldviews tell us what is likely or unlikely. What did Jews during the Babylonian exile or first-century Jews in Palestine under the heel of Rome expect of God?

Jesus said something quite startling to Phillip as recorded in John 14:9: "Anyone who has seen me has seen the Father. How can you say, 'Show us the Father'?" Jesus, the word made flesh, the only begotten Son, is the best representation we have of God. So, I would urge us to look to Jesus, his behavior, his words, and his life to improve our view of God. I would also point to the great parable of the prodigal son, which is really about the Father! God is like that! This exercise will help us to deal with some of the issues we have with God and improve our relationship with him, which is a form of healing. We may have to repent for our holding views of God that are unworthy of him. (There is also a list of Scriptures about the love of the Father at the end of this chapter.)

When young, I wandered like one of the lost boys of Peter Pan and was in passive-aggressive rebellion against my dad. I would act like the first son in Jesus' parable, who said he would go and help, but didn't. I also judged my mom and dad for various things, which I seemed to repeat in my own life. But the fourth commandment says, "Honor your father and your mother, so that you may live long in the land the LORD your God is giving you" (Ex. 20:12). As part of the Sermon on the Mount, Jesus tells us: "Do not judge, or you too will be judged. For in the same way you judge others, you will be judged, and with the measure you use, it will be measured to you" (Matt. 7:1). Jesus criticized the Pharisees for using a technicality in their oral tradition to avoid honoring their parents by taking care of them. If we have disobeyed or dishonored our father and mother, we need to repent and seek their forgiveness if this is possible. If we have judged them, we need to reconsider what we have done, so our lives can be long and blessed. The same goes for God, who in Malachi 1:6 tells the priests: "A son honors his father and a servant his master. If I am a father, where is the honor due me? If I am a master, where is the respect due me? says the LORD Almighty. It is you, O priests, who show contempt for my name."

Selected List of Scriptures on the Father's Love

1. "The compassionate and gracious God, slow to anger, abounding in love and faithfulness, maintaining love to thousands, and forgiving wickedness, rebellion and sin. Yet he does not leave the guilty unpunished." (Ex. 34:6)

2. "Yet the Lord set his affection on your forefathers and loved them, and he chose you, their descendants, above all the nations." (Deut. 10:15)

3. "Within your temple, O God, we meditate on your unfailing love." (Ps. 48:9)

4. "Have mercy on me, O God, according to your unfailing love; according to your great compassion blot out my transgressions." (Ps. 51:1)

5. "For as high as the heavens are above the earth, so great is his love for those who fear (reverence) him . . ." (Ps. 103:11)

6. "When Israel was a child, I loved him, and out of Egypt I called my son. I led them with cords of human kindness, with ties of love; I lifted the yoke from their neck and bent down to feed them." (Hos. 11:1)

7. "The parable of the prodigal son!" (Luke 15:11–24)

8. "For God so loved the world that he gave his one and only Son, that whoever believes in him shall not perish but have eternal life." (John 3:16)

9. "And hope does not disappoint us, because God has poured out his love into our hearts by the Holy Spirit, whom he has given us." (Rom. 5:5)

10. "How great is the love the Father has lavished on us, that we should be called children of God! And that is what we are!" (1 Job 3:1)

Issue 4 — Vows

Most of the vows found in the Holy Scriptures are made to God, but they are also to ones' self, and may include other human beings. In the Levitical codes, sacrifices were **often coupl**ed with the making of vows and their completion (Lev. 22:21, 27:2). When a man makes a vow of separation as a Nazarite, he must abstain from wine or grape juice and never let a razor touch his head (Num. 6:2). If we make vows or take oaths to obligate ourselves by a pledge, we must not break our pledge but do everything we promised promptly (Num. 30:2). Think about it! If a young woman living in her father's home makes a vow, and he hears it, he may annul or cancel it. But if he says nothing, the vow stands. Poor Jephthah vowed to sacrifice the first person coming out of his door after winning a battle — and it was his daughter (Judg. 11:34–39). However, Jesus tells us not to swear by God's throne, the Earth, or by our head; we should simply let our yes be yes and our no, no (Matt. 5:37). Having to say more comes from the devil.

According to the Sandfords[41] and others in the healing ministry, many people under adverse conditions may make rash promises or vows that seem to exert strong, lasting effects in their lives. One such vow could be to never let anyone near her again. Their bodies seem programmed, and unclean spirits may act as legalistic enforcers. Healing ministers, under God's leading may cancel that bad program and set the captive free after dealing with feelings and lies associated with the original events. Having considered some issues dealt with in the healing or transformation of our soul, let us now look at a contemporary pattern.

A Model for Contemporary Inner Healing

I presented Rita Bennett's simplified pattern[42] for small-group use during a workshop at the International Order of Saint Luke the Physician summer conference in Boise, Idaho.

1. **Four ways to begin**

   a. Ask the person if there is a recent or older troubling event or experience for which he or she would like prayer. WAIT.

   b. Ask the Holy Spirit to bring to the person's awareness a memory that needs to be prayed for, whether large or small, recent or long ago. WAIT.

   c. Begin with a question, such as, What situations have been bothering you lately? or Did you accept and love yourself when you were a child?

   d. Use an inventory, such as the one provided at Christian Healing Ministries, and begin there.[43]

2. **Encourage the person to describe the event clearly and to provide details.** Ask how the person felt or reacted, then WAIT and pray. Were there earlier experiences that felt the same?

3. **Invite Jesus**, who transcends space and time, to make his presence, love, peace, and truth known to the person as that memory is relived. Pray and WAIT.

4. **Team members may ask:**

   a. Was Jesus with you? Did he say or do something?

   b. Is there someone, including yourself or God, whom you need to forgive?

   c. Was there an old lie that you believed? Should you ask the Lord to reveal the truth? Pray and wait.

   d. Is there an old vow that needs to be renounced? Ask God to set the person free from that vow.

Encourage and bless the person. Invite the individual to return. Consider what he or she has shared **as** confidential!

Chapter 11

Effective Healing Ministry in the Context of Prayer

W hether someone receives healing ministry at an altar rail, in a chapel or auditorium, or even on a street corner, it is likely that there are others praying and interceding for him. When the granddaughter of church members at St. George's Anglican Church in Waynesburg, PA was born with severe respiratory problems, thousands of people were praying for her and interacting with the family via the hospital's online Care Pages. Two years ago, many people were interceding for Father Nigel Mumford, a popular speaker at healing missions and writer who was in Intensive Care recovering from severe pneumonia. Prayer, including intercession, is the larger context for focused healing ministry. I do not know the extent of the intercessions that those saints who are now in glory with Jesus are making for Christians on Earth, but I do believe in the statement of the Anglican collect: "O Almighty God, you have knit together your elect in one communion and fellowship in the mystical body of your Son Christ our Lord."[42] More crucial is the knowledge that according to Isaiah 53:12 Jesus bore the sin of many and made intercession for the transgressors—on the cross. Before that hour, Jesus often prayed alone, then provided us the model of the Lord's Prayer, and we have Jesus' great high-priestly prayer and intercession for current and future believers, as recorded by John. Because Jesus lives forever, he has a permanent priesthood. Therefore he is able to save completely those who come to God through him, because he always lives to intercede for them (Heb. 7:25).

James, after giving our third pattern of healing ministry, reminds us with the example of Elijah that the prayer of a righteous man is powerful and effective (James 5:16). Writing to Timothy, Paul urges believers to make prayers, intercessions, and thanksgivings for everyone —even evil kings (1 Tim 2:1). He tells us that the Holy Spirit helps us in our weaknesses. "We do not know what we ought to pray for, but the Spirit himself intercedes for us with groans that words cannot express" (Rom. 8:26). John, the elder, prayed that his friend would enjoy good health, with everything going well for him, even as his soul was getting along well (3 John 1:2). God motivates us to intercede for others, and then he incorporates our prayers in his action plans.

Within the New Testament, God has given us several commands and encouragements to pray. Jesus assumes that we will give alms, fast, and pray. We will certainly pray in the context of small groups and worship settings, but we shouldn't be putting on an act, like the hypocrites who Jesus parodied. He wants us to go into our room, close the door, and pray to our unseen Father (Matt. 6:6–7). Then our unseen Father in Heaven will reward us. God promises us that we will find him when we seek him with all our heart (Jer. 29:12–13). The parable of the persistent widow and the cynical judge encourages us to pray and never give up! Rather than being anxious, we should by prayer and petition, with thanksgiving, make all our requests to God (Phil. 4:6). (See also the contemporary books on intercession listed in the endnotes.[43, 44]

Even before the incarnation, God often used the prayers of his people, especially his chosen leaders, to save his people from God's wrath, provide food and water in the wilderness, and enable them to conquer the promised land. Isaac prayed for his barren wife, Rebecca, and she became pregnant with two jostling babies (Gen. 25:21). Hannah prayed and promised to give the son she desired to the Lord, then became pregnant and gave birth to Samuel, the future judge and prophet (1 Sam. 1). Zechariah prayed for Elizabeth to have a son but was silenced for his doubting, until John (the future baptizer) was born and ready to be named! Moses and David prayed successfully for plagues to be stopped. Both prophets, Elijah and his successor Elisha, prayed and did something like CPR until the child they were staying with was brought back to life by God. When Isaiah told King Hezekiah to get his things in order because he would die of a boil, the king wept bitterly and reminded God about his past faithfulness. Isaiah turned around, came back, and told the king that he had fifteen more years, with God providing a remedy and the confirming sign of the sun's shadow going backward on the steps (2 Kings 20).

When Solomon prayed at the dedication of the temple in Jerusalem, he said, "When a prayer or plea is made by any of your people Israel—each one aware of his afflictions and pains, and spreading out his hands toward this temple—then hear from Heaven, your dwelling place. Forgive, and deal with each man according to all he does" (2 Chron. 6:29–30). When Daniel pleaded with God and confessed his own and Israel's sins, while fasting and wearing sackcloth, the archangel Gabriel traveled swiftly, arriving at the time of the evening sacrifice (Dan. 9:3–22) and told him that he had been held up by the territorial spirit over Persia, until Michael the Archangel helped him. Do not forget also the blessings and curses in Deuteronomy 27–28 related to obedience or disobedience related to God's law and the promise that God would not put on his people the plagues and diseases of Egypt. He is Yahweh Rapha, the God who heals us (Ex. 15:26).

While we were looking in the previous chapters at the reactions of the Pharisees, law experts, and (occasionally) the Herodians to the healing ministry of Jesus, we found no instances where Jesus was prevented from healing someone, even on the Sabbath, or in any difficult or hostile setting. As far as we know, his success rate with those to whom he ministered was

100 percent. While he laid aside the use of some of his divine attributes (Phil. 2:5–11) at his incarnation and depended on the Holy Spirit for many of his works, Jesus was not only in constant touch with the heavenly Father but had never disobeyed or sinned against him, even under stresses that we cannot imagine. The rest of us cannot say that and need to live in such a way that we do not get in the way of the things God wants to do through us or for us, since we are imperfect clay vessels. All the healing examples we observe in the book of Acts indicate the working of God's Spirit in many lives, without hindrances, yet other people in need probably remained unhealed because they never came to Jesus or his disciples. Today we have many resources for making the conditions of our sick sisters and brothers known, yet fail to do so.

According to Mark 8:22–25, there was one occasion when Jesus required two touches for healing: In Bethsaida, the townspeople brought a blind man to Jesus and begged him to touch him. Jesus led the man outside of the village, presumably with his disciples tagging along, then actually spat on the man's eyes and put his hands on him! As often happens in contemporary healing prayer patterns, Jesus asked him whether he could see anything. The man looked up, probably wiping his face, and reported that he saw people like trees walking around. Obviously, he had once been able to see and knew that something was still wrong. Then Jesus laid his hands on the man a second time, and his eyes were opened, with full sight restored. Jesus told him not to go back into the village but return to his home. This was hardly a failure. In some cases, people who come to us for healing ministry will need more than one prayer session. Follow-up will be needed, when one ministry team is praying for dozens of people in a line after the usual evening healing message.

In the narrative of Mark, Jesus had already healed many people in Galilee before he returns to his home town of Nazareth with his disciples. On the Sabbath he goes to synagogue and is invited to speak after the reading of the law and prophets, but the amazed or skeptical reactions of his audience weren't encouraging. They couldn't understand where this ordinary carpenter had received the words they were hearing or the wisdom that had supposedly resulted in miracles (*dunamis*) in other towns. Joseph had probably died already, and Jesus was pegged as Mary's son, possibly a slur against his questionable parentage. This situation became a stumbling block, a scandal to them, and they took offense, which stopped them from coming to him or receiving anything. Jesus said to them, "Only in his hometown, among his relatives and in his own house is a prophet without honor" (Matt. 13:57). He could not perform any miracles there, except lay his hands on a few sick people and heal them (Mark 6:4). And he was amazed at their lack of faith. Willful, rigid unbelief can be a significant blockage to healing and salvation. At least the father with a demonized son (Matt. 17:14 and the parallels), after observing the disciples fail in setting the boy free, still asks Jesus to heal him if he can. As the father says that he believes but needs help with his unbelief, the boy is set free. In the epistle of James, when someone lacks wisdom, they should "ask God, who gives generously without finding fault and it will be given him" (James 1:5–8). But if they doubt at the same time, they will be double-minded and unstable, like the sea tossing back and forth, then receive nothing. In the context of healing, someone needs to have faith. Persons needing inner healing due to early traumas or abuse may have an inner unbelieving heart (Sandford)[45] due to no fault of their own, which also needs healing, followed by encouragement, before faith can blossom.

Sometimes using the phrase "if it be your will" in a prayer indicates an uncertainty about God's will when his written or prophetic word, a gift of faith, or the Holy Spirit, may have already informed us about God's particular will for the situation. We might instead say, "According to your will." In calling a judge in Israel to warfare, God was patient after telling Gideon, "Go in the strength you have and save Israel out of Midian's hand. Am I not sending you" (Judg. 6:14); Gideon had asked for a double-fleece test, then obeyed God and won a great victory with very few men! Asking the Holy Spirit to guide and empower us as we move into prayer, then watching what God does, is always appropriate.

As we move beyond the examples of healing in the Scriptures, after looking at the many reasons why Jesus healed, we should have a significant measure of faith and confidence in the ability and the willingness of God to heal us! Sometimes, however, we may not receive healing ourselves or be successful in healing ministry until we deal with a few roadblocks, curves, or dead ends along the way. We have already noted one: namely, unbelief or persistent doubt. Today, this may be related to various worldviews, some scientific or philosophical, that we absorbed, which deny the possibility of healing, or religious frameworks, which cause us to consistently view our sufferings, including illness or disease, as gifts from God.

One of the crucial blockages to the healing of our souls and bodies and our relationships with God and our neighbors is unforgiveness, which often brings along its relatives: anger, resentment, bitterness, and malice. It is also an important cause of several diseases. If we are not yet Christians, we must come to God, through Jesus Christ and his finished work of redemption on the cross, in repentance and faith. Until that occurs our sins are not yet covered or put away, and we are still facing God's wrath. We are like the servant who owed a tremendous amount of money, which he could never pay in a thousand years. Once we are set free from that tremendous debt, then we are to forgive our fellow servants the puny amounts they owe us. In the Lord's Prayer we ask God to forgive us our sins to the degree that we have forgiven others. Regularly, we need to confess our new sins so that they may be forgiven and our fellowship with God restored, and then be ready to forgive others unilaterally. "If we confess our sins, God is faithful and just and will forgive us our sins and purify us from all righteousness" (1 John

1:9). Our inner healing from the wounds others have afflicted on us will often remain uncompleted until we forgive even our enemies. Many of us have also stymied God's grace in our lives by refusing to believe all the good news and forgive ourselves! Some of God's promises do have conditions attached to them!

God wants us to intercede for other people and make petitions for ourselves. Without regular devotions, including Bible reading and prayer, we will tend to become discouraged, lose heart, and fall away from fellowship with God and other Christians. God wants us to be persistent in praying: "Keep on asking, and it will be given you; keep on seeking, and you will find; keep on knocking, and it will be opened to you" (Matt. 7:7; a continuous present). We are to be like the persistent widow in the parable because God isn't like the unjust callous judge. Jesus promises his presence among us when just two or three of us agree together in our asking (Matt. 18:19). Asking for healing of our diseases and infirmities is not the same as asking for resources to spend on our questionable pleasures (James 4:3). Every day we ask God for our daily bread and our daily forgiveness. Let's not refuse God's healing out of some false humility.

It is also important that we actually confess our specific sins to God regularly, receive God's forgiveness, and seek to lead a new life walking in his ways. One recent writer has correlated about 80 percent of chronic or incurable diseases rampant today with the sinful or rebellious states of our souls.[46]

Many of us are guilty of not doing the things that God has already told us to do, often out of fear masked as prudence. Others do the reverse. David said, "If I had cherished sin in my heart, the Lord would not have listened" (Ps. 66:18). Also, watch out for pride that we rarely notice in ourselves but that God detests: "God opposes the proud but gives grace to the humble" (1 Pet. 5:5). Asking for healing isn't prideful.

In the *Ministry Training Manual* by Randy Clark,[47] interested persons may find discussions of other hindrances to healing, including generational problems, curses, freemasonry, fear, unresolved guilt, unbroken inner vows, and ungodly soul ties. However, these also can be dealt with before praying for the physical condition about which the person came up for ministry. Some of these hindrances have little connection with the reported healing ministry of Jesus and the apostles.

I have gathered other hindrances to prayer, which may be applicable to healing situations. However, I do not believe that we should focus so much on possible reasons why people may not be healed that we become discouraged. Often, as we begin to pray for people, the percentages of immediate partial or complete healings may seem rather low. I may not hear about a certain healing for weeks then assume that nothing happened. . But rest assured: God will encourage, bless, and help us as we experiment in faith! Often God does something unrelated to our prayers.

Here is a list of other hindrances to prayer or receiving from God.

- Improper treatment of spouse: "Husbands, in the same way, be considerate as you live with your wives and teat them with respect as the weaker partner and as heirs with you of the gracious gift of life, so that nothing will hinder your prayers." (1 Pet. 3:7)

- Neglecting the poor: "If a man shuts his ears to the cry of the poor, he too will cry out and not be answered." (Prov. 21:13)

- Proud attitude: "God opposes the proud but gives grace to the humble." (James 4:6)

- Lack of persistence: Jesus told them a parable to the effect that they ought always to pray and not lose heart. (Luke 18:1)

- Passivity: After hearing Samuel's negative prophecy, Eli said: "He is the Lord; let him do what is right in his eyes" (1 Sam. 3:18).

- Not praying in unison with others: "If two of you shall agree on earth as touching anything that they shall ask, it shall be done for them of my Father which is in Heaven. For where two or three are gathered together in my name, there am I in the midst of them." (Matt. 18:19–20)

- Ingratitude: "Men shall be lovers of their own selves, covetous, boasters, proud, blasphemers, disobedient to parents, unthankful, unholy. . . . In everything give thanks; for this is the will of God in Christ Jesus concerning you." (2 Tim. 3:1, 1 Thess. 5:16)

- Cherishing sin in our hearts: "If I had cherished sin in my heart, the Lord would not have listened" (Ps. 66:18); "If anyone turns a deaf ear to the law, even his prayers are detestable." (Prov. 28:9)

- Doubting (asking for wisdom): "When he asks, he must believe and not doubt, because he who doubts is like a wave of the sea, blown and tossed by the wind. That man should not think he will receive anything from the Lord; he is a double-minded man, unstable in all he does." (James 1:6–8)

- Request that is outside of God's will: "This is the confidence we have in approaching God: that if we ask anything according to his will, he hears us. And if we know that he hears us—whatever we ask—we know that we have what we asked of him." (1 Job 5:14)

Henry Wright's book,[54] lists other blocks to healing: Following is a list of those that were new or different to me.

1. Ignorance or lack of knowledge (Isa. 5:13–14, Hos. 4:6)
2. No relationship with God according to knowledge (Mark 7:24–30)

3. The need to see a miracle and looking for signs and wonders (Matt. 27:38–44, Job 28–29, Rom. 10:17, John 4:46–48, Matt. 12:38–39)

4. Expecting God to heal on one's own terms (2 Kings 5:8–14)

5. Looking to man rather than to God (Jer. 17:5, 1 Cor. 12)

6. Looking to symptoms and not to the healer (Matt. 14:29)

7. Letting fear enter your heart (Job 3:24–26, 4:14–15; Rom. 8:15)

8. Not being honest and transparent (Prov. 16:18)

9. Robbing God in tithes and offerings (Mal. 3:8–11)

10. Sin of our parents (2 Sam. 12:13–14, 1 Kings 14:1–13)

Even though I have presented three patterns of healing based on the Holy Scriptures, believing them to be relevant vital standards for today, I realize that there are mysteries and treasures hidden in the reality of our triune God and his working through, around, and in us to bring about various types of healing, reconciliation, and wholeness. We have no rigid formulas or systems that could compel God to act in a certain desirable way. Christian ministers are not manipulating impersonal energy fields to obtain a desired effect— they are dependent on the Lord almighty as are physicians and other medical personnel using knowledge and methods obtained from our wonderful universe that God designed, created, and holds together.

The Earth is not as it once was in creation. It has been partially ruined by the effects of angelic rebellion and the fall of human beings. The first effect of that primeval sin was the loss of our spiritual life and relationship with God, followed by disease, weakness, disability, and physical death. The laws of sowing and reaping may be in operation for those for whom we pray if they have been acting according to the sinful nature, rather than by living according to the Holy Spirit and producing good fruit (Gal. 5:16–25). They may also be affected by the sins of the fathers and mothers.

That's why those engaged in healing prayer need the gifts of the Spirit, even to know how to pray. A person may come to us with a complaint of arthritis, when they actually need to forgive their sister or stop being jealous of their co-workers. If they repent, they may be healed physically at once. We don't need to know everything before we pray. If he chooses, God can make us aware of problems that need to be removed or shift the intention of our prayers toward his better way. Apparent medical problems or weaknesses can be simulated by spirits of infirmity or pain. Nevertheless, we go ahead and pray as God moves us. God is the healer, but he loves to include us in the process.

In some cases we cannot pinpoint the causes that led to a person's weakness, sickness, or disability. We are annoyed when bad things happen to seemingly good people or vice versa, and we fail to take the long view. If someone's final illness brings him to the point where he accepts Jesus Christ in his weakness, then dies and ends up with Jesus, that's gain! If he is turned from bitter to better, that brings joy! Let's welcome those who come for healing, listen, love, and see what the Lord will do, then send them off with a blessing. Let's get healed regularly ourselves and not be unhealed ministers who harm others, then use lists like mine to play the blame game on themselves or others. As we continue in prayer and ministry, we can learn from our successes, mistakes, and God's redeeming corrections. The Christian life, which includes Bible reading, study, and meditation; prayer; worship; sacraments; programs; and respect for godly authority, helps us in our calling. Jesus came that we might have more abundant life, with freedom to do the good things God has planned for us. In the end, all will be well for believers in Christ.

Chapter 12

The Discipling, Healing Church

W e have already considered the healing and deliverance ministries of Jesus, the apostles, and other Christian leaders,
which accompanied the preaching of the Gospel and the teaching of
the faith. Behind these ministries we find sincere Christians living
distinctive lives, praying strongly and faithfully, and engaging in
spiritual warfare (Ephesians 6) for the Church, in opposition to the
world, the flesh, and evil spiritual forces. In this chapter I want to
examine the characteristics of the early Church as a community of
believers, based on a few passages from the Book of Acts, selected
Epistle passages, and Word studies. I will also include some contemporary ideas about what makes the Church a healing fellowship.
In his recent work, Francis MacNutt gives salient reasons for the
later decline of healing in the Church through the Christian centuries
and its recent revival.[49]

Characteristics of the Churches in the Book of Acts

On the fiftieth day after Jesus' resurrection and ten days after his ascension, at the time of the celebration of the first fruits in Israel, the followers of Jesus, some 120 in number, "were all together in one place" (Acts 2:1). They were not only in spatial proximity to one another, having experienced Jesus' triumph over death and the grave, they were united in one purpose and ready to receive the gift that the Father had promised, namely, the baptism and the power of the Holy Spirit. After Pentecost, they would be Jesus' witnesses in widening circles outward from Jerusalem, even to farthest parts of the known world. On this day, the Holy Spirit became manifest as something like a powerful wind blowing through the building and beyond, followed by brilliant light or fire, separating into flamelets, resting over the heads of each person, not just Mary or the apostles. Simultaneously, they were filled with the Holy Spirit and began to speak in (known) tongues or languages that they had never learned in rabbinic or any other school. This sound and light show, as well as the hubbub of people speaking, drew a crowd of Jews who had come from various lands for the festival and were surprised to hear these Galileans speaking in their own languages as noted by Luke. This happened in proximity to the holy temple. Many of their listeners were surprised to hear these believers speaking about the mighty deeds of God. A few said they were drunk.

Peter quickly seized the opportunity by explaining that this event was a fulfillment of Joel's prophecy about God pouring out his spirit in the last days on many. Jesus was accredited by God but was handed over to them by God's purpose, and killed, but God raised him from the dead in agreement with David's prophecy, and exalted him to the right hand of God, where he now reigns. The stricken crowd was urged to repent, be baptized, and promised the gift of the Holy Spirit. Three thousand were added that day (Acts 2:1–40)!

Then, we find a brief, almost idyllic picture of the earliest, on-fire Church, soon after Pentecost. These (mostly new) Christian believers were warmly devoted to the teachings of the apostles, to the fellowship (koinonia), to the breaking of bread together, whether at an ordinary meal or in the remembrance of Jesus' last supper, and to their corporate or individual prayers. Simultaneously, they were overawed as many signs, such as were recorded by John much later, and wonders were occurring regularly as the apostles ministered among them. Often, these followers of Christ would consider their possessions and resources as being for the common good, then sell or pool them. Daily, they would pray in the appropriate temple courts, and then move from house to house, sharing common meals with tremendous joy and sincerity of heart. At this early stage, they enjoyed great favor among the common people, so that their numbers were increasing every day, not once per quarter. The reality of their Christian lives and God's kingdom was inviting and contagious.

After Peter and John heal the cripple at the temple gate and are persecuted for doing so, we find the same unity of heart and mind among the disciples according to Acts 4:32–35. God's grace was abundantly on them as the apostles kept on powerfully testifying about the resurrection of Jesus. No one was needy, because periodically the believers sold their possessions and then gave their profits to the apostles for distribution. Later, the first seven spirit-filled deacons were given this ministry of distribution for increasing numbers of widows, farther from Jerusalem. When Ananias and Sapphira sold a property and gave part of their profits to the apostles but misrepresented it as the whole and were caught, they both died! Early leaders of the Church were poor, not rich (Acts 3:6), yet they freely gave what they had received. The strong, glorious presence of the Lord in his new temple or body produced great awe. Centuries later, the wealthy medieval Church could neither say "Silver and gold have I none" nor "Get up and walk!"

Even in the Sanhedrin council, Peter and John spoke boldly about the death and resurrection of Jesus, their use of his name, and their intention to obey God rather than men. After being jailed and beaten but not executed, due to Gamaliel's wise counsel, they met with the Church, and everyone was refilled with the Holy Spirit. Even the death by stoning of Stephen, one of the seven, with Saul watching, and the subsequent persecution of Christians, led to the Gospel being preached in the rest of Judea, in Samaria by Philip, and northward to Antioch, where believers were first called Christians. Saul became a violent opponent of the Christians, arresting, jailing, even killing them, until Jesus appeared to him on the road to Damascus, where Saul intended to export his persecutions. Stopped cold, blinded, and shocked to discover that he had actually been persecuting the risen Jesus, the future apostle was healed, baptized in water, and filled with the Holy Spirit. Now called Paul, he spent time re-evaluating his whole life, and soon preached powerfully in Damascus about Jesus being the Messiah, then went as a missionary to the ends of the empire and the inhabited world (*oikumene*). The church enjoyed a time of peace, grew in numbers, living in the fear (awe) of the Lord (Acts 9:31).

The early Church and its leaders adapted rapidly to changing situations, cultures, and people as they fulfilled the great commission. After Philip's preaching and healing in Samaria, the apostle Peter, staying in Joppa, experienced a strange repeated vision of unclean creatures, which God told him to kill and eat. When he protested, the Lord told him not to call anything unclean that the Lord had made clean (Acts 10:15). Simultaneously, Cornelius, a Gentile, God-fearing Centurion, had been told in a vision to send for Peter and given the location where he could be found. When the men arrived, the Holy Spirit told Peter to go with them. When Peter arrived at the house of Cornelius, where many were gathered, and refused to be worshiped, he remarked: "It is against our law for a Jew to associate with a Gentile or visit him. But God has shown me that I should not call any man impure or unclean!" (Acts 10:28). This is an amazing statement, which paved the way for them to receive the good news about Jesus, who was anointed by the Spirit, did well, but was killed, then rose again. In the midst of his message, Peter's hearers came to faith and were filled with the Holy Spirit, and given the gift of tongues. Peter and his Jewish friends were amazed that God had given these Gentiles the Spirit, so they went ahead and baptized them! Peter had to explain his decision three times, but soon other Christians were preaching to Gentiles. Eventually, this new Jewish sect became predominantly Gentile, as the Gospel spread rapidly. Paul could even say that there was no longer Jew or Gentile, slave or free, male or female in the new humanity following Christ. The flexibility and adaptability of the early Church was surprising.

Antioch in Syria became the first missionary center to the wider world. Barnabas, the encourager, went to Paul's hometown of Tarsus, found him, and brought him to Antioch, where they regularly taught the disciples (Acts 11:25–27). When a prophet named Agabus spoke about a coming famine, they sent funds to the Church in Jerusalem. As the believers worshiped and fasted, the Holy Spirit spoke through a prophet to tell them to set apart (commission) Barnabas and Paul for the work God had for them (Acts 13:1–4). They prayed and fasted some more, laid hands on the missionaries, and sent them forth on what would be called Paul's first missionary trip. He usually spoke to the Jews and God-fearers first in the synagogue, quoting from the Hebrew Scriptures, and witnessing to the resurrection until ejected, then continued in houses or lecture halls.

Paul preached the same essential message but made it relevant to his varied hearers. In Athens, Paul used Greek poetry and an altar to an unknown god as his starting points. "He became all things to all men in order to save some" (1 Cor. 9:21–23). Meanwhile, the apostle James was killed by Herod Agrippa I but subsequently, due to fervent prayer, Peter was set free and protected by an angel.

Paul never spent more than two years in any city. As the congregations grew rapidly and stabilized, Paul and his growing number of lieutenants began appointing elders (presbyters) in every place, committing them to the Lord and new ministry with prayer and fasting. Other teachers and leaders appeared, included Priscilla and Aquila, who taught the way correctly to Apollo. When Paul encountered some disciples near Ephesus who had no experience with the Holy Spirit, having only received the Baptism of John, Paul immediately baptized then into Jesus' name and laid hands on them for the fullness of the Spirit. Even on the way to Jerusalem, arrest, imprisonment, then execution in Rome, Paul met with the Ephesian elders in Miletus, warning them to keep watch over themselves and their flocks (Acts 20:19–33) because savage wolves would attack and others within would distort the truth. As he stopped along the coastline of Palestine, Paul was warned by prophets about dangers ahead but resolutely moved forward. By the time Ephesians was written, Paul spoke about a fivefold leadership ministry of apostles, prophets, evangelists, pastors, and teachers to help all Christians come to maturity as they exercise gifts for ministry. The pastoral epistles even have lists of qualifications for elders, deacons, and presbyters. Patterns of ministry in the various congregations from Galatia to Macedonia were rapidly evolving. When possible, apostolic letters, collections of key Old Testament scriptures, then later complete Gospels were circulated to believers in various cities.

Since much of the focus of the Book of Acts is on the triumphant progress of the Gospel throughout the empire, the powerful role of the Holy Spirit of God, and the ministries of two apostolic figures, Peter and Paul, we do not see examples of the healing ministries of ordinary believers, except in the case of Ananias, though in places such as Corinth they certainly existed and were discussed in Paul's first letter to the church there. Speaking to the Galatians, Paul asks, "Does God give you his Spirit and work miracles among you, because you observe the law, or because you believe what you heard?" (Gal. 3:5). According to Hebrews 2:4, "God testified to the message of salvation by signs, wonders, and various miracles, and gifts of the Holy Spirit which were distributed according to his will." The healing ministry of leaders and others flourished because Christians were like flexible wineskins, responsive to the presence, power, and direction of the Holy Spirit.

Characteristics of the Churches in the Epistles

Paul and the other Epistle writers followed a standard Greek letter format with Senders first, then Recipients, followed by a

Thanksgiving, the Body of the letter, and final Greetings. Longer letters from Paul have a doctrinal section, followed by practical applications within the Body. In these letters we can see both positive and negative characteristics of the Church and the situations they were facing.

In his first letter to the Corinthians, Paul thanks God for his grace given to them, their knowledge and speaking, and the abundance of spiritual gifts among them, yet he also criticizes their dividing into cliques according to their favorite leaders, sexual immorality, taking fellow Christians to pagan courts, and their abuse of love feasts. Then, Paul emphasizes agape' love and the reality of the Body of Christ with the goal of reducing their charismatic chaos. He uses his own example of coming in weakness and trembling to preach nothing except the cross of Christ, which was accompanied by the demonstration of God's power (1 Cor. 2:1–4) and reminds them of their initial lack of wisdom, influence, and high standing. Amazingly, God can work through people like us in the midst of turbulent times!

In his second letter to the Corinthians Paul speaks of being led in procession, spreading the fragrance of Christ (2 Cor. 2:14–16) both to those being saved and those perishing. As a servant of Christ, he tried to put no stumbling block in their path toward Christ. He endured "troubles, hardships . . . beatings, imprisonments and riots; hard work, sleepless nights and hard work and his life was characterized by purity, patience and kindness in the Holy Spirit and in sincere love; in truthful speech and in the power of God; with weapons of righteousness . . . through glory and dishonor . . . genuine yet regarded as imposters; dying, and yet we live on; beaten, and yet not killed; sorrowful, yet always rejoicing, poor, yet making many rich; having nothing, and yet possessing everything" (2 Cor. 6:3–10). Unlike most of us, he could urge other people to imitate him as he imitated Jesus.

Paul's letter to the Galatians, probably written before the Jerusalem council, had no thanksgiving because Paul was so disturbed about their being influenced by the Judaizers, who told them that they must be circumcised and follow the Law of Moses. He says, "I am astonished that you are so quickly deserting the one who called you by the grace of Christ and are turning to a different Gospel—which is really no gospel at all!" (Gal. 1:6–7). Paul also urged them to live by faith, and then experience freedom in Christ and life in the spirit, rather than trying to satisfy their sinful natures (Gal. 3–5).

In what may actually be a circular letter to several churches but called the letter to the Ephesians, Paul praises God for choosing those who would become Christians even before creation, then providing them with a tremendous series of blessings that he lists in detail. Paul prays that the eyes of their hearts would be enlightened, so that they would realize the great things that God had done for them. As a prisoner, Paul urged them to live up to their calling in Christ, being patient and humble, maintaining the unity of the body, putting off old bad behaviors, and putting on new good behaviors, submitting to one another, and standing strong against the enemy.

Paul delights in and rejoices with joy as he writes to the Philippians. He refers to their partnership with him, their sharing of God's grace with him, their sincere prayers for him, obedience, and their consistent financial support of his ministry. He urges them to continue working out their salvation with fear and trembling, as God simultaneously works within them to decide and actually do God's will. He also urges them to think about things that are true, noble, right, pure, lovely, and admirable (Phil. 4:8–9). We certainly need that admonition today! Paul calls their most recent gift a fragrant and an acceptable offering pleasing to God. Likewise, in his letter to the Colossians, Paul thanks God for the big three (faith, hope, and love), then warns them about deceptive philosophy based only on human traditions, and urges them to put to death the things that belong to their earthy, fallen nature. He also reminds them of the pre-eminence of Christ, the first born over creation, which holds all things together in the universe, providing a space, time, and energy framework that scientists can explore.

In his early letters to the Thessalonians, Paul notes how the Gospel came with words, power, and the Holy Spirit, producing deep conviction in their hearts, and joy, resulting in their imitation of Christ and his apostle. The missionaries came with pure motives, not flattery, greed, or deception, and chose not to burden their converts. Paul boasts in their endurance, growing faith, and love, despite serious trials. In his final staccato commands, Paul urges the Thessalonians to pray continually, give thanks in all circumstances, and not to put out or quench the Spirit's fire or show contempt for prophecies.

In his first letter, Peter mentions the living hope of Christians, which is based on the resurrection of the dead and reminds them of their wonderful inheritance as members of a royal priesthood and a holy nation, even though they were suffering painful trials again.

James warns his hearers about the necessity for works that follow from faith, the dangers of the unruly tongue and inconsistent speech, and their failure to receive anything from God when they fight, fail to ask God, and spend what they do receive on their selfish pleasures (hedonism; James 4:1–3). They should draw near to God, repent of their double-mindedness, and resist the devil.

Such passages from the epistles give us some information about the conditions and problems of various early congregations, but we cannot directly correlate them with the success of healing or other ministries.

However, during Jesus' time of ministry among us and the first two centuries afterward, small groups, more than large congregational meetings and worship events, were the norm. Believers met often in homes, not dedicated Church buildings, until well into the third century, as Christianity became a legal religion. We have already seen this in the summary of Acts 2:42–47, in Acts 4:31, and Acts 5:12. That's where converts became disciples, formed strong relationships, and learned to minister. Many twelve-step programs and the Alpha USA course perform a similar function today. Hebrews 10:25 warns us not to give up meeting together but to encourage one another as the day of Christ's return approaches. Throughout Paul's letters to the various churches and in his use of the Body of Christ as an organic, living model for the Church, we find him speaking about each other and one another. We are to be devoted to one another in brotherly love (Rom. 12:10), accept one another (Rom 15:7), bear with each other (Col. 3:13), build each other up (1 Thess. 5:11), submit to one another out of reverence in Christ (Eph. 5:21), and spur one another toward love and good deeds (Heb 10:24). Evidently, there was an intensity among early believers largely missing today. The reality of agape love among such Christians coupled with their outreach to others changed an empire.

Surely, one additional, important factor in the strong Christian healing ministry during the first century was the consistent, verifiable reality of healing that the apostles and other disciples had experienced during the approximately three years of Jesus' ministry among them, which had modified their own views about the reality of God and his willingness, even eagerness to heal people. They expected God to heal and transform people by his grace and power—so he did. As the New Testament writings were read in various cities, copied, and given to others, including missionaries, they slowly became the standard (canon) by which later writings could be evaluated, then accepted or rejected. They testify to the power and gifts of the Holy Spirit, including healing within various early Church contexts. By the fourth century, various worldviews, alliances between church and state, and pagan invasions effectively shut down the healing ministry among large segments of organized but powerless Christianity. Later, theories about the seven sacraments, dispensed only by clergy, constrained the work of God. More recent developments in science and medicine have also shifted our expectations toward the functional healing of physical and mental disease through the work of physicians rather than Christian ministry. These changes were facilitated by new educational systems largely outside of the Church. Nevertheless, if one looks for it, there is still contemporary evidence that God is capable of and willing to intervene in our lives, resulting in our health and wholeness.

Contemporary healing events at Christ the King Spiritual Life Center in Greenwich, N.Y. (www.christ-the-king-center.org) or Servant Song Ministries in Waynesburg, PA (servantsongministries. org), accompanied by records of actual healings, may also supply us with useful information about the ways God works in various communities. *The Faith Factor: Is Religion Good for Your Health?* by Dr. Dale Matthews's highlights some of these.[50] Here is another contemporary list.

Contemporary Healing Congregations [51]
Positive Factors

- The environment is characterized by friendship, encouragement, and a real sense of community.
- There is an atmosphere of compassion, trust, and acceptance.
- There is a sense that God is at home (present) and active as the congregation worships him.
- The pastor and members pursue God, obey him, and seek their own healing.
- Members are willing to deal with the brokenness of human lives.
- The church is_a safe place for people to let down their guard.

Consider the Costs

- The congregation will need to increase budgets to support new ministries.
- Team members will need to be trained and scheduled for ministry appointments.
- Once the word gets out, a variety of new people will show up and provide us with new challenges and opportunities.

Additional Materials from C. Peter Wagner [52]

- Health is a major concern of people,
- Some needs for health and wholeness are not being met: Robert Schuller said, "Find a need and fill it."
- Participate in the Third Wave of the Holy Spirit through ministry, not dramatic experiences.
- God works through ordinary, obedient Christians who live the lifestyle of the Kingdom (reign) of God.
- It is God who heals. We do not manipulate God by magic. Be open for God to do whatever he wants through you or someone else.

We cannot go back to the early Church or its environment, but we can provide hospitality, acceptance, love, and openness to the Holy Spirit, which should lead to significant levels of healing among us today. Do we want to be a congregation or fellowship where God is regularly healing people? Are we willing to be one of them too?

Chapter 13

Selected Questions and Answers Regarding Healing

As I studied the New Testament, I wrote down approximately 175 questions that I attempted to answer with the help of the Scriptures, articles, and commentaries. In many cases these sources did not provide me with sufficient information to definitively answer my questions—but these questions were still worth thinking about. I have already covered many of them in earlier chapters of this book. Now, I present the following to you.

1. If we are born sinners in a damaged world and then harm others or ourselves with our attitudes, words, and deeds, are not sickness and disease the natural consequences of our thoughts and actions, or even of God's wrath? If so, should we ask for healing, or should we change ourselves?

a. Generally, without transformation, we tend to reap what we sow in proportion to the sowing, depending on environmental conditions. One seed could produce a full grown plant with many seeds in the head. The farmer who watches the wind and doesn't sow in faith will reap nothing. Job said that those who sow trouble reap trouble (Job 4:8), and Hosea observes that those who sow the wind reap the whirlwind (Hos. 8:7). Those who sow righteousness after preparing the ground to be receptive, may reap unfailing love (Hos. 10:12). Broadcast sowing the word by Jesus could result in multiplication where the ground is not hard, shallow, or weed covered (Matt. 13:3–7). When sowing tithes and offerings, puny giving leads to small results. In terms of our sins, sowing to please our sinful nature results in corruption or destruction; but if we sow to please the Holy Spirit, we will reap eternal life. An unknown native American elder described his struggles to understand the Bible. One dog inside him was mean and talked him into making bad choices, the other one was good and encouraged him to make good choices. They fought. Which one won? The one the elder fed the most. Some people are sick, diseased, or weak because of their sins, habits, and attitudes. God may not heal their physical condition until he deals with the condition of their soul and their behavior! We should not allow sin to reign in our mortal bodies (Rom. 6:13), for the wages of sin is death (Rom. 6:23), broken relationships with God and the people in our lives, and physical decline. This is depressing!

b. Yes, the law and the accuser condemn, while we try denial, but God The sacrificial, restoring work of Jesus Christ actually reaps our punishment, so that we are spared bad things we have earned, and get good things which we don't deserve. Then, with God indwelling our spirit, revealing himself to us, loving us and setting us free, there is a real possibility of significant repentance and change so that the laws of God, including sowing and reaping will actually work for our good. If we refuse to change, we may still reap disaster. Think about the work of Christ upon the cross.

2. Here is the type of question a physicist might ask: Are many of the events we observe in nature, some of which seem completely random, a consequence of the original creation or its corruption? Entropy and chaos are increasing; everything is going downhill, including our bodies. Is that simply the way it is? Are the paths of bullets, cancer-causing cells, or the growth of bacterial colonies governed only by natural

laws such as randomness? Does God never, rarely, or often intervene? Are our worldviews about such events askew? Our experiences with educational systems have significantly influenced our viewpoints. I definitely believe that God has intervened many times in my own life. Much of my healing has been in terms of the inner wounds of the past. Sometimes, God helps us do better in facing adversity, than we would if he were not there! The apostles and other early Christians, as well as many in third-world countries, have an easier time in believing that supernatural events, including miracles, do occur. Using double-blind scientific studies of the effects of intercession and the like may not convince hard-core naturalists. What about us? The incarnation, life, death, and resurrection of Jesus the Christ are important reasons for me to believe in healing, despite the chaos of life.

3. Did God directly cause the handicap, infirmity, or illness that we are seeking to heal as physicians and prayer warriors? Or is someone's condition more the result of corporate, family, or personal sin? Jeremiah asks, "Why have you afflicted us so that we cannot be healed?" (Jer. 14:19). In Deuteronomy 28, God promises blessings to a people who follow his commands but curses (e.g., the disease plagues of Egypt) for those who disobey. These are consequences of willful disobedience, but they do not strike every indi-

vidual. In Exodus 4:11, God states that he gives man his mouth, makes him deaf or mute, gives him sight, or makes him blind. Then he also gives sight to the blind and lifts up those who are bowed down (Ps. 146:8). Job states, "For he wounds, but he also binds up; he injures, but his hands also heal" (Job 5:18). In the Hebrew Scripture, sin can result in active punishment by God, which may take the form of disease. However, God can forgive all our sins and then heal all our diseases (Ps. 103:3). When Jesus and his disciples encountered the man born blind, Jesus refused to blame the blindness on the man's sin but said he would be healed to display (even to disbelieving, spiritually blind Pharisees) the work of God in his life. Similarly, Isaiah prophesied that the lame would leap like deer and the mute tongues sing for joy (Isa. 35:6). Since God is good, I do not believe that he afflicts us without a good purpose, and he has a wonderful way of turning things for good to those who are among his people. We may also find sickness and infirmities coming from several other sources. I have often wanted to know why things happen, but I wouldn't comprehend God's ways and I often have to be content with his word and the personal help of the Spirit of truth.

4. Along the same line, with several books on deliverance in my office, I have wondered how often an unclean or evil spirit is responsible for illness or disease. C. S. Lewis, in

his famous work *The Screwtape Letters,*[53] warns us against completely dismissing the possibility of the involvement of evil spirits, or of focusing too much attention on evil and making it seem equal with God. Temptations from the world, the flesh, and the devil are normal. In his summary to Cornelius and friends (Acts 10:38–41), Peter says, "God anointed Jesus of Nazareth with the Holy Spirit and power, and how he went around doing good and healing all who were under the power of the devil, because God was with him." This may well refer both to healings and deliverance. The woman in the synagogue who could not stand erect had been bound by Satan for eighteen years (Luke 13:16). Satan sifted Peter like wheat, took over Judas, caused Ananias and Sapphira to lie about their donations, and gave Paul a persistent thorn in the flesh. Satan still wields disaster, disease, and death to some extent. Among God's people who encountered Jesus, there seemed to be as many who were oppressed by demons as those who were simply ill. In some cases, demonization and physical ailments are mentioned in the same sentence, so I think it likely that a significant but unknown percentage of illnesses may be caused by or triggered by unclean spirits. If we are deceived or guided by unclean spirits, we will often do things that violate God's law, resulting in our being judged by God. In false cults or religions, demons may give apparent healings but leave the person in worse shape spiritually. There are many alternate versions even of laying on of hands, including therapeutic touch.

5. Some Christian denominations, leaders, and teachers deny that a Christian can be demonized, although that individual certainly can be tempted or harassed from the outside. One of their key Scriptures might be, "Therefore, if anyone is in Christ, he is a new creation; the old has gone, the new has come!" (2 Cor. 5:17). There is also "We know that anyone born of God does not continue to sin; the one that was born of God keeps him safe, and the evil one cannot harm him" (1 John 5:18). Why do I disagree? In chapter 7 on deliverance, we note instances where the person having a demon was probably a part of God's first people, having received circumcision and having taken on himself the burden of the Law. In ancient Israel, King Saul was temporarily changed into a different man by God's spirit as he joined the prophets, but he reverted to jealousy and malice regarding David being governed by another spirit. Another Saul was the rising star of the Pharisees who persecuted Christians until he was stopped cold by God. Ananias and Sapphira were among the believers until they lied about their giving. Of course, one can argue that they were or were not born-again believers. The following two models might be helpful in this regard.

a. The apostle Paul speaks to believers gathered together, then individual Christians by themselves as temples of the Holy Spirit. If we think about Herod's holy temple in Jerusalem at the time of Jesus, we could begin with the most holy inner room, where only the high priest on the solemn Day of Atonement could enter with the required sacrifices to appear before the ark in the glory of God. One mistake, one intruder, and a dead person would be hauled out by the rope. But as we move outward through the court of priests, the court of men, the court of women, to the court of Gentiles, we find less holiness, less known presence of God, and increasing corruption, along with business operations. In past centuries, with shrines to false gods in temple rooms the whole temple was corrupt. Jesus told his contemporaries that they had made his Father's house a den of thieves! So within us, as the new temple, there could be holiness within our own spirit, indwelled by the Holy Spirit yet weak wills or ungodly thinking in our souls and disease in our bodies, allowing some influence or control from the world, the flesh, and the devil.

b. If we look at the conquest of Palestine by the liberated but sinful people of God under Joshua, we see first a crucial triple series of events: circumcision, crossing the river Jordan at full flood, and the destruction of Jericho by trumpet blasts and shouting! There were great triumphs, discouraging defeats, tricks, and assimilations, so very gradually the land became theirs! But as you may know, they never possessed the entire land without temptations to worship other gods, harassing enemies even invasions, while true prophets regularly warned them. Could that be the way humans are? Does the Holy Spirit have the run of our own territory? Or does the enemy hide in our dark, messy closets or basements? Has he taken advantage of our hurts or sinful reactions and sins to get inside and harass or condemn us? We need God's help throughout our lives to become that Holy temple which God sees in us and not be hypocritical.

6. In the Book of Common Prayer's rite of Baptism, adult candidates promise to renounce Satan and all the spiritual forces of wickedness, the evil powers of this world, and all sinful desires that draw us away from the love of God.[54] How does the flesh or the sinful nature affect our health and wholeness? For the first people of God, the covenant mark was in the flesh by circumcision (Gen. 17:3). We should depend on God, rather than the flesh, for strength. The Word became flesh and tented among us (Job 1:14). We cannot keep the law because of the weakness of our sinful

nature, with sinful passions bearing fruit for death (Rom. 7:5) and making us displeasing to God. Rather, we are to clothe ourselves with the Lord Jesus Christ, and not think about gratifying wrong desires. Such decisions will lead to life. According to Romans 1, being given over to sinful desires, including sexual impurity, degrades our bodies and leads to negative health effects or even death. Our old self was crucified so that sin might not reign in us but rather that we offer ourselves to God and become healthy. If we are filled with the Holy Spirit, walking in his ways, and ministering to others, we should have true freedom (Gal. 5:16). In 1Thessalonians 5:23, Paul prays that "our whole being: spirit, soul and body be kept blameless at the coming of our Lord." The old nature, though being executed and dying, tries to trick us into paying it attention and obedience, prolonging its demise and harming us. We cannot find a direct, cause-effect statement, but walking along God's path rather than experimenting with the seven deadly sins will lead to enhanced or maintained health, which is better than repeatedly getting sick and then being healed until the next episode.

7. Are there times when we should simply accept chronic physical illnesses or disabilities as being God's will rather than seeking to be healed? People usually mention Paul's "thorn in the flesh" (2 Cor. 12:7–10) as an appropriate

example of persistent sickness or weakness. Also, what does it mean when Paul speaks about being given over to death outwardly in his body through the things he suffers, yet being made new in his spirit (2 Cor. 4:10–12)? Paul certainly had outstanding visions, perhaps even while he was being beaten almost to death. To keep him from being conceited because of his revelations he was given a constant irritation, a thorn sticking in him that was a messenger of the adversary (Satan). It could actually be a steady spiritual attack of temptation or accusation, or some physical condition, such as malaria or painful, weak eyes. Paul prayed three times with determination and faith for relief, but the Lord said no. Instead, the Lord told Paul that his grace would be sufficient: God's strength was made perfect in or through the human condition of weakness or inability. Then, Paul's attitude reverses itself so that he can even boast about his weaknesses, so that he might be strong in Christ. But he then speaks more about insults, hardships, and persecutions that he experiences in abundance, and even catalogues them (2 Cor. 11:16–30). He is a broken clay pot through whom the glory of God can shine (2 Cor. 4:7). I don't think that we can develop a case for passive resignation to illness from Paul's messenger or Timothy's weak stomach, sickened by bad water. Despite his circumstances and weakened, wounded body, the apostle Paul accomplished more than any other Christian of any century. God may delay our physical healing until he deals with something within our soul that is more important for our future wholeness. Our relationships with God and with our neighbors are quite important!

8. Years ago, a lady from a nearby parish dreamed that she saw me sitting in a jail cell, not realizing that the door was unlocked! In her dream, I walked out of the cell, but I sometimes went back. The relevant question asked of the invalid at Bethesda is: Do you want to be healed? Will our healing from physical, mental, or spiritual disease and addictions lead to true wholeness and our being able to walk out of our freedom to fulfill God's good plans for us? Will we allow (John 8:31–33) Jesus to set us free to obey and use everything we have for God's glory? Paul in Galatians tells us to stand firm in our freedom and not to submit again to a yoke of slavery to sin, or to fall under hollow and deceptive philosophies based only on human traditions! We are called to serve one another in love. Jesus' mission is to do good, heal, and set free those under the power of the Devil (Acts 10:38). Each of us should cry, "Lord, set me free from my prison, that I may praise your name" (Ps.142:7).

9. What impact should the parable of the Good Samaritan and the description of the judgment of the sheep and goats (Matt. 25) have on Christians, including those in the healing

ministry? After a law expert asks Jesus to tell him what he must do to inherit eternal life, Jesus asks him what the law says and how he interprets it. The expert quotes the two great commandments about loving God with our whole selves and our neighbors as ourselves, and then Jesus urges him to do them in order to receive life. But the law expert needs to know who his neighbors are—for surely he cannot love everyone. Then Jesus tells him a story about a man who had been robbed and wounded on the Jericho road (Luke 10:30–37). When a priest saw the wounded, bleeding man, he quickly crossed to the other side of the road and completed his trip. A Levite, who may have just served at the temple, did the same. But a Samaritan, of mixed Jewish-pagan background and considered unclean by Jews, took pity on the man, just as Jesus had taken pity on the leaderless crowds. He performed first aid, using bandages, oil, and wine and then took the victim to what passed for an inn, continued to help him, and left additional money for his care. Then, Jesus asks the lawyer a different question: Which of these three do you think *was a neighbor* to the man who fell into the hands of the robbers? When the expert admits that it was the Samaritan who did so, Jesus tells him to do likewise! The real question is this: Is there someone to whom we can be good Samaritans, rather than driving by in the other lane? If we have an opportunity to perform life-saving first aid for someone and pray to for that person, will we do so? Will the Good Samaritan laws encourage us to do so?

10. In Revelation 20:11 there is a somber picture of the great white throne judgment of all the dead according to the things they had done in this life as recorded in God's books. If Matthew 25 were the only passage available to us about the way that Jesus would carry out this judgment of the people and nations of this world, we could only guess where we would be, after he sorts us out. The sheep on his right hand were invited to enjoy their inheritance in God's kingdom because when Jesus was hungry they gave him something to eat, when he was thirsty they gave him something to drink, when he was a stranger they invited him in, when he needed clothes they gave him some, when he was sick they looked after him, and when he was in prison they visited him! These righteous, giving ones are not able to remember when they had done such things for Jesus. Jesus tells them that whatever they had done for the least of Jesus' brothers (meaning his needy followers) they had actually done for him. By contrast, the goats on Jesus' left side, about to depart into eternal fire, had not done anything to help Jesus when he, in the person of his followers, had been suffering! In shock, they ask Jesus when they had not fed, clothed, or visited him. They just had not noticed needy Christians, just

as Dives in the story of Lazarus had not seen the beggar at his gates (Luke 16:19–31). For people who have not been given an opportunity to make a personal commitment to Christ but have come into contact with secretive believers, could their reactions and actions make a difference in their final destiny? How are we doing? James also warns us about telling a person in need to be warm and clothed, when we won't do anything to help them!

11. After the Jewish authorities accuse Jesus of using an evil power to fight evil, he warns them about the real danger of attributing the good work of the Holy Spirit to evil, which can grieve, quench, or stifle the Holy Spirit and his healing work. This is in addition to people becoming inflexible wineskins, who cannot handle the new wine. Was this common among the "people of the land"? No. Examine chapter 5 and you may well agree with me. The Spirit-filled early church seemed very responsive to the work of the Holy Spirit. But through the centuries, the church not only became more organized but began limiting the work of the Holy Spirit to seven sacramental channels. In practice we have denied the goodness of certain works of the Holy Spirit, including various gifts, which are outside our own artificial boundaries, or we may even ignore the Holy Spirit altogether. The importance of healing in the Gospel and early church life are often ignored, with such ministries treated as a sideshow.

Some theories deny the need for or the reality of Christian healing today as a sign of the presence and activity of the Holy Spirit in validating the good news about Jesus Christ, since we have the Bible.

12. According to First Corinthians 10–11, our attitudes and behaviors when we gather together for a love feast or the remembrance of Jesus' last supper in the sacrament, can result in sickness, even death, rather than healing and wholeness. The Church at Corinth was not only in the process of dividing into various factions, each with their favorite leaders, but had members ranging from poverty and slavery to wealth. In their ordinary meals together or even communion services, they ate or drank in selfish ways, not thinking of all Christians as part of the Body of Christ, the church, and providing for them. They also may have treated the consecrated unleavened bread and wine as ordinary, not considering the reality of Christ's holy presence with them. Paul solemnly recited the very early traditions of the Last Supper, which they were to repeat, thereby remembering and proclaiming the Lord's death until his return. All of us come to the communion table as sinners who have received forgiveness and eternal life based on the completed work of Christ. We should examine ourselves, then confess our sins and make sure that we have dealt with the people we have offended, before receiving communion or healing prayer.

Without faith we may fail to receive the benefits associated with being in fellowship with one another and with our Lord, at his table.

13. Some contemporary speakers urge us to speak and act as if we have already been healed, even though the evidence of our senses or that of medical tests indicate that we are not. Is this consistent with New Testament healing?

    a. In several cases, we do find that Jesus and the apostles told people to act in a way consistent with their being healed. The paralytic was told to get up and walk, the man with the shriveled hand was told to stretch it out, the ten lepers were told to head toward the priests and were healed on the way, and the blind man at Jericho was told to receive his sight. The lame man at Bethesda was asked if he wanted to get well, then was told to pick up his mat and walk, as was the lame beggar at the beautiful gate who encountered Peter and John, and the lame man in Lystra. We also find that friends were told that those they cared about were healed and obeyed Jesus' commands to return. The father of the little girl who had just died was encouraged by Jesus to have faith, and she was raised. In these cases, the individuals were simply obeying commands with good results! Therefore, if God tells us that we are healed or should do something, we should obey. If a person receives a word of knowledge that someone has been healed of a certain condition, then the Lord can quicken the appropriate person to act and experience healing.

b. Is it appropriate for us to say we are healed before we experience healing? Is it a cop out to say "Heal me if it is your will" when we could say "According to your will"? I often say that I am being healed, while still feeling kidney pain. Again I think of the definition of faith in Hebrews 11: "Now faith is being sure of what we hope for and certain of what we do not see." The gift of faith in the context of healing can be a strong assurance that one will or is being healed, which encourages one to receive that healing.

c. What we say makes a difference to ourselves and others. On his deathbed King David said, "The Spirit of the Lord spoke through me; his word was on my tongue." In Proverbs we find: "Reckless words pierce like a sword, but the tongue of the wise brings healing. . . The tongue that brings healing is a tree of life, but a deceitful tongue crushes the spirit . . . The tongue has the power of life and death" (Prov. 12:18, 15:4, 18:21). Paul said, "It is written: I believed; therefore I have spoken" (2 Cor. 4:13). Facing death, weeping, and praying, Hezekiah prayed further and was promised fifteen more years by Isaiah, then was given a sign to prove that the promise would be fulfilled! We can also attest that God's promises are "yes" in Christ. When we are speaking by the Spirit, we can affirm the unseen reality that God is working in us or another person for healing, while the manifestation of that healing may be immediate or progressive. Sometimes our own worldviews or theories from the past can tell us what God is likely to do through prayer, the laying on of hands, anointing, and the ministry of physicians and other health-care providers. I believe that God usually intends to heal us until he calls us home. To express faith in the God who heals is good, even if we do not receive some of the things we ask for.

14. What were the possibilities for healing and wholeness in the first century, other than through Jesus and the early church? Speaking only of physical healing, the Greeks were already moving toward what we now call scientific medicine, although early theories about balancing the four humors were seriously lacking. In many Greek cities there were healing places associated with the god Asclepius. In Epidaurus, sick persons would dream in special rooms and then would be given a message about their condition and its cure. The oath of Hippocrates involved a promise to do no harm. In far-away Judea, simple remedies and substances were common

in folk medicine: avoiding certain foods according to the Mosaic law, with priests diagnosing skin diseases or rashes, and physicians setting broken bones. Theories often attributed diseases to the wrath of God or to attacks from Satan's forces. Many physicians tried vainly to help the woman who was hemorrhaging, as she spent everything she had for these so-called cures without any improvement. Nevertheless, the Wisdom of Sirach 38 (Appendix B) gives a very modern assessment of physicians, as well as God's provisions of medicines, while urging us also to confess our sins and to pray. Within a short time after the death and resurrection of Jesus, others claimed to have healing powers similar to those of Jesus. Even the spittle of Roman emperors was said to heal people. Practically speaking, few people were healed and life seemed "nasty, brutish, and short." The ministry of Christians, who were effective in healing ministry, arose out of love and compassion, not often found elsewhere, and the hospital movement later arose out of this Judeo-Christian worldview.

15. How can we think of health in Biblical terms, consistent with the early Mediterranean culture of Israel? For help with this, I turned to a book by the physician John Wilkinson, *The Bible and Healing*. Using examples from the Scriptures, Wilkinson defines health as consisting of well-being, righteousness, obedience, strength, fertility, and longevity.[55]

He also stresses having the right relationships with God, with ourselves, with our neighbors, and with our environment; the focus is not on the functional operation of various organs and systems. In his discussion of health in the New Testament, Wilkinson stresses health as life, blessedness, holiness, and maturity.[56] The way we think about such things in our present Western society is quite different. This area is worth exploring further.

16. How should we regard our body and its need for healing? I am not thinking of the fallen or sinful nature, sometimes called the flesh, but that which would be studied in a biology or medical classroom. I recognize the wonderful cells, organs, and systems that work for many years before something goes seriously wrong or injury happens. Paul uses the analogy of the human body to indicate how, in the church, when one part suffers, all do. Inevitably, our bodies move toward death and dissolution. This natural body is perishable, weak, and, at times, dishonored (1 Cor. 15:42–44). The resurrection body will be spiritual, imperishable, glorious, and powerful. We care for our present body, sometimes to excess, seeking some ideal and may rightly feel uncertain about our future if we are not followers of Christ. He urges us to seek first the reign of God in our lives, promising to take care of our other needs, such as food, housing, and clothing. Using a startling analogy, he tells us to cut off anything that

is leading us into sin, even if it is a hand or an eye. We find
it difficult to decide the point where we stop trying to save
or protect our life (Matt. 16:25), much less lose it for Christ.
I believe that it is good for us to seek healing by going to
physicians, therapists, and technicians, but also by going
to prayer warriors, church elders, and those with spiritual
gifts. We should also be prepared to deal with other issues
that may be the real cause of our problems, including emotional wounds, unforgiveness, anger, jealousy, and broken
relationships with others! Do we want to be whole in every
area of our lives? Since God has provided for healing, let's
come boldly to the throne of grace and to our brothers and
sisters in the medical professions, but let us keep perspective and recall how the early Christians lived godly, faithful
lives and willingly died for the Gospel.

17. When there is more than one account of a healing in the
Gospels, they sometimes differ. How should we think
about these differences? I had a recent automobile acci-
dent involving two cars, one passenger, and two witnesses.
Thankfully, nobody was hurt significantly, but each of us
had different viewpoints and experiences about what happened, each of which went into the police report. Many
people, including the apostles and other disciples, observed
Jesus' healing and deliverance ministry, then oral traditions about these encounters were circulated, written down,

and arranged later by the writers of the Gospels. Read the introduction in Luke 1 to see one description of the process by which the Gospels appeared. The earliest Gospel of Mark, based on the preaching of Peter, joined with an oral or written tradition called Q contained the sayings of Jesus, along with other traditions, may have been used and edited by Matthew and Luke, with John providing a largely different but authentic account. In essentials all the accounts of the healings of Jesus agree. The action-packed Gospel of Mark provides one healing event after another in the second chapter, while Matthew shortens the accounts to make room for five sizable blocks of teaching. Luke emphasizes the work of the Holy Spirit, and John covers seven significant and unique signs, along with the seven "I am" statements of Jesus. The fact that there are different versions, rather than a single homogenized version, actually gives us more confidence in these accounts of healing in a largely oral, storytelling culture. However, some scholars use various problems and difficulties along with their favorite theories to reach very negative conclusions about the truthfulness of the Gospels. Of course, we would like all our questions answered: Were there two blind persons in Jericho or one? Did Jesus or the Pharisees ask the question? When did the synagogue ruler know that his daughter had died? We would also like to know why Jesus did things that seem strange to us! But we do have to work with the riches that we have been given! There are more manuscripts, translations, and early quotes for the New Testament, written within fifty years of the events, than for any major writings within the same time period! God made sure that these accounts were preserved for us!

My inquiring mind wants to know the answers; but I really want to know Christ, just as I am already known by him.

Chapter 14

Summing Up New Testament Healing

While reading and studying contemporary books on the Christian healing ministry, I rejoiced that many people had been healed but noticed that some doctrines and practices seemed significantly different from those found in the New Testament, or even completely novel. In the International Order of St. Luke the Physician (OSL), the initial training of associate members involves studying healing events found in the canonical Gospels and reading three basic books on Christian healing from an approved book list while joining other OSL members in a nearby chapter to participate in healing ministry.

At least three times in my own experience, individuals participating in OSL meetings, conferences or retreats have introduced, recommended or used healing practices featuring energy manipulations along with a significantly different view of god. The mid-Atlantic region of OSL only uses healing patterns or methods that arise from members' relationship with God through Jesus Christ—our Savior, Lord, and Healer, as presented in the New Testament. At the same time, OSL members affirm scientific research leading to increased knowledge of human beings and effective medical treatments and therapies, which, I believe, also involve the provision and guidance of God.

I recognize that many of the things we do or say in the context of a particular church denomination or Christian organization are not found in the Bible. But are they legitimate developments from the Bible? Are they compatible with ancient Christian doctrines and statements, such as the Nicene Creed? Do they glorify Jesus the Christ and allow for the work of the Holy Spirit? Are we building on the true foundation, which is Jesus Christ (1 Cor. 3:10–15)? What type of materials are we using? Would they stand up to a fiery test, or be consumed? Will there be a heavenly reward for a job well done when we see Jesus? In this book I have presented key features of the New Testament's description of healing for your thoughtful consideration as a sound flexible pattern for Christian healing. By learning about genuine biblical healing practices in a Christian context, I hope that you will not only use them with growing confidence but be able recognize and avoid those which arise from other religious systems or the occult just as a treasury agent handles and becomes very familiar with our new currency, until counterfeits are quickly spotted.

Here are some core beliefs that are supported by this study of the healing ministry of Jesus and his earliest disciples. The contemporary models for healing that I provide in chapter 9 are consistent with them.

1. Healing is an important part of the Gospel message as proclaimed and demonstrated by Jesus and his disciples.
2. Our need for healing arises from our fallen nature, influences from previous generations, temptations from the world and the devil, and our own history of failure.
3. As God works powerfully among us, we can be healed physically, set free from demonic oppression or inner wounds from the past, and brought into new and improved relationships with God, our families, and our neighbors.
4. Through Jesus Christ, God desires to save, sanctify, transform, and heal us. His powerful agent in healing is the blessed Holy Spirit, who gives good gifts for ministry to believers.
5. The faith of those seeking healing, along with that of their friends and ministers of healing, is a significant factor in healing.
6. By following or modifying biblical models, contemporary Christians can be effective in healing or other ministries within the Body of Christ. However, they are always dependent on the action of God, who is the true healer. God often chooses to use the Body of Christ to deliver good things.

During my 34 years of teaching physics at Penn State University–Fayette Campus, I often found myself frustrated that even simple demonstrations and experiments could go awry. In the last ten years of my teaching practice, we attached electronic sensors to a computer, by which we could generate graphs of speed versus time or sound patterns almost instantaneously—but noise could ruin the results. Using a simplified theory allowed us to calculate possible results but they weren't always accurate. Back in 1974, after I had struggled for weeks to find the mistake in a research computer program, God showed me, two minutes before class, what was wrong in a single line of a thousand punched card program! God not only knew about the problem but cared enough to help me in my distress.

He is even more willing to guide and help us in the context of healing prayer for someone in need. After all, it is God who is the healer, not us. We observe, read, learn, and begin to use a healing pattern like the ones I have presented and discussed in previous chapters. We are delighted as we notice how God touches and heals people, and our own trust in God increases. At times, nothing seems to be happening, but God is working quietly at some depth within the person. In inner healing, it is not unusual to invite the Lord to meet the person who is seeking help, and then find ourselves surprised and awed by the things the great physician says and does. We certainly cannot control or manage God almighty! He might do a new thing (Isa. 43:19). There is something of an adventure in praying for healing.

However, we need to be under new management! If Jesus is in the car of our lives, where is he? Are we storing him in the trunk for emergencies? Is he in the back seat, on our right, or driving while we are the passengers, sitting relaxed or hitting our imaginary brakes?

At a healing service I attended east of Pittsburgh, I went up for the healing of a minor problem, but I heard the woman who was ministering say, "Get out of my way!" This was a warning from God that I should not interfere with His use of lay persons in the ministry because of my pride or my jealousy of others. If we need healing ourselves, we should take advantage of the opportunities for healing which God offers us and not hang back. The fact that God may use us powerfully even while we are struggling in one area with sin or weakness is not an excuse to remain the same. The new birth is a beginning, not the end. Healing ministry should be regularly available in the Church in a public place with teams of at least two persons of both genders, with various talents and gifts praying. Confidentially is very important.

Our devotional life should include all kinds of prayer—adoration, thanksgiving, self-offering, intercessions for others, and petitions for ourselves. We can participate in Christian fellowship, various forms of worship, and small groups including Bible studies. Our church leaders, whether pastors, teachers, bishops, elders, or evangelists, should be honored and heeded. We are accountable to them as well as to God (Rom. 13:1–7).

In 2 Corinthians 4, Paul says, "Therefore, since through God's mercy we have this ministry, we do not lose heart. Rather, we have renounced secret and shameful ways; we do not use deception, nor do we distort the word of God. On the contrary, by setting forth the truth plainly we commend ourselves to every man's conscience in the sight of God." I want men and women, boys and girls to enter into a saving relationship with Jesus Christ; but I also want them to be healed by the great physician. The Christian healing ministry should be available in every congregation, regardless of brand. In today's society, many need healing: the chronic physical ailments of some are related to the condition of their soul and spirit or the result of spiritual attack. People who are active in Christian congregations and ministries are significantly healthier than those who are just cultural Christians. As a result, Christians have something important to contribute to our well-being. The law of love requires us to care for everyone, using the resources, abilities, and gifts we have for the benefit of others. To whom, can we be neighbors?

Through the love of God the Father, the grace and giving of God the Son, and the power of the Holy Spirit, the restoration of that healing ministry which once flourished among early Christians in close connection with the preaching of the good news about Jesus Christ, has once again burst forth to the delight of many with new wine in new wineskins. We have the opportunity now to participate in the works God has planned for us. As we are healed, let us share with others what we have received. To God be the glory, great things he has done. Amen.

Appendix A

Important Epistle Passages Related to Healing and Wholeness

1. Romans

a. **Rom. 8:11** "And if the Spirit of him who raised Jesus from the dead is living in you, he who raised Christ from the dead will also give life to your mortal bodies through his Spirit, who lives in you."

b. **Rom. 12:1** "Therefore, I urge you, brothers, in view of God's mercy, to offer your bodies as living sacrifices, holy and pleasing to God—this is your spiritual act of worship. Do not conform any longer to the pattern of this world, but be transformed by the renewing of your mind. . . . We have different gifts, according to the grace given us. If a man's gift is prophesying, let him use it in proportion to his faith . . ."

2. 1 Corinthians

a. 1 Cor. 2:4 "My message and my preaching were not with wise and persuasive words, but with a demonstration of the Spirit's power."

b. 1 Cor. 12:4 "There are different kinds of gifts, but the same Spirit. There are different kinds of service, but the same Lord. There are different kinds of working, but the same God works all of them in all men. Now to each one the manifestation of the Spirit is given for the common good. To one there is given through the Spirit the message of wisdom, to another the message of knowledge by means of the same Spirit, to another faith by the same Spirit, to another gifts of healing by that one Spirit, to another miraculous powers, to another prophecy, to another distinguishing between spirits, to another speaking in different kinds of tongues, and to still another the interpretation of tongues. All these are the work of one and the same Spirit, and he gives them to each one, just as he determines."

c. 1 Cor. 12:27 "Now you are the body of Christ, and each one of you is a part of it. And in the church God has appointed first of all apostles, second prophets, third teachers, then workers of miracles, also those having gifts of healing, those able to help others, those with gifts of administration, and those speaking in different kinds of tongues. Are all apostles? Are all prophets? Are all teachers? Do all work miracles? Do all have gifts of healing? Do all speak in tongues? Do all interpret? But eagerly desire the greater gifts."

d. 1 Cor. 15:42 "So will it be with the resurrection of the dead. The body that is sown is perishable, it is raised imperishable; it is sown in dishonor, it is raised in glory; it is sown in weakness, it is raised in power; it is sown a natural body, it is raised a spiritual body."

3. 2 Corinthians

a. 2 Cor. 12:7 "To keep me from becoming conceited because of these . . . revelations, there was given me a thorn in my flesh, a messenger of Satan, to torment me. Three times I pleaded with the Lord to take it away from me. But he said to me, 'My grace is sufficient for you, for my power is made perfect in weakness.' Therefore I will boast all the more gladly about my weaknesses, so that Christ's power may rest on me."

4. Galatians

a. Gal. 5:1 "It is for freedom that Christ has set us free. Stand firm, then, and do not let yourselves be burdened again by a yoke of slavery. . . . So I say, live by the Spirit, and you will not gratify the desires of the sinful nature. . . . But the fruit of the Spirit is love, joy, peace, patience, kindness, goodness, gentleness and self-control."

5. Ephesians

a. Eph. 5:18 "Do not get drunk on wine, which leads to debauchery. Instead, be filled with the Spirit. Speak to one another with psalms, hymns and spiritual songs. Sing and make music in your heart to the Lord, always giving thanks to God the Father for everything, in the name of our Lord Jesus Christ."

b. **Eph. 6:10** "Finally, be strong in the Lord and in his mighty power. Put on the full armor of God so that you can take your stand against the devil's schemes. For our struggle is not against flesh and blood, but against the rulers . . . and against the spiritual forces of evil in the heavenly realms. . . . Stand firm then, with the belt of truth buckled around your waist, with the breastplate of righteousness in place, and with your feet fitted with the readiness that comes from the Gospel of peace. In addition, take up the shield of faith, with which you can extinguish all the flaming arrows of the evil one. Take the helmet of salvation and the sword of the Spirit, which is the word of God. (The warfare) And pray in the Spirit on all occasions with all kinds of prayers and requests. . . . be alert and always keep on praying for all the saints."

6. I Thessalonians

a. **1 Thess. 5:16** "Be joyful always; pray continually; give thanks in all circumstances, for this is God's will for you in Christ Jesus. Do not put out the Spirit's fire; do not treat prophecies with contempt. Test everything. Hold on to the good."

7. **2 Timothy**

    a. **2 Tim. 1:6** "I remind you to fan into flame the gift of God, which is in you through the laying on of my hands. For God did not give us a spirit of timidity, but a spirit of power, of love and of self-discipline."

    b. **2 Tim. 3:16** "All Scripture is God-breathed and is useful for teaching, rebuking, correcting and training in righteousness, so that the man of God may be thoroughly equipped for every good work."

8. **Hebrews**

    a. **Heb. 4:12** "For the word of God is living and active. Sharper than any double-edged sword, it penetrates even to dividing soul and spirit, joints and marrow; it judges the thoughts and attitudes of the heart."

    b. **Heb. 11:1** "Now faith is being sure of what we hope for and certain of what we do not see."

9. **James**

    a. **James 4:7** "Submit yourselves then to God. Resist the devil, and he will flee from you. Come near to God and he will come near to you. Wash your hands, you sinners, and purify your hearts, you double-minded."

    b. **James 5:14** "Is any one of you sick? He should call the elders of the church to pray over him and anoint him with oil in the name of the Lord. And the prayer offered in faith will make the sick person well; the Lord will raise him up.

If he has sinned, he will be forgiven. Therefore confess your sins to each other and pray for each other so that you may be healed."

10. 1 Peter

    a. 1 Pet. 2:24 "He himself bore our sins in his body on the tree, so that we might die to sins and live for righteousness; by his wounds you have been healed."

11. 1 John

    a. 1 John 1:8 "If we confess our sins, he is faithful and just and will forgive us our sins and purify us from all unrighteousness."

Appendix B

The Old Testament and the Apocryphal Healing Scriptures

1. **Gen. 17: 21** "But my covenant I will establish with Isaac, whom Sarah will bear to you by this time next year." (God promises to end Abraham's barrenness.)

2. **Gen. 20:17** "Then Abraham prayed to God, and God healed Abimelech, his wife and his slave girls so they could have children again, for the LORD had closed up every womb in Abimelech's household because of Abraham's wife Sarah."

3. **Ex. 15:26** "He said, 'If you listen carefully to the voice of the LORD your God and do what is right in his eyes, if you pay attention to his commands and keep all his decrees, I will not bring on you any of the diseases I brought on the Egyptians, for I am the LORD, who heals you. [I am the Lord your physician.]'"

4. **Ex. 20:12** "Honor your father and your mother, so that you may live long in the land the LORD your God is giving you."

5. **Ex. 23:25** "Worship the LORD your God, and his blessing will be on your food and water. I will take away sickness from among you, and none will miscarry or be barren in your land. I will give you a full life span."

6. **Leviticus 13:1–46** and 14:1–32 covers the treatment of diseases, and Leviticus 15:1–33 covers healthy living.

7. **Num. 12:1–15** Covers the healing of Miriam's leprosy:

8. **Num. 16:46–48** "Then Moses said to Aaron, 'Take your censer and put incense in it, along with fire from the altar, and hurry to the assembly to make atonement for them. Wrath has come out from the LORD; the plague has started.' So Aaron did as Moses said, and ran into the midst of the assembly. The plague had already started among the people, but Aaron offered the incense and made atonement for them. He stood between the living and the dead, and the plague stopped."

9. **Num. 21:4** "They traveled from Mount Hor along the route to the Red Sea, to go around Edom. But the people grew impatient on the way; they spoke against God and against Moses, and said, 'Why have you brought us up out of Egypt to die in the desert? There is no bread! There is no water! And we detest this miserable food!' Then the LORD sent venomous snakes among them; they bit the people and many Israelites died. The people came to Moses and said, 'We sinned when we spoke against the LORD and against you. Pray that the LORD will take the snakes away from us.' So Moses prayed for the people. The

LORD said to Moses, 'Make a snake and put it up on a pole; anyone who is bitten can look at it and live.' So Moses made a bronze snake and put it up on a pole. Then when anyone was bitten by a snake and looked at the bronze snake, he lived."

10. **Num. 23:19** "God is not a man, that he should lie, nor a son of man, that he should change his mind. Does he speak and then not act? Does he promise and not fulfill?"

11. **Deut. 4:39** "Acknowledge and take to heart this day that the LORD is God in Heaven above and on the earth below. There is no other. Keep his decrees and commands, which I am giving you today, so that it may go well with you and your children after you and that you may live long in the land the LORD your God gives you for all time."

12. **Deut. 7:9** "Know therefore that the LORD your God is God; he is the faithful God, keeping his covenant of love to a thousand generations of those who love him and keep his commands. . . . If you pay attention to these laws and are careful to follow them, then the LORD your God will keep his covenant of love with you, as he swore to your forefathers. He will love you and bless you and increase your numbers. He will bless the fruit of your womb, the crops of your land—your grain, new wine and oil—the calves of your herds and the lambs of your flocks in the land that he swore to your forefathers to give you. You will be blessed more than any other people; none of your men or women will be childless, nor any of your livestock without

young. The LORD will keep you free from every disease. He will not inflict on you the horrible diseases you knew in Egypt, but he will inflict them on all who hate you."

13. **Deut. 30:19** "This day I call Heaven and earth as witnesses against you that I have set before you life and death, blessings and curses. Now choose life, so that you and your children may live and that you may love the LORD your God, listen to his voice, and hold fast to him. For the LORD is your life, and he will give you many years in the land he swore to give to your fathers, Abraham, Isaac and Jacob."

14. **1 Kings13:4-6** Covers the man with a withered hand

15. **1 Kings 17:20** "Then he cried out to the LORD, 'O LORD my God, have you brought tragedy also upon this widow I am staying with, by causing her son to die?' Then he stretched himself out on the boy three times and cried to the LORD, 'O LORD my God, let this boy's life return to him!' The LORD heard Elijah's cry, and the boy's life returned to him, and he lived. Elijah picked up the child and carried him down from the room into the house. He gave him to his mother and said, 'Look, your son is alive!'"

16. **2 Kings 4:28–37** Healing of child.

17. **2 Kings 5:1** "Now Naaman was commander of the army of the king of Aram. He was a great man in the sight of his master and highly regarded, because through him the LORD had given victory to Aram. He was a valiant soldier, but he had leprosy.

Now bands from Aram had gone out and had taken captive a young girl from Israel, and she served Naaman's wife. She said to her mistress, 'If only my master would see the prophet who is in Samaria! He would cure him of his leprosy.' Naaman went to his master and told him what the girl from Israel had said. 'By all means, go,' the king of Aram replied. 'I will send a letter to the king of Israel' So Naaman left, taking with him ten talents of silver, six thousand shekels of gold and ten sets of clothing." "The letter that he took to the king of Israel read: 'With this letter I am sending my servant Naaman to you so that you may cure him of his leprosy.' As soon as the king of Israel read the letter, he tore his robes and said, 'Am I God? Can I kill and bring back to life? Why does this fellow send someone to me to be cured of his leprosy? See how he is trying to pick a quarrel with me!' When Elisha the man of God heard that the king of Israel had torn his robes, he sent him this message: 'Why have you torn your robes? Have the man come to me and he will know that there is a prophet in Israel.' So Naaman went with his horses and chariots and stopped at the door of Elisha's house. Elisha sent a messenger to say to him, 'Go, wash yourself seven times in the Jordan, and your flesh will be restored and you will be cleansed.' But Naaman went away angry and said, 'I thought that he would surely come out to me and stand and call on the name of the LORD his God, wave his hand over the spot and cure me of my leprosy.' Naaman's servants went to him and said, 'My father, if the prophet had told you to do some great thing, would you not have done it? How much more, then, when he tells you, "Wash and be cleansed"!' So he went down and dipped himself in the Jordan seven times, as the man of God had told him, and his flesh was restored and became clean like that of a young boy. Then Naaman and all his attendants went back to the man of God. He stood before him and said, 'Now I know that there is no God in all the world except in Israel. Please accept now a gift from your servant.'"

18. **2 Kings 20:1–11** Hezekiah healed of terminal illness and his life extended.

19. **2 Chron. 7:14** "If my people, who are called by my name, will humble themselves and pray and seek my face and turn from their wicked ways, then will I hear from Heaven and will forgive their sin and will heal their land. Now my eyes will be open and my ears attentive to the prayers offered in this place. I have chosen and consecrated this temple so that my Name may be there forever. My eyes and my heart will always be there."

20. **2 Chron. 16** King Asa died because he did not seek healing from God, but only went to doctors.

21. **2 Chron. 30:18** "But Hezekiah prayed for them, saying, 'May the LORD, who is good, pardon everyone who sets his heart on seeking God—the LORD, the God of his fathers—even if he is not clean according to the rules of the sanctuary.' And the LORD heard Hezekiah and healed the people."

22. **Ps. 30:2** "O LORD my God, I called to you for help and you healed me."

23. **Ps. 91:9–10, 16** "If you make the Most High your dwelling— even the LORD, who is my refuge—then no harm will befall you, no disaster will come near your tent. With long life I will satisfy him and show him my salvation."

24. **Ps. 103:1** "Praise the LORD, O my soul; all my inmost being, praise his holy name. Praise the LORD, O my soul, and forget not all his benefits— who forgives all your sins and heals all your diseases, who redeems your life from the pit and crowns you with love and compassion."

25. **Ps. 107:19–20** "Then they cried to the LORD in their trouble, and he saved them from their distress. He sent forth his word and healed them; he rescued them from the grave."

26. **Ps. 147:3** "He heals the brokenhearted and binds up their wounds."

27. **Prov. 3:7–8** Tells how to be healthy.

28. **Prov. 4:20** "My son, pay attention to what I say; listen closely to my words. Do not let them out of your sight, keep them within your heart; for they are life to those who find them and health to a man's whole body. Above all else, guard your heart, for it is the wellspring of life. Put away perversity from your mouth; keep corrupt talk far from your lips."

29. **Prov. 12:18** "Reckless words pierce like a sword, but the tongue of the wise brings healing."

30. **Prov. 14:30** "A heart at peace gives life to the body, but envy rots the bones."

31. **Prov. 16:24** "Pleasant words are a honeycomb, sweet to the soul and healing to the bones."

32. **Prov. 15:4, 30** "Wholesome talk leads to health."

33. **Eccles. 5:14** "All his days he eats in darkness, with great frustration, affliction and anger."

34. **Eccles. 7:17** "Do not be overwicked, and do not be a fool—why die before your time.

35. **Isa. 6:10** "Make the heart of this people calloused; make their ears dull and close their eyes. Otherwise they might see with their eyes, hear with their ears, understand with their hearts, and turn and be healed."

36. **Isa. 19:22** "The LORD will strike Egypt with a plague; he will strike them and heal them. They will turn to the LORD, and he will respond to their pleas and heal them."

37. **Isa. 32:3** "Then the eyes of those who see will no longer be closed, and the ears of those who hear will listen. The mind of the rash will know and understand, and the stammering tongue will be fluent and clear."

38. **Isa. 33:24** "No one living in Zion will say, 'I am ill'; and the sins of those who dwell there will be forgiven."

39. **Isa. 35:5** "Then will the eyes of the blind be opened and the ears of the deaf unstopped. Then will the lame leap like a deer,

and the mute tongue shout for joy. Water will gush forth in the wilderness and streams in the desert."

40. **Isa. 41:10** "Fear not, for I am with you; be not dismayed, for I am your God; I will strengthen you, I will help you, I will uphold you with my righteous right hand."

41. **Isa. 53:4** "Surely he took up our infirmities and carried our sorrows, yet we considered him stricken by God, smitten by him, and afflicted. But he was pierced for our transgressions, he was crushed for our iniquities; the punishment that brought us peace was upon him, and by his wounds we are healed."

42. **Isa. 58:8–9** "Then your light will break forth like the dawn, and your healing will quickly appear; then your righteousness will go before you, and the glory of the LORD will be your rear guard."

43. **Jer. 17:14** "Heal me, O LORD, and I will be healed; save me and I will be saved, for you are the one I praise."

44. **Jer. 8:14** "Why are we sitting here? Gather together! Let us flee to the fortified cities and perish there! For the LORD our God has doomed us to perish and given us poisoned water to drink, because we have sinned against him. We hoped for peace but no good has come, for a time of healing but there was only terror. Is there no balm in Gilead? Is there no physician there? Why then is there no healing for the wound of my people?"

45. **Jer. 30:17** "For I will restore health to you, and your wounds I will heal, declares the Lord, because they have called you an outcast: 'It is Zion, for whom no one cares!'"

46. **Lam. 3:33** "Though he brings grief, he will show compassion, so great is his unfailing love For he does not willingly bring affliction or grief to the children of men."

47. **Ezek. 34:4** "You have not strengthened the weak or healed the sick or bound up the injured. You have not brought back the strays or searched for the lost."

48. **Dan. 4** Covers the sickness and healing of Nebuchadnezzar.

49. **Hos. 5:13** "When Ephraim saw his sickness, and Judah his sores, then Ephraim turned to Assyria, and sent to the great king for help. But he is not able to cure you, not able to heal your sores."

50. **Hos. 6:1, 7:1** "Come, let us return to the LORD. He has torn us to pieces but he will heal us; he has injured us but he will bind up our wounds. After two days he will revive us; on the third day he will restore us, that we may live in his presence. . . . whenever I would heal Israel, the sins of Ephraim are exposed and the crimes of Samaria revealed. They practice deceit, thieves break into houses, bandits rob in the streets."

51. **Mal. 4:2** "'But for you who revere my name, the sun of righteousness will rise with healing in its wings. And you will go out and leap like calves released from the stall. Then you will trample down the wicked; they will be ashes under the soles of

your feet on the day when I do these things,' says the LORD Almighty."

52. Ex. 15:26 "I am the Lord who heals you." (Jehovah–Rapha)

53. Wisdom of Sirach 38: 1 "Honour the doctor for his services, for the Lord created him. His skill comes from the Most High, and he is rewarded by kings. The doctor's knowledge gives him high standing and wins him the admiration of the great. The Lord has created medicines from the earth, and a sensible man will not disparage them. Was it not a tree that sweetened water and so disclosed its properties? The Lord has imparted knowledge to men, that by their use of his marvels he may win praise; by using them the doctor relieves pain and from them the pharmacist makes up his mixture. There is no end to the works of the Lord, who spreads health over the whole world. My son, if you have an illness, do not neglect it, but pray to the Lord, and he will heal you. Renounce your faults, amend your ways, and cleanse your heart from all sin. Bring a savoury offering and bring flour for a token and pour oil on the sacrifice; be as generous as you can. Then call in the doctor, for the Lord created him; do not let him leave you, for you need him. There may come a time when your recovery is in their hands; then they too will pray to the Lord to give them success in relieving pain and finding a cure to save their patient's life. When a man has sinned against his Maker, let him put himself in the doctor's hands."

Appendix C

Healing Words

1. **From the Hebrew Scriptures:** Rapha (Strong's Number 7495) is translated as "heal, make healthful," with other forms meaning "remedy," "healing," or "health." It appears more than sixty times and can be used for God's healing or that of man.[57]According to Hebrew Honey,[58] it signifies sewing together, a mending of bodies, hearts, homes, and nations torn by sin. "And with his stripes we are healed (Isa. 53:5). Rapha is used for curing a wounded person (Isa. 19:22), for forgiveness (Hos. 14:4), and ineffective comforters (Job 13:4), and the Lord, who heals broken hearted people (Ps.147:3). The word is used for making bad waters wholesome, for medicine (Jer. 46:11) and health (Prov. 3:8). In many cases it is God who directly causes misfortunes and disease or brings about healing during interactions with his rebellious or obedient people and their enemies. This is greatly different than our western, biochemical view about diseases.

2. From the New Testament Scriptures: Resources are the *Complete Word Study Dictionary: New Testament* by Spiros Zodhiates[59] and the *Theological Dictionary of the New Testament*, translated by Geoffrey W. Bromiley.[60]

    a. Therapeuō: In secular Greek the word means to serve, care for the sick, treat, or cure. The common New Testament use is for the real healing that the Messiah brings, which is more than medical treatment. Jesus has great power to heal the sick (Luke 7:21), which includes driving out demons and curing defects with a word, and often includes the laying on of hands. With Jesus, God's kingdom or reign has broken into our suffering world. (Matt. 4:23, 8:7, 16, 9:35, 10:1, 12:10, 15,22, 17:16, 18; Mark 3:2, 10, 15, 6:5, 5:15, 6:7, 18, 7:21, 8:2, 9:1, 6; Acts 4:14, 5:16, 8:7; Rev. 22:2)

    b. Iaomai, to heal; *iasis,* healing; *iatros,* healing: Ancient healing methods were a mix of limited medical knowledge, folk remedies, superstition, and religion. By the sixth century B.C.E., the Greeks were establishing a somewhat scientific basis. Sleeping and dreaming in the temple of Aesclepius was supposed to result in a diagnosis and cure. There is little about physicians in the Old Testament, but Asa (2 Chron. 16:12) is censured for only resorting to a human physician, not God. Jesus is the great healer-physician, who heals by declaration

or command as he responds to our pleas. In one case,
Paul groups sickness with other sufferings (Rom. 8:28)
or misfortunes, and he suffered with some thorn in the
flesh, which may have been illness. (Matt. 8:8, 13, 9:12,
13:15, 15:28; Mark 5:29; Luke 4:18, 23, 5:17, 6:17,
7:7, 8:43, 13:32; John 14:4, 17:1; Acts 3:11, 4:22, 9:34,
10:38, 28:8, 37)

c. *Katharizō*; to cleanse, purify; *katharōs*, clean, pure:
This group denotes physical, moral, and religious clean-
ness or purity. In the Old Testament, Worship of other
gods, participation in their rites, deliberate sins, conditions with bleeding, and certain skin diseases defile
one and separate the person from God's people and the
place of worship. Priests functioned to certify purity and
restore people after sacrifices. Jesus said that the attitudes of our sinful hearts defile, not forbidden foods and
cleansed several lepers and the woman who touched
him in the crowd. The blood of Christ, offered once for
all, cleanses us from the guilt of sin and provides for its
defeat. (Matt. 8:2, 10:8, 23:25; Mark 1:40; Luke 4:27,
5:12, 7:22, 17:14; Acts 10:15, 11:15; 2 Cor. 7:1; Eph.
5:26; Titus 2:14; Heb. 9:14; James 4:8,; 1 John 1:7)

d. *Sōzō*, to save; *Soteria*, salvation: Although this word
is predominantly used for spiritual salvation by faith
in Christ, a restoration of our relationship with God; it

is also employed for our healing and wholeness, which results from the work of Christ. This use occurs sixteen times in the New Testament. (Matt. 9:21; Mark 3:4, 5:23, 5:28, 5:34, 6:50, 10:52; Luke 8:36, 48, 17:19, 18:42; John 11:12; James 5:15)

3. Since the four Gospels were written by several authors to various groups of Christians in the Roman Empire from 60 C.E. to 95 C.E., I am not certain that their words for sickness and healing were used in the same way, or properly translated into our western scientific culture. John Pilch[61] has demonstrated the cultural difference between contemporary medical curing of disease and Christian healing of illness within a Judean first-century community, where separation is an important consequence of certain diseases. Because we Americans are highly individualistic, future oriented, set on mastering nature, and optimistic about our own human nature, we may not understand first-century Mediterranean peasants who focus on the present, on relationships at the same level, and are subjugated to nature. The persons whom Jesus healed would have considered their illnesses and alienation from society to have been caused by God, spirits, or antagonistic humans. There may be greater similarities between those healed by Jesus or the apostles and twentieth-century Egyptian peasants, than between them and physicians at the Mayo Clinic.

Appendix D

Scriptures about the Grace and Giving of Our Lord Jesus

These scriptures remind us about two crucial characteristics of Jesus the Christ, which are demonstrated most clearly in his death on the cross for our sins.

- **Matt. 10:1** "He called his twelve disciples to him and gave them authority to drive out evil spirits and to heal every disease and sickness. Heal the sick, raise the dead, cleanse those who have leprosy, drive out demons. Freely you have received, freely give."

- **Matt. 11:28** "Come to me, all you who are weary and burdened, and I will give you rest."

- **Matt. 20:28** "Just as the Son of Man did not come to be served, but to serve, and to give his life as a ransom for many."

- **Matt. 27:50** "When Jesus had cried out again in a loud voice, he gave up his spirit."

- **Mark 14:22** "While they were eating, Jesus took bread, gave thanks and broke it, and gave it to his disciples, saying, 'Take it; this is my body.' Then he took the cup, gave thanks and offered it to them, and they all drank from it."

- **Luke 4:18** "The Spirit of the Lord is on me, because he has anointed me to preach good news to the poor. He has sent me to proclaim freedom for the prisoners and recovery of sight for the blind, to release the oppressed."

- **John 1:14–17** "The word became flesh and made his dwelling among us. We have seen his glory, the glory of the One and Only, who came from the Father, full of grace and truth. From the fullness of his grace we have all received one blessing after another."

- **John 4:14** "Whoever drinks the water I give him will never thirst. Indeed, the water I give him will become in him a spring of water welling up to eternal life."

- **John 10:11** "I am the good shepherd. The good shepherd lays down his life for the sheep. . . . I know my own and my own know me. . . . I have other sheep, that are not of this fold; I must bring them also, and they will heed my voice. So there shall be one flock, one shepherd."

- **John 17:12–17** "I protected them and kept them safe by that name you gave me. . . . I have given them your word. . . . Sanctify them by the truth, your word is truth."

- **Acts 5:31** "God exalted him (Jesus) to his own right hand as prince and savior that he might give repentance and forgiveness to Israel."

- **Acts 14:3** "Paul and Barnabas spent considerable time there, speaking boldly for the Lord, who confirmed the message of his grace by enabling them to do miraculous signs and wonders."

- **Acts 15:11** "We believe it is through the grace of our Lord Jesus that we are saved, just as they are."

- **Acts 20:24** "I consider my life worth nothing to me, if only I may finish the race and complete the task the Lord Jesus has given me—the task of testifying to the Gospel of God's grace."

- **Rom. 1:7** "To all in Rome who are loved by God and called to be saints: Grace and peace to you from God our Father and from the Lord Jesus Christ."

- **Rom. 5:15** "But the gift is not like the trespass. For if the many died by the trespass of the one man, how much more did God's grace and the gift that came by the grace of the one man, Jesus Christ, overflow to the many! . . . how much more will those who receive God's abundant provision of grace and of the gift of righteousness reign in life through the one man, Jesus Christ [Head of the new humanity]."

- **2 Cor. 8:9** "For you know the grace of our Lord Jesus Christ, that though he was rich, yet for your sakes he became poor, so that you through his poverty might become rich." [See Philippians 2:5 –11.)

- **2 Cor. 13:14** "May the grace of the Lord Jesus Christ, and the love of God, and the fellowship of the Holy Spirit be with you all."

- **Gal. 1:4** "Who gave himself for our sins to rescue us from the present evil age, according to the will of our God and Father. . . . I am astonished that you are so quickly deserting the one who called you by the grace of Christ and are turning to a *different Gospel*."

- **Gal. 2:20** "I have been crucified with Christ and I no longer live, but Christ lives in me. The life I live in the body, I live by faith in the Son of God, who loved me and gave himself for me."

- **Eph. 2:5, 7** "But because of his great love for us, God, who is rich in mercy, made us alive with Christ even when we were dead in transgressions—it is by grace you have been saved. In order that in the coming ages he might show the incomparable riches of his grace, expressed in his kindness to us in Christ Jesus."

- **Eph. 4:7** "But to each one of us grace has been given as Christ apportioned it."

- **Eph. 5:25** "Husbands, love your wives, just as Christ loved the church and gave himself up for her."

- **1 Tim. 1:14** "The grace of our Lord was poured out on me abundantly, along with the faith and love that are in Christ Jesus."

- **2 Tim. 1:9** "Who has saved us and called us to a holy life—not because of anything we have done but because of his own purpose and grace. This grace was given us in Christ Jesus before the beginning of time. You then, my son, be strong in the grace that is in Christ Jesus."

- **1 Pet. 1:13** "Therefore, prepare your minds for action; be self-controlled; set your hope fully on the grace to be given you when Jesus Christ is revealed."

- **2 Pet. 3:18** "But grow in the grace and knowledge of our Lord and Savior Jesus Christ. To him be glory both now and forever!"

- **Jude 21** "Keep yourselves in God's love as you wait for the mercy of our Lord Jesus Christ to bring you to eternal life."

- **Rev. 21:6** "I am the Alpha and the Omega, the Beginning and the End. To him who is thirsty I will give to drink without cost from the spring of the water of life."

Table of Abbreviations for the Books of the Bible

New Testament Book		Old Testament Books	
Acts	Acts	Amos	Amos
Colossians	Col.	Chronicles	Chron.
Corinthians	Cor.	Daniel	Dan.
Ephesians	Eph.	Deuteronomy	Deut.
Galatians	Gal.	Ecclesiastes	Eccles.
Hebrews	Heb.	Esther	Est.
James	James	Exodus	Ex.
John	John	Ezekiel	Ezek.
Jude	Jude	Ezra	Ezra
Luke	Luke	Genesis	Gen
Mark	Mark	Habakkuk	Hab.
Matthew	Matt.	Haggai	Hag.
Peter	Pet.	Hosea	Hos.
Philemon	Philem.	Isaiah	Isa.
Philippians	Phil.	Jeremiah	Jer.
Revelation	Rev.	Job	Job
Romans	Rom	Joel	Joel

Thessalonians	Thess.	Jonah	Jonah
Timothy	Tim.	Joshua	Josh.
Titus	Titus	Judges	Judg.
		Kings	Kings
		Lamentations	Lam.
		Leviticus	Lev.
		Malachi	Mal.
		Micah	Mic.
		Nahum	Nah.
		Nehemiah	Neh.
		Numbers	Num.
		Obadiah	Obad
		Proverbs	Prov.
		Psalms	Ps.
		Ruth	Ruth
		Samuel	Sam.
		Song of Solomon	Song
		Zechariah	Zech.
		Zephaniah	Zeph.

End Notes

1. International Order of St. Luke the Physician, *The Healing Ministry of Jesus: Initial Study Project for Associate Members in the International Order of St. Luke the Physician.* (San Antonio, Texas: International Order of St. Luke the Physician, 2002).

2. R. J. S. Barrett-Lennard, *Christian Healing After the New Testament.* (Lanham, MD: University Press of America. 1994).

3. J. Wilkinson, *The Bible and Healing.* (Grand Rapids, MI: Eerdmans, 1998).

4. *iaomai* (pronounced ee-ah'-om-ahee), meaning "I heal, generally of the physical, sometimes of spiritual, disease."

5. agápe Love, affectionate regard, benevolence, sacrificial gift love of God, demonstrated by Christ and described in 1 Corinthians 13.

6. *dunamis* (Greek, pronounced doo'-nam-is), meaning (a) physical power, force, might, ability, efficacy, energy, meaning; (b)

plural: powerful deeds, deeds showing (physical) power, marvelous works

7. *logos* (Greek; pronounced **loh**-gos,-gohs,**log**-os). In Christianity, the word "logos" refers to the creative or divine word of God, incarnate in Jesus; the second person of the Trinity incarnate but also something said, message or preaching.

8. William Lane, *The Gospel According to Mark* (Grand Rapids, MI: Wm B. Eerdmans, 1975), 75.

9. *phobos* (Greek) meaning "fear" or "terror" or "reverence and awe of God."

10. International Order of St. Luke the Physician. *The Healing Ministry of Jesus: Initial Study Project for Associate Members in the International Order of St. Luke the Physician* (San Antonio, Texas: International Order of St. Luke the Physician, 2002), 53–56.

11. Hector Avalos, *Health Care and the Rise of Christianity* (Peabody, MA: Hendrickson, 1999), 51,102.

12. Francis MacNutt, *The Healing Reawakening: Reclaiming Our Lost Inheritance.* (Grand Rapids, MI: Chosen, 2005.)

13. Joel Green, Scot McKnight, and I. Howard Marshall, eds. *Dictionary of Jesus and the Gospels* (Downers Grove, IL: InterVarsity Press, 1984), 716–719

14. Rodney Whitacre, *John*, (Downers Grove, IL: InterVarsity Press 1999)], 185.

15. Herold Weiss, "The Sabbath in the Synoptic Gospels," *Journal for the Study of the New Testament* 38, no.12 (1990): 13–27.

16. Herold Weiss, "The Sabbath in the Fourth Gospel," *Journal of Biblical Literature* 110 no. 2 (1991): 311.

17. Yong-Eui Yang, *Jesus and the Sabbath in Matthew's Gospel* (Oxford: Continuum International Publishing Group, 1997).

18. Gerd Theissen and Annette Merz, *The Historical Jesus: A Comprehensive Guide* (Minneapolis, MN: Augsburg Fortress Publishers, 1998], 368–369.

19. Johannes Beutler, *Judaism and the Jews in the Gospel of John* [Rome, Italy: Pontifico Istituto Biblico, 2006).

20. Frederick Fyvie Bruce, *The Gospel of John* (Grand Rapids, MI: Wm. B. Eerdmans, 1983), 212.

21. C. S. Lewis, *The Screwtape Letters* (Harper San Francisco, CA: Harpers, 1996), 173.

22. Jerry Robeson and Carol Robeson, *Strongman's His Name* (New Kensington, PA: Whitaker House, 1987), 8.

23. Kurt Struckmeyer, "Traditional Interpretations," *Mustard Seed School of theology*, accessed March 22, 2010, http://follow-ingjesus.org/vision/traditional_interpretations.htm.

24. Walter Wink, *Engaging the Powers: Discernment and Resistance in a World of Domination* (Minneapolis, MN: Augsburg Fortress Publishers, 1992).

25. Kurt Struckmeyer, http://followingjesus.org/vision/reign_god.htm.

26. John Piper, *What Jesus Demands from the World* (Wheaton, IL: Crossway Books, 2006).

27. John Loren Sandford, *Transforming the Inner Man* (Lake Mary, FL: Charisma House, 2007), 145–178.

28. Alexander Balmain Bruce, *The Training of the Twelve* (Grand Rapids, MI: Kregel, 1988), 99.

29. Bill Johnson, *When Heaven Invades Earth: A Practical Guide to a Life of Miracles* (Shippensburg, PA: Treasure House, 2003), 23.

30. Mike Endicott, *Rediscovering Kingdom Healing* (Bradford on Avon Wiltshire, Great Britain: Terra Nova, 2006).

31. Morton Kelsey, *Healing and Christianity* (Minneapolis, MN: Augsburg Fortress Publishers, 1995).

32. Francis MacNutt, *The Healing Reawakening* (Grand Rapids, MI: Chosen, 2005).

33. Amanda Porterfield, *Healing in the History of Christianity* (Oxford: Oxford University Press, 2005).

34. Morton Kelsey, *Healing and Christianity* (Minneapolis, MN: Augsburg Fortress Publishers, 1995),145–150.

35. Peter H. Davids, *The New International Greek Testament Commentary on the Epistle of James* (Grand Rapids, MI: Wm. B. Eerdmans, 1982), 2–9.

36. Michael Evans, *Learning to Do What Jesus Did* (Winter Park, FL: Archer-Ellison, 1996], 3–6.

37. Neil T. Anderson, *The Bondage Breaker* (Eugene, OR: Harvest House, 2000), 222–225.

38. R. Otto, *The Idea of the Holy* trans. John W. Harvey (Oxford: Oxford University Press, 1958).

39. Ronald H. Nash, *Worldviews in Conflict* (Grand Rapids, MI: Zondervan,1992).

40. James W. Sire, *The Universe Next Door: A Basic Worldview Catalog* (Downers Grove, IL: InterVarsity Press, 1988).

41. John Sandford and Paula Sandford, *The Transformation of the Inner Man* (Plainsfield, NJ: Bridge, 1982), 191–206

42. Rita Bennett, *You can be Emotionally Free* (Old Tappan, NJ: Revell, 1982), 104-106.

43. Francis MacNutt, *School of Healing Prayer Level 1 Student's Manual* (Jacksonville, FL: Christian Healing Ministries, 1999), 62-63

44. *The Book of Common Prayer* (New York, NJ: Church Publishing, 1979], 244–2445.

45. Sheets Dutch, *Intercessory Prayer: How God Can Use Your Prayers to Move Heaven and Earth* (Ventura, CA: Regal Books, 1996).

46. Jim Goll, *The Lost Art of Intercession* (Shippensburg, PA: Revival Press, 1997).

47. John Sandford, Loren Sandford, and Paula Sandford, *Transforming the Inner Man* (Charisma House, Lake Mary, FL, 2007), 25.

48. Henry Wright, *A More Excellent Way: Be in Health* (New Kensington, PA: Whitaker House, 2009).

49. R. Clark, *Global Awakening Ministry Training Manual* (Mechanicsburg, PA: Global Awakening, 2007).

50. Henry Wright, *A More Excellent Way: Be in Health,* (New Kensington, PA: Whitaker House, 2009), 303–365.

51. Francis MacNutt, *The Healing Reawakening: Reclaiming Our Lost Inheritance* (Grand Rapids, MI: Chosen, 2005).

52. Dale A. Matthews, *The Faith Factor: Proof of the Healing Power of Prayer.* With Connie Clark (New York, NY, Viking, 1998).

53. Doug Murren, *Churches that Heal: Becoming a Church that Mends Broken Hearts and Restores Shattered Lives* (West Monroe, LA: Howard Books, 1999), 39–54.

54. C. Peter Wagner, *How to Have a Healing Ministry in Any Church*, ed. Mary Beckwith (Ventura, CA: Regal Books, 1988), 37–132.

55. C. S. Lewis, *The Screwtape Letters* (New York, NY: HarperCollins, 1996), pp. ix–x.

56. *Book of Common Prayer*, 302.

57. John Wilkinson, *The Bible and Healing* (Edinburgh: Handsel Press, 1998), 11.

58. John Wilkinson, *The Bible and Healing: A Medical and Theological Commentary* (Edinburgh: Handsel Press, 1998), 22–26.

59. R. Laird Harris, Gleason L. Archer, and Bruce Waltke, *Theological Wordbook of the Old Testament*, vol.2 (Chicago, IL: Moody, 1980), 857.

60. Al Novak, *Hebrew Honey: A Simple and Deep Word Study of the Old Testament* (Houston, TX: Countryman, 1965], 121–122.

61. Spiros Zodhiates, ed., *The Complete Word Study Dictionary: New Testament* (Chattanooga, TN: AMG, 1992], 731–732.

62. Gerhard Kittel and Gerhard Friedrich, eds., *Theological Dictionary of the New Testament*. trans. Geoffrey W. Bromiley (Grand Rapids, MI: Wm. B. Eerdmans, 1985] 332, 344–348.

63. John J. Pilch, *Healing in the New Testament: Insights from Medical and Mediterranean Anthropology* (Minneapolis, MN: Augsburg Fortress, 2000], 4–12, 104.

CPSIA information can be obtained at www.ICGtesting.com
Printed in the USA
BVOW07s0646251114

376584BV00002B/13/P